The

# OREGON

## Weather Book

*A State of Extremes*

The

# OREGON

## Weather Book

*A State of Extremes*

George H. Taylor & Raymond R. Hatton

**Oregon State University Press**
**Corvallis**

Cover photos by Bruce B. Johnson (http://www.oregonphotos.com/)

**Library of Congress Cataloging-in-Publication Data**
Taylor, George H., 1947-
The Oregon weather book / George H. Taylor, Raymond R. Hatton. — 1st ed.
  p.  cm.
Includes bibliographical references and index.
ISBN 0-87071-467-8 (alk. paper)
1. Oregon—Climate. 2. Weather. I. Hatton, Raymond R., 1932-  . II. Title.
QC984.06T39   1999
551.69795—dc21                                                         99-35418
                                                                              CIP

**Oregon State University Press**
101 Waldo Hall
Corvallis OR 97331-6407
541-737-3166 •fax 541-737-3170
http://osu.orst.edu/dept/press

# Contents

# Foreword

No matter where you go, you always take the weather with you.

Now, when you go, you can bring along the weather insights of George Taylor and Raymond Hatton, two men whose understanding and enthusiasm for Oregon's broad range of weather—its subtleties, marvels, and extremes—can hardly be overstated.

My own fascination—okay, fanaticism—with the weather in general and that of Oregon in particular really didn't begin until I moved to the Pacific Northwest in 1981, although I do have fond memories of walking in hip-deep snow during a humungous snowstorm in Delaware when I was five years old.

Oh sure, I had chased a few thunderstorms across the cornfields of northern Illinois. And I had enjoyed the dampness of a Pennsylvania summer (Oregonians know wet, but they don't know humid, hot wet until they've spent an August in western Pennsylvania). But driving across Portland's Fremont Bridge in August of 1981 on the day the temperature hit 107°, I knew I had stepped into some real heat.

The contrast was even more startling; that morning, I had woken up in Bellingham, Washington; the temperature was 50° and it was misting outside. But then again, it was always 50° and misting in Bellingham.

Before I moved to Portland in 1985, I had already gone camping on the Oregon coast, where I had spent days hunkered into a sand dune near Garibaldi watching the clouds stream overhead in heaps and layers, and wishing for more sun.

For the past ten years, I have been given the grand opportunity to travel around the state, reporting for *The Oregonian* on forest fires in eastern and southern Oregon, 50-foot snowfalls at Crater Lake, and hurricane-like windstorms on the coast and in the Willamette Valley.

There is one 12-hour period in this weather life, though, that stands out like a shaft of skittering lightning, blotting out what had come before, and illuminating what was to come.

In August 1993 I was given the assignment (okay, I begged, cajoled, and wheedled for it) the sixth annual Star Party sponsored by the Rose City Astronomers in the Ochoco National Forest outside Prineville. Gentle winds played over the short canyons and riverine draws on the way to the site, a piece of rocky, very open and exposed scabland at about 5,000 feet.

After finding a suitable place to pitch my tent, I did what everybody else did: waited for it to get dark. But there was no stargazing on that first night. By 7 p.m., the skies to the south had grown ominously dark. Rain began to fall in wind-driven sheets, interspersed with blasts of hail and snow pellets. But it was the lightning—twelve hours of soul-freezing columns of fire and electric buzz bombs—that made me start to question my sanity in being there.

Before that night, lightning had been something that stood off across the mountains, or spit out of the bottom of a thundercloud over a flat field. This was something else. This lighting was alive and devilishly close, so close that it stood out at times less than 20 feet away, as thick as a tree trunk and shivery bright.

I still have a cassette tape I recorded that night, an interview with an amateur astronomer that goes along normally for a few seconds, and then—zzzzzzbzzzappp!—the tape is interrupted by our shouts and screams, part joy, part terror, but all awe.

After six hours, we thought it would never end. At ten hours, we decided we didn't want it to end, even though one well-placed dagger of voltage blew the top off a 100-foot Ponderosa pine about 50 yards away. Miraculously, no one was injured.

After stuffing my waterlogged tent into the back of the car, I drove down into town for a hotel room. The storm still raged for a few hours more, and later that night the gates of heaven opened under clear, cool skies.

When I asked George Taylor recently why he wrote this book, he talked of a chance meeting with a publisher he knew, and that it was just something he always wanted to do, but never got around to. Don't believe it. He and Ray Hatton wrote this book for me, and for every other weather-loving one of us.

—*Stuart Tomlinson*
June 1999
Portland

# Preface

Oregon's weather and climate have played a major role in shaping the demographics, economics, and ecology of the state. The variety of the climates in Oregon is remarkable. There are coastal mountains with enough rain (up to 200 inches per year) to support rain forests, high mountain peaks that receive upwards of 500 inches per year of snow, parched deserts with as little as 5 inches a year of precipitation, and nearly every climate regime between those extremes. This sheer variety, coupled with strong reliance on natural resources (agriculture, forestry, and hydroelectric power, for example), has kindled a strong interest in weather and climate among Oregonians. In addition, the people of Oregon are very fond of outdoor recreation, and find that fishing, hunting, skiing, camping, and bicycling are also very much affected by weather and climate.

Oregon Climate Service receives about six thousand requests for weather and climate information each year, mostly from within Oregon. Our Web page receives another forty thousand "hits" every week. While many requesters need specific information (*"How much rain was there last month?" "How strong were the winds on February 15?"*), many need contextual information; for example, *"How did this year compare with past years?" "What was the wettest year ever?"* Others wish to understand why we get the weather and climate that we experience. There are also many "weather nuts" who love discussing the weather and will read whatever they can on the subject. In my experience, there are probably more of the latter per capita in Oregon than in any other state.

Several years ago, I was talking with my friend Kelly Redmond of the Western Regional Climate Center. Kelly is now the Western Regional Climatologist, and preceded me as State Climatologist for Oregon (he departed in 1989). Kelly mentioned that several climate people in other states had written books on their states' weather history, and suggested that such a book would have a wide audience in Oregon.

The more I thought about that, the more I liked the idea. Then one day I saw Jeff Grass, the Director of OSU Press, in the locker room at the gym (Jeff and I are both runners). I asked Jeff what he thought about an Oregon Weather Book, and he enthusiastically suggested I write a proposal. The Press liked the proposal, and requested a sample chapter. They liked that, and the next thing I knew I had signed a contract to produce this book.

In the meantime, I spoke with Ray Hatton. I've known Ray for years, mostly because I've provided him with a lot of data for his research projects and books. I told him of my book idea and he told me that he had planned to do such a book for many years; in fact, he had many files of historical information, photos, and anecdotes that could be used. So Ray and I agreed to co-author this book.

The reader will notice that the material in this book is not necessarily "geographically balanced." Much of this is because Oregon weather history information is not balanced. Regions with cities and high population (especially western Oregon interior valleys) have provided much more extensive historical material than some of the sparsely populated areas of the state, especially east of the Cascades. The photos in the book are particularly heavily westside oriented, and a rather large number are from the Corvallis area. That's primarily because we found a treasure-trove of photos in the Oregon State University Archives, thanks to the assistance of Larry Landis and Elizabeth Nielsen. And the photos were available royalty-free, unlike many of the possible photo sources we found. It was too good to resist.

We hope you enjoy the book. Feel free to provide us with comments and suggestions, especially if you feel we've left out significant weather events that should have been included. It is our hope that we can continue to update this book periodically in the years ahead.

—*George H. Taylor*
Corvallis, Oregon
June 1999

I have been interested in weather ever since the early 1940s when, in England, several continuous days with blizzard conditions resulted in 10- to 18-foot snow drifts which caused school closures that lasted three weeks! Weather conditions (which on almost any day of the year vary greatly from one region to another) interest me from a professional point of view, since I have taught "Weather and Climate" courses at Central Oregon Community College in Bend, and for a practical reason, as I often take hiking excursions into the Cascades or to the High Desert.

It is the regional variations, along with the diverse physical geography of the state, that make the weather throughout Oregon so fascinating. Although, for the most part, the weather in Oregon does not have the ferocity and severity of weather elements in, say, the Plains states, over the years Oregon has experienced severe floods, raging blizzards, and damaging winds, among other weather phenomena. As a result, weather events have greatly impacted the lives of Oregonians.

*The Oregon Weather Book* identifies, explains, and discusses various weather phenomena as they have related to the state. My task has been to describe, from a human interest point of view, selected weather events that have occurred in Oregon. It is my hope that this book will give readers a more complete knowledge of Oregon's weather from a historical and geographic perspective.

—*Raymond R. Hatton*

# Acknowledgments

I am blessed with an outstanding wife, Cindy, and three wonderful children, John, Annie, and Tim. Every day I'm grateful for each of you.

My mother, Elinor, is chiefly responsible for encouraging my curiosity about science and academics and has always been my #1 cheerleader. Thanks, Mom! I only wish my late father could be here to share in the joy of his son's first book. He'd be very proud. I miss you, Dad.

My sisters, Eileen, Marlene, and Judi, and brother Ken have been a big part of my life. They have all helped me stay grounded and realistic (if I'd been an only child, Mom would've spoiled me rotten!) Jack and Jenny Yates, my in-laws, are more like a Dad and Mom to me, and Becky and Dave Cameron have become my sister and brother, rather than just marriage relations.

Several individuals have helped immensely in my professional growth by providing opportunities. Einar Hovind hired me twice. The first time, he gave me my first glimpse of meteorology. Years later, he hired me again as a professional. Einar, you embody grace and kindness and I'll always be grateful. Alan Eschenroeder saw something in an inexperienced, just-graduated kid and hired me to my first "professional" job. He was a wonderful mentor and role model. Steve Esbensen offered me the State Climatologist position even though I was new to Oregon and didn't know Molalla from Yoncalla. Steve provided just the right blend of freedom and assistance.

Kelly Redmond of the Western Regional Climate Center, my predecessor as the State Climatologist, continues to help and inspire me. His were big shoes to fill, and I'm not sure I'm worthy even now. Dick Reinhardt, WRCC Director, has also been very supportive of my office. Phil Pasteris and Greg Johnson of the USDA Natural Resources Conservation Service have supported Oregon Climate Service for many years, and have become very good friends as well.

I have been blessed with kind, talented co-workers at Oregon Climate Service. Chris Daly, Wayne Gibson, Chris Hannan, and Tye Parzybok (alphabetically) are my very effective full-time team. Current support staff includes Joy Aikin, Nate DeYoung, Jen McCannell, and Corinne Ruth. In the past, dozens of assistants have worked here. I'll just acknowledge a few: Lexi Bartlett, the first "data babe" and a co-author of many reports; Holly Bohman and Luke Foster, who worked on early data searches and tables for this book; and Mandy Matzke, who's been with us for four summers. Holly, in particular, played a major role in getting this book started.

Warren Slesinger of OSU Press very capably guided us through the initial process of doing a book. Warren's colleague Jo Alexander has done an amazing job of taking an inconsistent manuscript and making it much better than it was before. Jo, you're the greatest!

My wonderful pals Ron Adler and Gordon Morrell have been a big inspiration to me. Ron is my running buddy and, as an accomplished author, has given me much inspiration and advice. Gordon was my business partner for six years and taught me a great deal about business, life, and personal relationships.

Larry Landis and Elizabeth Nielsen of OSU Archives spent a lot of time going through their files looking for weather-related pictures, many of which appear in this book. We are indebted to them for their hard work and cheerful service.

Bruce Johnson supplied the color photos for the cover and also gave me a lot of good advice and feedback on descriptions of weather events, particularly cold weather.

And finally, Jesus Christ is my Lord, Savior, Rock, and Shepherd. I give Him glory, honor, and thanks for His role in my life.

*—George Taylor*


Most of the information for my contribution to this manuscript came from newspaper accounts that date back to 1861. As most of these newspapers are on microfilm, I relied on the services of libraries. Thanks are extended to the various staff members of the microfilm department of the Knight Library at the University of Oregon in Eugene where, several years ago, I was engaged in research on Oregon's weather and climate.

More recently, in following up the earlier research, I used the library at Central Oregon Community College in Bend. Particular thanks to Central librarians JoAnne Cordis and Janet Mutchie, who greatly facilitated my reasearch.

Special thanks to my wife, Sylvia, who typed my original manuscript, then patiently waded through the many changes and revisions that I subsequently made.

*—Raymond R. Hatton*

# Introduction

Oregon. Weather. The words are inextricably linked in the minds of those who live here, and those who don't. "It rains all the time there." "I couldn't stand to live in place that gets so little sunshine." "I saw the most amazing clouds there." On and on, statement after statement, impression after impression . . . all of them weather-related. We hear them all the time. And so we thought it was time to collect, compile, sort, and organize what we knew about the history of weather in Oregon—what's happened in the past—as well as the causes of the weather we experience—why we get the weather we get.

We should distinguish right away between weather and climate. Weather can be defined as "the state of the atmosphere on a given day or at a given moment in time," while climate comprises long-term averages of weather conditions (say, a 30-year average of annual precipitation in Burns, or the probability of a dry day on July 12 in Salem). Our favorite distinction between "weather" and "climate," however, came from a 7-year-old named Amy. Author Taylor had been asked to speak to her Sunday School class about his job. He asked the children, "Does anyone know the difference between weather and climate?" After a few cute but very inaccurate answers, Amy raised her hand and said, "weather is what you get and climate is what you're supposed to get." He had never heard a better, more concise distinction between the two.

Several years later, during an uncharacteristically wet summer in western Oregon, the phrase, "It's summer and it's not supposed to be wet!" seemed all too common. That summer, what we got was not what we were supposed to get, but something much more extreme. This book is mostly about extremes, rather than averages, because extremes are much more interesting, and they exert a very strong influence. Extreme floods are the primary cause of change in river systems. A few extreme windstorms cause nearly all of the wind-related damage. And the wettest several days in the year account for a sizable percentage of the annual precipitation total.

This book is a history of significant weather events, as well as a guide to the mechanisms that create and govern Oregon's weather. We also explore some common perceptions about weather in our state, and attempt to teach the reader how to predict the weather with greater accuracy. It is our hope that readers will assist us in expanding the list of interesting weather events in Oregon by sending in their own weather stories—an information sheet for such purposes is included in the Appendix.

Mark Twain was once quoted as saying, "Everybody talks about the weather but nobody does anything about it" (*Remembered Yesterdays*, Robert Johnson). We hope that by doing something about it, we can give you more to talk about!

# Oregon Weather Records

| | | |
|---|---|---|
| **Highest temperature: 119°F** | Pendleton | July 29, 1898 |
| | Prineville | August 10, 1898 |
| **Lowest temperature: -54°F** | Seneca | February 10, 1933 |
| | Ukiah | February 9, 1933 |
| **Wettest day: 11.65 inches** | Port Orford 5E | November 19, 1996 |
| **Wettest month: 52.78 inches** | Glenora | December 1917 |
| **Wettest year: 204.12 inches** | Laurel Mountain | 1996 |
| **Driest year: 3.33 inches** | Warm Springs Reservoir | 1939 |
| **Greatest 1-day snowfall: 39 inches** | Bonneville Dam | January 9, 1980 |
| **Greatest 1-month snowfall: 313 inches** | Crater Lake | January 1950 |
| **Greatest annual snowfall: 903 inches** | Crater Lake | 1950 |
| **Highest wind speed: 131 mph** | Mt. Hebo | October 12, 1962 |
| **Lowest pressure: 28.51 inches** | Astoria | December 12, 1995 |

—Port Orford 5E is the station 5 miles east of Port Orford

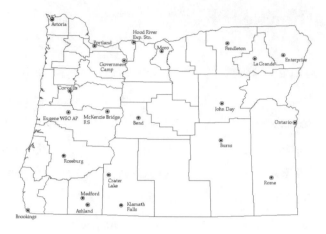

## Selected NOAA Weather Reporting Stations in Oregon

| Station name | Station number | Latitude (N) Degrees | Minutes | Longitude (W) Degrees | Minutes | Elevation (feet) | County |
|---|---|---|---|---|---|---|---|
| Ashland | 304 | 42 | 13 | 122 | 43 | 1780 | Jackson |
| Astoria WSO AP | 328 | 46 | 9 | 123 | 52 | 10 | Clatsop |
| Bend | 694 | 44 | 4 | 121 | 19 | 3650 | Deschutes |
| Brookings | 1055 | 42 | 3 | 124 | 16 | 70 | Curry |
| Burns WSO AP | 1175 | 43 | 34 | 118 | 57 | 4140 | Harney |
| Corvallis St Univ | 1862 | 44 | 37 | 123 | 12 | 230 | Benton |
| Crater Lake NPS Hq | 1946 | 42 | 54 | 122 | 7 | 6480 | Klamath |
| Detroit Dam | 2292 | 44 | 43 | 122 | 15 | 1220 | Marion |
| Enterprise 2 S | 2675 | 45 | 24 | 117 | 16 | 3880 | Wallowa |
| Eugene WSO AP | 2709 | 44 | 7 | 123 | 13 | 360 | Lane |
| Government Camp | 3402 | 45 | 18 | 121 | 45 | 3980 | Clackamas |
| Hood River Exp Stn | 4003 | 45 | 40 | 121 | 31 | 500 | Hood River |
| John Day | 4291 | 44 | 25 | 118 | 57 | 3060 | Grant |
| Klamath Falls 2 SSW | 4506 | 42 | 12 | 121 | 46 | 4100 | Klamath |
| La Grande | 4622 | 45 | 19 | 118 | 4 | 2760 | Union |
| McKenzie Bridge RS | 5362 | 44 | 10 | 122 | 7 | 1480 | Lane |
| Medford WSO AP | 5429 | 42 | 22 | 122 | 52 | 1310 | Jackson |
| Moro | 5734 | 45 | 28 | 120 | 43 | 1870 | Sherman |
| Ontario | 5160 | 43 | 58 | 117 | 1 | 2230 | Malheur |
| Pendleton WSO AP | 6546 | 45 | 40 | 118 | 51 | 1490 | Umatilla |
| Portland WSO AP | 6751 | 45 | 36 | 122 | 36 | 20 | Washington |
| Rome 2 NW | 7310 | 42 | 52 | 117 | 39 | 3410 | Malheur |
| Roseburg KQEN | 7331 | 43 | 12 | 123 | 21 | 470 | Douglas |

# PART 1

# Large-scale Influences on Oregon's Weather and Climate

O regon's weather and climate result from an interplay of warm and cold air, marine and continental air, and the large-scale circulation of the atmosphere. On any given day, one or more of these influences may predominate, but over longer periods of time they become more consistent. The climate is affected by the general circulation of the atmosphere on a planetary scale; but local weather conditions can be very significantly affected by regional and local influences.

## General Circulation of the Atmosphere

The circulation of the atmosphere is driven by differences in temperature between the tropics and the poles. Since the sun shines more directly on the tropical latitudes, temperatures there are consistently warm throughout the year. Near the poles, however, the sun's rays are much less direct. This is especially true in winter, when the sun is very low on the horizon (in mid-winter, above the Arctic and Antarctic Circles, the sun does not rise at all). Summer temperatures in these latitudes are generally quite mild, however, due to a higher sun angle and very long days.

In the atmosphere, temperature differences create air flow. The atmosphere continually attempts to reach equilibrium, with warm air moving to colder areas and cold air to warmer, keeping the atmosphere in a somewhat steady, though imbalanced, state. Were it not for this fact, the tropics would get warmer and warmer and the poles colder and colder. The greater the difference in temperature, the greater the tendency for temperature balance to occur, and thus the greater the north-south air flow.

North-south temperature differences also result in changes in wind speeds. In general, the greater the temperature difference, the higher the wind speeds. Winds are caused by differences in atmospheric pressure, which generally coincide with differences in temperature. The highest temperature differences (which occur in winter) thus produce the highest wind speeds (on a global basis). In mid-latitudes, where Oregon lies, these winds blow generally from west to east.

Often there is a very strong demarcation line between the colder polar air and warmer tropical air. The more sudden the transition, and the greater the difference in temperature, the stronger the winds tend to be. The strongest winds of all occur in the upper atmosphere above these transition areas, and are known as "jet streams." Typical jet streams are swift air currents hundreds (or even thousands) of miles long, less than 100 miles wide, and less than a mile thick. Speeds often exceed 115 mph and sometimes surpass 275 mph. The highest speeds usually occur at the top of the troposphere, the lowest layer in the atmosphere, at roughly 40,000 feet above sea level. The jet stream is also significant because (1) it delineates the "line" between the cold polar and warm tropical air; and (2) it represents the path along which storms tend to travel, and thus is often called the "storm track."

# Seasonal Changes

North-south variations in temperature are not constant throughout the year, however. In winter, the temperature difference between the equator and the pole is very high. In the Northern Hemisphere, consider, for example, Guayaquil, Ecuador (very near the equator) and Fairbanks, Alaska. In July, Guayaquil's average temperature is 79°F and Fairbanks' is 63°F, a difference of 16°F. In January, on the other hand, the difference is huge: steady Guayaquil averages 78°F and Fairbanks -10°F, a difference nearly six times larger than in July. These differences are typical of winter months, and promote very active movement of warm air northward and cold air southward. Greater temperature differences also cause a more vigorous jet stream, yielding more storms and stronger west-to-east winds than during the warm season.

In summer, on the other hand, the temperature difference between the tropics and polar regions reaches an annual minimum. The prevailing west-to-east winds decrease in intensity and high pressure forms at the surface over the eastern Pacific west of Oregon. The only real temperature contrast is between the perpetually frozen polar regions and high latitudes, such as Fairbanks. Thus, the jet stream and storm track remain far to the north of Oregon, and are usually rather passive. Another result of the lower temperature gradient is that the tropics and poles have very little influence on Oregon's weather due to reduced north-south circulation. During summer, most of Oregon's weather comes from locations at similar latitudes, such as the North Pacific (see Figure 1).

Figure 2 shows the typical position of the high pressure area offshore during summer, as well as average wind directions surrounding the high; a corresponding high off the east coast of the U.S. brings warm, moist air from the subtropics, causing the often uncomfortable

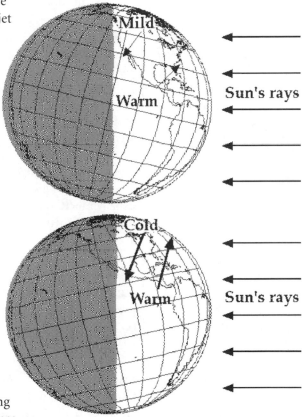

*Figure 1. Seasonal changes in the angle of the sun's rays and resulting effects on temperatures and circulation. In the Northern Hemisphere summer (top), high-latitude temperatures are mild, and north-south air flow minimal because of low temperature gradient. In winter (bottom), very cold polar temperatures cause a large temperature gradient and thus very active north-south air flow.*

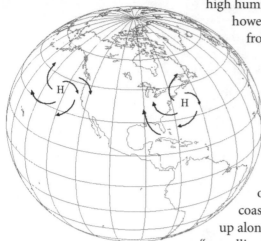

*Figure 2. Typical position of the semi-permanent high-pressure cells over the North Atlantic and North Pacific in summer, and resultant wind directions.*

high humidity for which that area is renowned. Oregon, however, is affected predominantly by cooler air from the North Pacific.

Ocean surface currents off Oregon respond primarily to surface winds, just as they do throughout the world. The clockwise air flow around the oceanic summer high-pressure cell leads to a southward-moving current along the West Coast. "Coriolis" acceleration caused by the earth's rotation deflects surface water to the right—offshore—as it travels southward along the coast. As a result, cool subsurface water is pulled up along the shoreline, a process known as "upwelling." This cool water is rich in nutrients, supporting abundant marine life. It also exerts a strong influence on the coastal summer climate, causing it to be generally very mild (sometimes downright cold!), with frequent fog and cool sea breezes.

## Oregon Climate and the Seasons

As the seasons change, so does Oregon's climate.

Inland during summer the daytime air temperatures are usually much warmer than along the coast. High temperatures in the Willamette Valley and in much of eastern Oregon average in the low 80s, but in some low-elevation valleys temperatures 5-10°F higher are common (Medford, Pendleton, Roseburg, and Ontario are often the warmest cities in Oregon during summer). The warm inland temperatures create low pressure near the surface, which strengthens the offshore-onshore pressure gradient and helps to maintain the typical sea breeze circulation.

At night in summer, the land cools off much more quickly than does the water, which remains nearly the same temperature. In most cases, onshore minimum temperatures are lower than ocean temperatures. For example, the average low temperature in July in Salem is 50.9°F, which is cooler than average ocean temperatures at that time of year. This reversal of the temperature gradient causes a pressure gradient shift as well, with lower pressure offshore and higher pressure onshore. The result is an offshore, or "land" breeze blowing generally from east to west at night. These nighttime summer land breezes are typically much weaker than daytime sea breezes because the temperature/pressure gradients are much lower at night than during the day.

As autumn approaches there are strong changes in atmospheric circulation in the Northern Hemisphere. Offshore, the subtropical high-pressure cells move southward and become weaker. Southward-flowing coastal currents weaken and eventually stop, and are replaced by winter currents that flow northward along the coast. Upwelling no longer occurs.

As the season progresses to winter, the storm track becomes more active and migrates south. In October, Washington is often hit with storms which merely brush by Oregon. But October is a big transition month in Oregon. Early in the month, mild "Indian summer" days are common, and the probability of precipitation in western Oregon is only about 30%. By the end of the month, however, early winter has usually arrived. Precipitation probabilities have risen to 60%, temperatures have dropped considerably, and there is a 50-50 chance that the first frost of the season has occurred.

As winter progresses, the month of greatest precipitation steadily moves southward. In northern Washington, October is generally the wettest month; in Oregon, December and January are the wettest, while in California the maximum average occurs in February.

As the season further progresses to spring, the most active weather zone (the storm track) begins to slowly move back toward high latitudes and decrease in intensity. This is a very gradual process, taking several months to complete, during which time the frequency of storms diminishes. Sometimes spring seems agonizingly long, and compared with autumn it is very slow indeed. While the autumn transition lasts about a month (the month of October), spring extends from the end of February until late May or early June, at least in western Oregon.

## Air Masses

An air mass is a large body of air that has similar moisture and temperature characteristics. Oregon is affected by air masses arriving from each compass direction, and our weather results largely from the nature and origin of the air mass that is present at any given time. There are six primary source regions for Oregon air masses (Figure 3 shows their approximate location relative to Oregon). The air masses, and their typical influence on Oregon weather, are:

**Pacific.** Western Oregon is dominated by Pacific marine air. This is consistently true near the coast, often true in the Willamette Valley, but less true as one moves farther inland. Nonetheless, storms from the Pacific produce the vast majority of Oregon's precipitation and the influence of mild maritime air causes temperatures to be much more moderate, by and large, than they are in inland states. Oregon is often under the influence of weather from this direction for weeks at a time in winter, with storm after storm affecting the area. Typically, storms arrive here about every three days.

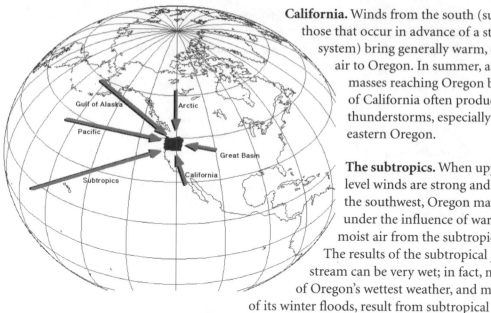

*Figure 3. Air masses affecting Oregon, and their source regions.*

**California.** Winds from the south (such as those that occur in advance of a storm system) bring generally warm, dry air to Oregon. In summer, air masses reaching Oregon by way of California often produce thunderstorms, especially in eastern Oregon.

**The subtropics.** When upper-level winds are strong and from the southwest, Oregon may be under the influence of warm, moist air from the subtropics. The results of the subtropical jet stream can be very wet; in fact, most of Oregon's wettest weather, and many of its winter floods, result from subtropical moisture. Recent examples include the very large floods of February and November, 1996 (see Flood chapter). Many people call these subtropical air masses the "Pineapple Express," since they appear to originate near Hawaii, although often the moisture comes from beyond Hawaii, much farther south and west. The mild air raises freezing levels (sometimes over 10,000 feet), causing snow to melt rapidly. Combined with high rainfall, the snowmelt contributes significantly to big flood events.

**Gulf of Alaska.** Occasionally the upper-level winds bring modified polar air into Oregon from the northwest. This is air from the Arctic regions, tempered slightly by the North Pacific, but still cold and damp.

**Inland polar regions.** Oregon's coldest temperatures occur when cold, dry air from the Arctic moves into the state. Most of the time, the Cascades and other mountain ranges prevent this air from reaching western Oregon, and the coldest temperatures remain east of the Cascades. Occasionally, however, the arctic air penetrates the westside areas, either through the Columbia Gorge or by way of Puget Sound, producing cold, often snowy weather.

**Great Basin.** During summer, air from the Great Basin can be hot and dry (if it comes from the east or southeast) or warm and moist (if it brings moisture from the south by way of Arizona or Nevada). Winter air from this direction is cold and dry (although generally milder than the arctic air masses).

# PART 2

# Weather Elements

# Precipitation

**M**oist air moving into Oregon from the Pacific brings abundant precipitation (by definition, rain or melted snow and ice) to the Oregon coast. As a result, coastal areas average 70-90 inches a year at sea level, and some of the Coast Range peaks approach 200 inches per year. As air crosses the Coast Range and drops into the Willamette Valley, it warms slightly and gets a bit drier, and annual precipitation is reduced to about 30-60 inches per year. The steep ascent up the very high Cascades barrier cools the air, causing condensation (and precipitation) averaging 80 to 120 inches per year, much of it in the form of snow. By the time Pacific air reaches eastern Oregon, most of the water has already fallen as rain or snow in western Oregon. For that reason, most of Oregon east of the Cascades is rather dry: valley locations generally receive 8-15 inches of precipitation per year, while the highest peaks exceed 30 inches (a few get more than 50 inches). Figure 4 shows an idealized cross-section of Oregon, illustrating the generalized west-to-east distribution in precipitation.

## Seasonal Characteristics

Unlike subtropical regions, where the wet season tends to occur during summer, the mid-latitude coastal areas and inland valleys of Oregon receive the bulk of their annual precipitation during winter. In western Oregon, the wettest months are generally from November through March. Although significant precipitation can occur during the warm season, average totals during those months are generally lower than during winter. East of the Cascades, however, the seasonal distribution is quite different. Relatively

*Figure 4. Cross-section of Oregon, showing west-to-east distribution of precipitation.*

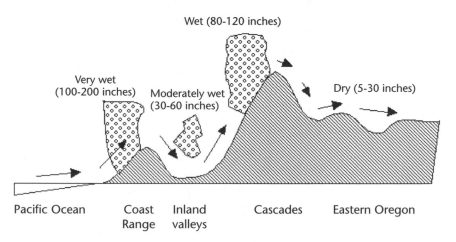

Wet (80-120 inches)

Very wet (100-200 inches)

Moderately wet (30-60 inches)

Dry (5-30 inches)

Pacific Ocean   Coast Range   Inland valleys   Cascades   Eastern Oregon

low winter totals are nearly matched by rain from summer thunderstorms, which are much more common than in western areas. Thus, much of eastern Oregon receives almost uniform precipitation throughout the year.

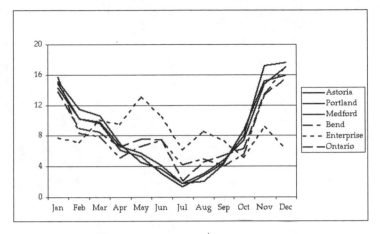

This is illustrated in Figure 5, which shows the percentage of annual precipitation occurring each month at six sites throughout the state. Notice how all three western Oregon stations (Astoria, Medford, and Portland) have similar distributions, with very low precipitation in the warm season, while the three eastern Oregon locations (Bend, Enterprise, and Ontario) receive significant precipitation during late spring and summer. Table 1 shows the actual monthly average precipitation for selected Oregon cities. Table 2 shows the percentage of average annual precipitation that occurs each month.

*Figure 5. Percentage of the average annual precipitation occurring each month at Astoria, Bend, Enterprise, Medford, Ontario, and Portland, based on 1961-1990 averages.*

## Spatial Distribution

The most important factors influencing annual average precipitation in the region are elevation and distance from the coast. Locally, elevation is the most important factor; on a regional basis, however, distance from the coast becomes increasingly important.

Although air masses in the Northwest contain sufficient amounts of water to allow precipitation to occur at sea level and over flat terrain, the effects of the mountain ranges—known as orographic influences—on precipitation are very significant. The primary effect is to cause precipitation to increase with elevation, so in general, the higher the elevation, the greater the precipitation. Orographic effects typically operate at large spatial scales, responding to smoothed topographic features rather than detailed variations in terrain. Thus, a major terrain barrier such as the Coast Range or Cascades results in abundant orographic precipitation, even though small ridges and valleys embedded in a mountain range may not show demonstrable effects.

There are many methods of interpolating precipitation from monitoring stations to grid points. Some provide estimates of acceptable accuracy in flat terrain, but none have

*Significant progress in mapping precipitation has recently been achieved through the development of PRISM (Precipitation-elevation Regressions on Independent Slopes Model) by Chris Daly of Oregon State University. PRISM is an analytical model that uses point data and a digital elevation model to generate gridded estimates of monthly and annual precipitation. PRISM is uniquely suited to regions with mountainous terrain, because it incorporates a conceptual framework that allows the spatial scale and pattern of orographic precipitation to be quantified and generalized (Daly et al. 1994). PRISM is currently being used to produce new precipitation maps for every state in the U.S.*

**Table 1. Average precipitation in selected Oregon stations (by climate zone). Total monthly precipitation (inches)**

| Zone | Station | County | Elev. (ft) | Jan | Feb | Mar | Apr | May | Jun | Jul | Aug | Sep | Oct | Nov | Dec | Ann |
|---|---|---|---|---|---|---|---|---|---|---|---|---|---|---|---|---|
| 1 | Astoria | Clatsop | 10 | 10.00 | 7.59 | 7.07 | 4.61 | 3.02 | 2.40 | 1.16 | 1.33 | 2.91 | 5.73 | 10.05 | 10.55 | 66.42 |
| 1 | Brookings | Curry | 70 | 10.85 | 9.03 | 9.49 | 5.30 | 3.64 | 1.55 | .53 | 1.31 | 2.15 | 5.84 | 11.52 | 12.23 | 73.44 |
| 2 | Corvallis | Benton | 225 | 6.82 | 5.04 | 4.55 | 2.56 | 1.95 | 1.23 | .52 | .87 | 1.51 | 3.11 | 6.82 | 7.72 | 42.70 |
| 2 | Eugene | Lane | 364 | 7.03 | 5.38 | 5.17 | 3.60 | 2.20 | 1.22 | .46 | .80 | 1.32 | 3.35 | 7.51 | 7.86 | 45.90 |
| 2 | Portland | Multnomah | 20 | 5.35 | 3.68 | 3.54 | 2.39 | 2.06 | 1.48 | .63 | 1.09 | 1.75 | 2.66 | 5.34 | 6.13 | 36.10 |
| 3 | Ashland | Jackson | 1750 | 2.37 | 1.72 | 1.95 | 1.61 | 1.29 | .91 | .32 | .58 | .95 | 1.60 | 2.82 | 3.06 | 19.18 |
| 3 | Medford | Jackson | 1300 | 2.69 | 1.93 | 1.82 | 1.16 | 1.00 | .58 | .26 | .52 | .86 | 1.49 | 3.23 | 3.32 | 18.86 |
| 3 | Roseburg | Douglas | 465 | 5.13 | 3.70 | 3.56 | 2.24 | 1.43 | .83 | .43 | .73 | 1.24 | 2.23 | 5.36 | 5.47 | 32.35 |
| 4 | Detroit Dam | Marion | 1220 | 12.79 | 10.24 | 9.42 | 6.54 | 4.87 | 3.27 | .90 | 1.60 | 3.56 | 6.42 | 13.21 | 13.98 | 86.80 |
| 4 | Government Camp | Hood River | 3980 | 13.65 | 10.01 | 8.92 | 7.15 | 4.75 | 3.42 | 1.13 | 1.83 | 3.90 | 6.13 | 11.92 | 14.01 | 86.82 |
| 4 | McKenzie Bridge RS | Lane | 1478 | 9.88 | 7.33 | 7.03 | 5.02 | 3.58 | 2.59 | .85 | 1.44 | 2.93 | 5.08 | 10.01 | 10.76 | 66.50 |
| 5 | Crater Lake | Klamath | 6475 | 9.66 | 7.78 | 8.09 | 4.60 | 3.01 | 1.98 | .68 | 1.29 | 2.38 | 4.75 | 10.56 | 10.84 | 65.62 |
| 5 | Silver Lake RS | Lake | 4380 | .89 | .68 | .76 | .63 | .86 | .85 | .50 | .61 | .58 | .63 | 1.20 | 1.10 | 9.29 |
| 6 | Hood River | Hood River | 500 | 4.56 | 3.59 | 2.50 | 2.47 | 1.10 | .91 | .44 | .27 | .64 | 2.69 | 5.95 | 5.28 | 30.40 |
| 6 | Moro | Sherman | 1870 | 1.49 | .98 | 1.04 | .78 | .77 | .59 | .28 | .47 | .54 | .75 | 1.66 | 1.74 | 11.09 |
| 6 | Pendleton | Umatilla | 1492 | 1.51 | 1.14 | 1.16 | 1.04 | .99 | .64 | .35 | .53 | .59 | .86 | 1.58 | 1.63 | 12.02 |
| 7 | Bend | Deschutes | 3660 | 1.83 | .97 | .92 | .60 | .77 | .86 | .49 | .58 | .47 | .65 | 1.57 | 1.99 | 11.70 |
| 7 | Burns | Harney | 4140 | .81 | 1.17 | 1.60 | .80 | 1.07 | .67 | .52 | .43 | .62 | .78 | 1.41 | 1.41 | 11.29 |
| 7 | Klamath Falls | Klamath | 4098 | 1.81 | 1.28 | 1.35 | .75 | .85 | .69 | .35 | .62 | .55 | 1.07 | 1.97 | 2.23 | 13.52 |
| 8 | Enterprise | Wallowa | 3880 | 1.26 | 1.17 | 1.65 | 1.55 | 2.15 | 1.72 | 1.00 | 1.40 | 1.19 | .84 | 1.50 | 1.00 | 16.43 |
| 8 | John Day | Grant | 3063 | 1.15 | .82 | 1.12 | 1.21 | 1.56 | 1.40 | .53 | .95 | .84 | .92 | 1.47 | 1.40 | 13.37 |
| 8 | La Grande | Union | 2755 | 1.96 | 1.47 | 1.48 | 1.42 | 1.61 | 1.43 | .63 | .92 | .97 | 1.24 | 1.86 | 1.86 | 16.85 |
| 9 | Ontario | Malheur | 2145 | 1.33 | .87 | .82 | .63 | .73 | .72 | .20 | .44 | .53 | .61 | 1.30 | 1.50 | 9.68 |
| 9 | Rome | Malheur | 3410 | .58 | .50 | .83 | .69 | 1.01 | 1.05 | .36 | .46 | .58 | .55 | .82 | .63 | 8.06 |

Averages are based on 1961–1990 data

## Table 2. Percentage of annual precipitation each month

| Zone | Station | County | Elev. (ft) | Jan | Feb | Mar | Apr | May | Jun | Jul | Aug | Sep | Oct | Nov | Dec |
|---|---|---|---|---|---|---|---|---|---|---|---|---|---|---|---|
| 1 | Astoria | Clatsop | 10 | 15 | 11 | 11 | 7 | 5 | 4 | 2 | 2 | 4 | 9 | 15 | 16 |
| 1 | Brookings | Curry | 70 | 15 | 12 | 13 | 7 | 5 | 2 | 1 | 2 | 3 | 8 | 16 | 17 |
| 2 | Corvallis | Benton | 225 | 16 | 12 | 11 | 6 | 5 | 3 | 1 | 2 | 4 | 7 | 16 | 18 |
| 2 | Eugene | Lane | 364 | 15 | 12 | 11 | 8 | 5 | 3 | 1 | 2 | 3 | 7 | 16 | 17 |
| 2 | Portland | Multnomah | 20 | 15 | 10 | 10 | 7 | 6 | 4 | 2 | 3 | 5 | 7 | 15 | 17 |
| 3 | Ashland | Jackson | 1750 | 12 | 9 | 10 | 8 | 7 | 5 | 2 | 3 | 5 | 8 | 15 | 16 |
| 3 | Medford | Jackson | 1300 | 14 | 10 | 10 | 6 | 5 | 3 | 1 | 3 | 5 | 8 | 17 | 18 |
| 3 | Roseburg | Douglas | 465 | 16 | 11 | 11 | 7 | 4 | 3 | 1 | 2 | 4 | 7 | 17 | 17 |
| 4 | Detroit Dam | Marion | 1220 | 15 | 12 | 11 | 8 | 6 | 4 | 1 | 2 | 4 | 7 | 15 | 16 |
| 4 | Government Camp | Hood River | 3980 | 16 | 12 | 10 | 8 | 5 | 4 | 1 | 2 | 4 | 7 | 14 | 16 |
| 4 | McKenzie Bridge RS | Lane | 1478 | 15 | 11 | 11 | 8 | 5 | 4 | 1 | 2 | 4 | 8 | 15 | 16 |
| 5 | Crater Lake | Klamath | 6475 | 15 | 12 | 12 | 7 | 5 | 3 | 1 | 2 | 4 | 7 | 16 | 17 |
| 5 | Silver Lake RS | Lake | 4380 | 10 | 7 | 8 | 7 | 9 | 9 | 5 | 7 | 6 | 7 | 13 | 12 |
| 6 | Hood River | Hood River | 500 | 15 | 12 | 8 | 8 | 4 | 3 | 1 | 1 | 2 | 9 | 20 | 17 |
| 6 | Moro | Sherman | 1870 | 13 | 9 | 9 | 7 | 7 | 5 | 3 | 4 | 5 | 7 | 15 | 16 |
| 6 | Pendleton | Umatilla | 1492 | 13 | 9 | 10 | 9 | 8 | 5 | 3 | 4 | 5 | 7 | 13 | 14 |
| 7 | Bend | Deschutes | 3660 | 16 | 8 | 8 | 5 | 7 | 7 | 4 | 5 | 4 | 6 | 13 | 17 |
| 7 | Burns | Harney | 4140 | 7 | 10 | 14 | 7 | 9 | 6 | 5 | 4 | 5 | 7 | 12 | 12 |
| 7 | Klamath Falls | Klamath | 4098 | 13 | 9 | 10 | 6 | 6 | 5 | 3 | 5 | 4 | 8 | 15 | 16 |
| 8 | Enterprise | Wallowa | 3880 | 8 | 7 | 10 | 9 | 13 | 10 | 6 | 9 | 7 | 5 | 9 | 6 |
| 8 | John Day | Grant | 3063 | 9 | 6 | 8 | 9 | 12 | 10 | 4 | 7 | 6 | 7 | 11 | 10 |
| 8 | La Grande | Union | 2755 | 12 | 9 | 9 | 8 | 10 | 8 | 4 | 5 | 6 | 7 | 11 | 11 |
| 9 | Ontario | Malheur | 2145 | 14 | 9 | 8 | 7 | 8 | 7 | 2 | 5 | 5 | 6 | 13 | 15 |
| 9 | Rome | Malheur | 3410 | 7 | 6 | 10 | 9 | 13 | 13 | 4 | 6 | 7 | 7 | 10 | 8 |

Averages are based on 1961-1990 data

been able to adequately explain the complex variations in precipitation that occur in mountainous regions. Inadequacies in these methods are typically overcome by adding numerous estimated "pseudo-stations" to the data set and tediously modifying the resulting output by hand. Even then, there is no provision for easily updating precipitation maps with new data or developing maps for other years or months.

Figure 6 shows a simplified map of annual average precipitation in Oregon. As can be seen, the immediate coastal areas are quite wet (averaging 60 to 80 inches per year), but much higher precipitation amounts occur somewhat inland at higher elevations.

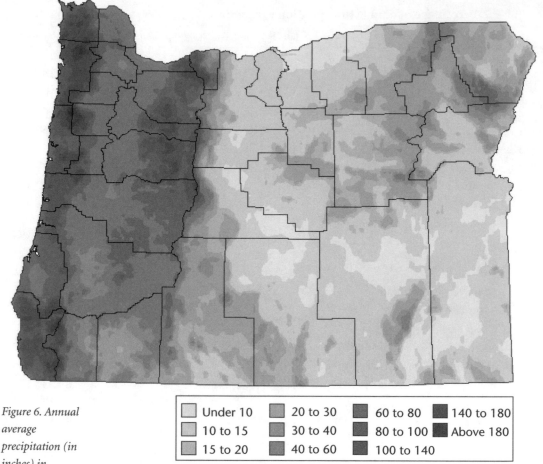

*Figure 6. Annual average precipitation (in inches) in Oregon (1960-1990 averages).*

| | | | |
|---|---|---|---|
| Under 10 | 20 to 30 | 60 to 80 | 140 to 180 |
| 10 to 15 | 30 to 40 | 80 to 100 | Above 180 |
| 15 to 20 | 40 to 60 | 100 to 140 | |

## Long-term Distribution

Precipitation in Oregon can vary significantly from year to year. However, the records indicate a number of longer-term cyclical patterns, with relatively dry years and relatively wet years bunched together. Figure 7 shows annual precipitation at Astoria since 1855. Two lines are shown: the thinner represents annual total for the Water Year, October through September, ending on the year shown, while the thicker line is a 5-year (centered) running average of the annual values. The annual variations are clearly seen, as are the multi-year trends. For example, the early 1930s had a number of wet years in a row, causing a notable peak in the 5-year values. Other unusually wet periods occurred around 1880, 1900, 1920, and 1950. Recent years have been among the driest on record, with the lowest 5-year average during the entire period.

Although many of the long-term trends at other sites in the study area are somewhat different from Astoria's, one fact is common to the whole state: every site experiences periods of generally wet conditions and generally dry conditions spanning multiple years. In addition, variations from one year to the next tend to be fairly large.

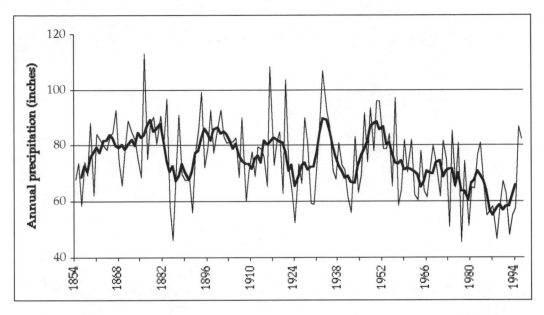

# Stream Flows

*Figure 7. Water year precipitation, Astoria, 1854-1996. Thin line shows annual totals, thick line 5-year running averages.*

Especially on an annual basis, undisturbed stream flows are highest during the wettest years, and reach their minimum values during dry periods. During this century, many of the rivers and streams in the state have been dammed, for hydroelectric or flood control purposes (or both). This has served to make stream flows more uniform, by mitigating the highest flows in winter and spring and maintaining higher minimum flows in summer and autumn.

Over the past fifty years, increases in reservoir storage capacity on the Columbia River system have intercepted the huge spring snowmelt peak, reducing the large late spring pulse of fresh water emptied into the sea near Astoria, and through this delay increasing the amount of fresh water sent to the sea in autumn and early winter. The freshwater plume that used to travel south on summer ocean currents has been reduced, and the northward-flowing plume in winter has increased. Decreases in salinity along the coast have consequently been noted as far as six hundred miles north of the mouth of the Columbia River. The consequences to estuarine environments are unknown.

# Frequency of Precipitation

Although the entire state can be considered "wet" by most standards, sites in the south experience significantly fewer days with measurable precipitation than those farther north. Table 3 shows the average number of days with measurable precipitation for stations throughout the state.

Table 3. Average number of days with measurable precipitation (.01 inch or more).

| Station | Zone | Jan | Feb | Mar | Apr | May | Jun | Jul | Aug | Sep | Oct | Nov | Dec | Year |
|---|---|---|---|---|---|---|---|---|---|---|---|---|---|---|
| Astoria WSO AP | 1 | 22 | 19 | 21 | 18 | 15 | 12 | 8 | 8 | 10 | 15 | 21 | 22 | 190 |
| Brookings | 1 | 17 | 16 | 18 | 13 | 9 | 6 | 4 | 5 | 6 | 11 | 18 | 18 | 141 |
| Corvallis | 2 | 19 | 17 | 18 | 15 | 12 | 7 | 3 | 4 | 8 | 13 | 20 | 21 | 158 |
| Eugene WSO AP | 2 | 17 | 15 | 16 | 12 | 10 | 6 | 3 | 4 | 6 | 10 | 17 | 18 | 134 |
| Portland WSO AP | 2 | 18 | 15 | 17 | 14 | 12 | 9 | 4 | 5 | 8 | 12 | 19 | 19 | 151 |
| Ashland | 3 | 12 | 11 | 12 | 10 | 8 | 6 | 2 | 3 | 5 | 8 | 14 | 14 | 105 |
| Medford WSO AP | 3 | 13 | 11 | 12 | 10 | 7 | 5 | 2 | 3 | 4 | 7 | 14 | 14 | 101 |
| Roseburg KQEN | 3 | 18 | 15 | 17 | 14 | 9 | 6 | 2 | 3 | 6 | 10 | 18 | 18 | 137 |
| Detroit Dam | 4 | 20 | 18 | 20 | 18 | 15 | 10 | 5 | 5 | 9 | 13 | 21 | 21 | 176 |
| Government Camp | 4 | 20 | 18 | 20 | 18 | 15 | 10 | 5 | 6 | 9 | 13 | 20 | 20 | 172 |
| McKenzie Bridge | 4 | 16 | 14 | 16 | 14 | 11 | 8 | 4 | 5 | 7 | 9 | 15 | 16 | 137 |
| Crater Lake | 5 | 17 | 16 | 19 | 14 | 10 | 8 | 3 | 5 | 6 | 10 | 17 | 18 | 142 |
| Silver Lake | 5 | 13 | 11 | 12 | 8 | 7 | 6 | 4 | 4 | 5 | 7 | 13 | 13 | 103 |
| Hood River Exp Stn | 6 | 16 | 14 | 14 | 12 | 8 | 6 | 3 | 4 | 6 | 10 | 18 | 17 | 128 |
| Moro | 6 | 11 | 9 | 11 | 8 | 7 | 5 | 3 | 4 | 4 | 7 | 13 | 11 | 91 |
| Pendleton WSO AP | 6 | 12 | 11 | 11 | 9 | 7 | 6 | 3 | 4 | 5 | 6 | 12 | 12 | 96 |
| Bend | 7 | 10 | 7 | 8 | 6 | 5 | 5 | 3 | 4 | 4 | 5 | 9 | 10 | 75 |
| Burns WSO | 7 | 9 | 9 | 13 | 8 | 9 | 6 | 3 | 4 | 5 | 6 | 12 | 10 | 99 |
| Klamath Falls | 7 | 11 | 9 | 11 | 7 | 6 | 5 | 2 | 3 | 3 | 6 | 11 | 12 | 86 |
| Enterprise 2 S | 8 | 11 | 11 | 14 | 12 | 13 | 11 | 7 | 7 | 7 | 7 | 14 | 10 | 120 |
| John Day | 8 | 11 | 9 | 10 | 10 | 10 | 9 | 3 | 5 | 5 | 7 | 11 | 12 | 101 |
| LaGrande | 8 | 12 | 9 | 12 | 11 | 10 | 9 | 4 | 5 | 6 | 8 | 11 | 11 | 108 |
| Ontario | 9 | 9 | 8 | 8 | 6 | 6 | 6 | 2 | 3 | 4 | 5 | 10 | 10 | 76 |
| Rome 2 NW | 9 | 4 | 3 | 4 | 4 | 4 | 4 | 2 | 2 | 3 | 3 | 5 | 4 | 41 |

Values represent 1961-1990 averages.

# Temperature

## Seasonal and Diurnal Characteristics

The strong marine influence near the coast causes both seasonal and diurnal temperatures to be mild and relatively uniform there compared with inland areas. In Oregon there is a gradual transition from the mild, wet coastal sites to the drier, more extreme inland valleys. The biggest climatic transition occurs at the Cascade crest. The Cascades effectively divide Oregon into two states: the generally wet, relatively mild western third and the mostly dry, more extreme eastern two-thirds. Table 4 lists temperature parameters for three Oregon sites at the same latitude: Newport, on the coast; Corvallis, in the Willamette Valley between the Coast Range and Cascades; and Madras, east of the Cascades. The Coast Range causes temperatures in Corvallis to be more extreme than those at Newport, while the additional barrier of the Cascade Mountains causes Madras to be even more extreme than Corvallis.

**Table 4. Comparison of temperature charateristics at a coastal site (Newport), a western valley location (Corvallis) and an eastern location (Madras), all at about the same latitude.**

| Parameter | Newport | Corvallis | Madras |
|---|---|---|---|
| Mean maximum in warmest month | 65.1 | 81.2 | 87.2 |
| Mean minimum in coldest month | 50.0 | 33.0 | 21.1 |
| Days with maximum 90°F or more | 0.5 | 13.5 | 33.3 |
| Days with maximum 32°F or less | 0.6 | 2.7 | 13.8 |
| Record high temperature | 100 | 108 | 112 |
| Record low temperature | 1 | -14 | -40 |
| Annual heating degree days @ 65°F | 5132 | 4818 | 6444 |
| Annual cooling degree days @ 65°F | 0 | 203 | 277 |

## Long-term Characteristics

Like precipitation, temperature shows significant year-to-year variations as well as noticeable longer-term trends. Figure 8 shows annual average temperatures in Corvallis since 1889. This location has several distinct advantages for evaluation of long-term temperature trends: there has been very little urban development near the station; data records are seldom missing; and there have been very few station relocations.

Corvallis data show a trend that is commonly seen in U.S. stations that are not subject to local biases, such as urban growth: the warmest temperatures of the century occurred in the late 1930s and early 1940s. This was followed by a cooler period in the next several decades, and warming in the last twenty years; however, temperatures have remained below those observed sixty years ago.

Figure 9 shows U.S. average temperatures from 1895 to 1997 for all Historical Climate Network (HCN) stations. HCN stations (of which Corvallis is one) are long-term, reliable observing sites which have had few moves and little or no nearby changes that would interfere with the recorded data. Notice the similarity between the Corvallis trend and the nationwide data.

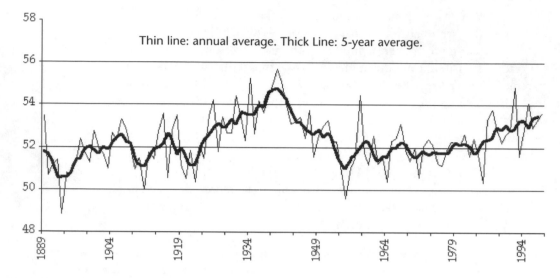

*Figure 8. Annual average temperatures in Corvallis, 1889-1997 (Oregon Climate Service).*

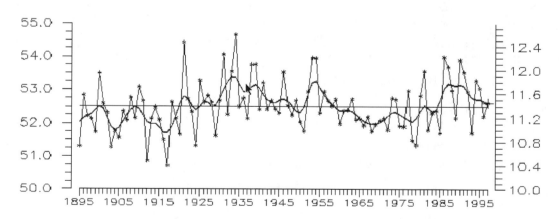

*Figure 9. U.S. annual average temperatures, 1895-1997 (National Climatic Data Center).*

# Winds

Local winds in Oregon are dominated by large-scale pressure patterns over the North Pacific and onshore. During winter (and, to a lesser extent, autumn and spring), frequent storms reach the area from the west, greatly influencing winds and other weather elements. Summer months see fewer strong storms, and are more typically characterized by sea and land breezes.

When the state is under the influence of cyclonic storms, large-scale winds tend to follow a particular pattern, although local terrain influences, and the location and intensity of the storms, can alter this pattern significantly. A typical succession prior to and following the arrival of a storm is as follows:

—As the storm approaches, winds begin to blow from the south or southeast. Wind speeds generally increase as the front associated with the storm gets nearer. For most coastal areas, these pre-frontal periods produce the highest wind speeds observed during the year.

—If passage of a warm front occurs, wind direction often changes, approaching from the southwest. Wind speeds may not change significantly.

—Passage of the cold front causes a sudden increase in pressure, decrease in wind speeds and temperature, and change in wind direction. Post-frontal winds are generally from the west and often gusty. Localized disturbances such as thunderstorms often produce local wind effects. These are generally miniature versions of the patterns described here: southerly winds prior to arrival, west winds following passage.

—As the frontal system continues moving eastward, high pressure builds onshore, causing steady decreases in wind speeds and gustiness. If storms are very close together, this step may be skipped entirely.

—Impending arrival of another storm system causes south winds to blow (see first step above) and the process repeats.

During summer, the North Pacific High, a quasi-stationary area of high pressure off the coast, exerts a significant influence on weather in the western U.S. The High moves northward in summer as the jet stream weakens and moves toward the pole. As a result, Pacific storms, which are already less vigorous than those in winter, tend to be diverted to the north.

Several times each year, very strong winds hit the coast. Wantz and Sinclair (1981) have published estimates of extreme winds in the Northwest. They estimate that speeds along the coast (sustained for an average of one minute and recurring on average every two years) are as high as 56 mph, while fifty-year events would produce winds of approximately 74 mph. Peak gusts would be about 40% higher. The most damaging storm in recent decades was the Columbus Day storm of October 11-13, 1962, which affected the entire state. During that storm, Naselle, Washington, reported a peak gust of 160 mph, while Mt. Hebo, Oregon, reported 131 mph and Portland, Oregon (Morrison St. Bridge), 116 mph. The storm caused an estimated $250 million and took fifty lives.

Fortunately, the Columbus Day storm was a very rare event. Storms of much lesser magnitude, however, can cause major damage, especially along the coast. This can include the downing of large trees ("wind throw") and other property damage. Although some areas near the coast are sheltered by the terrain, most of the coastal vicinity is quite exposed to wind damage during strong storms.

# Humidity

The presence of the Pacific, combined with generally mild temperatures, causes average relative humidity along the coast and in most western Oregon valleys to be quite high. Table 5 shows average relative humidities at several National Weather Service stations.

**Table 5. Average relative humidity (percent), monthly and annual**

| Station/time | J | F | M | A | M | J | J | A | S | O | N | D | Year |
|---|---|---|---|---|---|---|---|---|---|---|---|---|---|
| *Astoria* | | | | | | | | | | | | | |
| 0400 LST | 86 | 87 | 88 | 89 | 90 | 90 | 90 | 91 | 91 | 90 | 88 | 87 | 89 |
| 1000 LST | 84 | 82 | 78 | 74 | 74 | 75 | 75 | 77 | 75 | 81 | 83 | 85 | 79 |
| 1600 LST | 78 | 74 | 71 | 69 | 70 | 71 | 69 | 70 | 69 | 73 | 77 | 80 | 73 |
| 2200 LST | 85 | 86 | 86 | 85 | 85 | 85 | 86 | 88 | 88 | 88 | 87 | 86 | 86 |
| *Eugene* | | | | | | | | | | | | | |
| 0400 LST | 92 | 92 | 92 | 91 | 91 | 90 | 88 | 88 | 89 | 94 | 93 | 93 | 91 |
| 1000 LST | 88 | 86 | 78 | 71 | 66 | 63 | 57 | 60 | 65 | 80 | 87 | 89 | 74 |
| 1600 LST | 80 | 73 | 64 | 58 | 54 | 49 | 38 | 39 | 43 | 62 | 79 | 84 | 60 |
| 2200 LST | 91 | 90 | 86 | 83 | 82 | 79 | 73 | 73 | 77 | 88 | 92 | 92 | 84 |
| *Medford* | | | | | | | | | | | | | |
| 0400 LST | 90 | 88 | 86 | 84 | 83 | 79 | 74 | 75 | 79 | 86 | 92 | 91 | 84 |
| 1000 LST | 88 | 83 | 73 | 63 | 56 | 48 | 45 | 47 | 53 | 69 | 87 | 89 | 67 |
| 1600 LST | 71 | 57 | 50 | 45 | 39 | 33 | 26 | 27 | 29 | 43 | 68 | 76 | 47 |
| 2200 LST | 87 | 82 | 75 | 70 | 65 | 59 | 51 | 52 | 60 | 76 | 88 | 89 | 71 |
| *Pendleton* | | | | | | | | | | | | | |
| 0400 LST | 81 | 79 | 74 | 71 | 69 | 66 | 54 | 54 | 61 | 72 | 79 | 82 | 70 |
| 1000 LST | 78 | 71 | 59 | 51 | 47 | 42 | 34 | 36 | 42 | 55 | 72 | 78 | 55 |
| 1600 LST | 75 | 65 | 49 | 42 | 37 | 32 | 23 | 26 | 32 | 46 | 69 | 78 | 48 |
| 2200 LST | 80 | 77 | 69 | 63 | 58 | 52 | 39 | 41 | 51 | 66 | 78 | 81 | 63 |
| *Portland* | | | | | | | | | | | | | |
| 0400 LST | 85 | 86 | 86 | 86 | 85 | 84 | 82 | 94 | 87 | 90 | 88 | 87 | 86 |
| 1000 LST | 82 | 80 | 73 | 69 | 66 | 65 | 62 | 64 | 67 | 78 | 82 | 83 | 73 |
| 1600 LST | 75 | 67 | 60 | 55 | 53 | 49 | 45 | 45 | 48 | 62 | 74 | 78 | 59 |
| 2200 LST | 83 | 81 | 78 | 75 | 73 | 71 | 68 | 70 | 75 | 94 | 84 | 85 | 77 |

LST = Local Standard Time

Relative humidity is only part of the picture, however. In general, the air over Oregon actually holds relatively small amounts of moisture, at least compared with some other parts of the U.S. Relative humidity is the actual amount of water vapor, compared with how much the air can hold when it's "saturated." And air is saturated when it is holding all the water vapor it can possibly hold. If air is saturated, the relative humidity is 100%.

But saturation depends on air temperature. The warmer the air, the more water the air can hold before reaching saturation. Think of a sponge: the bigger the sponge, the more water it can hold. And warmer air is like having a bigger sponge.

Off the coast of Oregon, the water is always cool (or downright cold). Thus the air over the water is also cool, and its capacity to hold water vapor is restricted. Evaporation is also reduced by the cool water temperatures—the cooler the water, the less evaporation there is. But the water off the southern and eastern U.S. is *much* warmer, especially in summer. Warm water and warm air result in high rates of evaporation, and a high capacity to hold water vapor (a "big sponge").

The best way to actually measure this is by means of "dew point" (or dew point temperature), which represents the actual amount of water vapor in the air. Dew point tells us precisely how much water vapor is in the air, and he greater the amount of water vapor, the higher the dew point. In western Oregon, typical dew points are in the 40s and 50s. In Florida or Georgia, they're often in the 70s. There's more than twice as much water vapor in the air when the dew point is 70 than when it's 50. And that's why it feels so sticky in the east during the summer.

**Table 6. Average monthly dew point (°F).**

| City | Jan | Feb | Mar | Apr | May | Jun | Jul | Aug | Sep | Oct | Nov | Dec |
|---|---|---|---|---|---|---|---|---|---|---|---|---|
| **Portland** | **33** | **36** | **37** | **41** | **46** | **50** | **53** | **54** | **51** | **47** | **40** | **36** |
| **Medford** | **32** | **34** | **35** | **38** | **42** | **46** | **49** | **49** | **45** | **43** | **37** | **34** |
| **Pendleton** | **24** | **30** | **30** | **34** | **40** | **42** | **43** | **43** | **41** | **39** | **33** | **29** |
| Miami | 57 | 59 | 61 | 63 | 68 | 72 | 73 | 74 | 74 | 69 | 63 | 58 |
| Atlanta | 34 | 34 | 39 | 48 | 57 | 65 | 68 | 67 | 62 | 51 | 40 | 34 |
| St. Louis | 22 | 25 | 30 | 42 | 52 | 62 | 66 | 64 | 56 | 46 | 33 | 26 |
| Washington, D.C. | 25 | 25 | 29 | 40 | 52 | 61 | 65 | 64 | 59 | 48 | 36 | 26 |
| New York | 22 | 23 | 27 | 38 | 47 | 57 | 62 | 62 | 56 | 46 | 35 | 26 |
| Boston | 19 | 19 | 25 | 34 | 44 | 55 | 60 | 60 | 53 | 44 | 34 | 22 |
| Minneapolis | 6 | 10 | 20 | 32 | 43 | 55 | 60 | 59 | 50 | 40 | 25 | 13 |

But though dew point is a precise measure of water vapor, relative humidity can be misleading. Consider a rainy winter day in Oregon (easy to imagine), with a temperature of 36°F and 100% relative humidity; thus, a dew point of 36. Now compare that with a hot, dry summer day in Death Valley, with a temperature of 122°F and a bone-dry relative humidity of 7%. If we computed the dew point we'd find it to be 37. But wait, that's *higher* than on the rainy Oregon day. There is actually *more* water vapor in the air on a hot summer day in Death Valley than on a rainy winter day in Oregon, even though the relative humidity is much, much lower in Death Valley.

Table 6 shows average monthly dew point in Oregon and at several stations in the eastern half of the United States. Notice in particular the contrast in the summer dew points.

# Cloud Cover and Solar Radiation

Near the coast, there is frequent and persistent cloud cover throughout the year. However, cloudiness often drops significantly within a few miles of the coast, especially during the warm season, as a result of air temperature increases. During winter, when the area is dominated by large-scale storm systems, cloud cover tends to be much more uniform throughout the area.

Table 7 shows average monthly cloud cover at stations throughout Oregon. Table 8 shows the percentage of possible sunshine for three sites: Portland and Roseburg in western Oregon and Baker in extreme eastern Oregon.

## Table 7. Average cloud cover (percent) for Oregon stations

| Site | Jan | Feb | Mar | Apr | May | Jun | Jul | Aug | Sep | Oct | Nov | Dec | Ann |
|------|-----|-----|-----|-----|-----|-----|-----|-----|-----|-----|-----|-----|-----|
| Astoria | 85 | 84 | 81 | 81 | 77 | 78 | 67 | 66 | 63 | 74 | 80 | 86 | 77 |
| Baker | 69 | 67 | 63 | 59 | 57 | 50 | 28 | 28 | 38 | 45 | 60 | 67 | 53 |
| Burns | 76 | 72 | 67 | 63 | 61 | 50 | 25 | 34 | 33 | 49 | 65 | 73 | 56 |
| Eugene | 85 | 81 | 79 | 72 | 67 | 62 | 36 | 44 | 49 | 71 | 83 | 89 | 68 |
| Klamath Falls | 84 | 66 | 64 | 59 | 67 | 43 | 13 | 29 | 25 | 43 | 65 | 75 | 51 |
| La Grande | 81 | 79 | 80 | 64 | 47 | 58 | 20 | 36 | 40 | 58 | 71 | 85 | 61 |
| Meacham | 85 | 84 | 80 | 76 | 62 | 61 | 31 | 39 | 47 | 65 | 80 | 84 | 67 |
| Medford | 82 | 76 | 72 | 66 | 69 | 48 | 21 | 23 | 33 | 56 | 75 | 86 | 58 |
| North Bend | 86 | 76 | 75 | 66 | 59 | 61 | 46 | 56 | 55 | 63 | 73 | 82 | 67 |
| Pendleton | 82 | 80 | 72 | 66 | 61 | 52 | 26 | 33 | 40 | 57 | 77 | 84 | 61 |
| Portland | 85 | 84 | 82 | 77 | 60 | 68 | 46 | 53 | 56 | 72 | 81 | 89 | 72 |
| Redmond | 80 | 70 | 70 | 56 | 73 | 53 | 15 | 34 | 30 | 45 | 68 | 72 | 51 |
| Roseburg | 87 | 84 | 80 | 72 | 50 | 57 | 30 | 38 | 48 | 71 | 85 | 89 | 67 |
| Salem | 83 | 82 | 79 | 73 | 68 | 65 | 40 | 47 | 51 | 69 | 80 | 88 | 69 |
| Sexton Summit | 77 | 77 | 77 | 68 | 70 | 48 | 23 | 28 | 35 | 56 | 73 | 77 | 58 |
| Troutdale | 81 | 84 | 86 | 72 | 62 | 68 | 49 | 52 | 52 | 75 | 81 | 87 | 71 |

## Table 8. Monthly percent of possible sunshine

| Site | Jan | Feb | Mar | Apr | May | Jun | Jul | Aug | Sep | Oct | Nov | Dec | Ann |
|------|-----|-----|-----|-----|-----|-----|-----|-----|-----|-----|-----|-----|-----|
| Baker | 41 | 49 | 56 | 61 | 63 | 67 | 83 | 81 | 74 | 62 | 46 | 37 | 60 |
| Portland | 24 | 32 | 37 | 47 | 51 | 47 | 67 | 61 | 58 | 38 | 29 | 21 | 45 |
| Roseburg | 26 | 30 | 39 | 49 | 52 | 61 | 79 | 74 | 68 | 42 | 25 | 20 | 50 |

# Snow

Snow is relatively rare along the immediate coastlinethroughout the state; as one moves inland or to higher elevations, the amount of snowfall reported per year increases steadily. For example, Laurel Mountain, in the Coast Range at 3590 feet above sea level, averages 110 inches of snow per year. Assuming a ratio of snow to water of 10:1, this represents about 10% of Laurel Mountain's average annual precipitation of 116 inches. Newport, at sea level, averages 1.57 inches of snowfall, which would represent only 0.2% of its annual average of 72.04 inches.

In the Willamette Valley, Portland Airport averages 36.12 inches of precipitation and 5.44 inches of snow, so the water in the snow represents 1.5% of the annual average. Government Camp, near Mt. Hood (at about 4,000 feet in elevation) gets an average of 86.03 inches of precipitation and 278 inches of snow, so the snowfall there makes up about 32% of the total precipitation.

The mildness of the Willamette Valley and other western Oregon inland valleys means snow is rare. In the Cascades, however, snow is frequent and significant. Eastern Oregon also receives a significant percentage of its winter precipitation in the form of snow, although the lower annual precipitation makes the actual snowfall amounts much lower than in the Cascades. Table 9 lists average monthly and annual snowfall at various Oregon stations.

Figure 10 shows the average annual snowfall (1961-90 averages) across Oregon. While the Cascades, and mountains in northeast and southwest Oregon, show up as expected, it may surprise many to see the high amounts in the Coast Range; despite their proximity to the ocean, the higher peaks in the Coast Range (in excess of 3,000 feet in some places) pick up significant snowfall amounts.

*The National Weather Service defines several categories of snowfall, based on the rate of fall and the prevailing winds or visibility:*

**Snow flurries.** *Light snow falling for short durations. No accumulation or just a light dusting is all that is expected.*

**Snow showers.** *Snow falling at varying intensities for brief periods of time. Some accumulation is possible.*

**Squalls.** *Brief, intense snow showers accompanied by strong, gusty winds. Accumulation may be significant. Snow squalls are best known in the Great Lakes region.*

**Blowing snow.** *Wind-driven snow that reduces visibility and causes significant drifting. Blowing snow may be snow that is falling and/or loose snow on the ground picked up by the wind.*

**Blizzard.** *Winds over 35 mph with snow and blowing snow reducing visibility to near zero.*

**Table 9. Average monthly and annual snowfall (in inches) at Oregon stations.**

| Station | Zone | Jan | Feb | Mar | Apr | May | Jun | Jul | Aug | Sep | Oct | Nov | Dec | Ann. |
|---|---|---|---|---|---|---|---|---|---|---|---|---|---|---|
| Astoria WSO AP | 1 | 2.2 | .4 | .4 | .1 | | | | | | | .2 | 1.4 | 4.7 |
| Brookings | 1 | .2 | .3 | .1 | | | | | | | | | .1 | .4 |
| Corvallis | 2 | 2.2 | 1.3 | .2 | | | | | | | | .2 | 1.6 | 5.7 |
| Eugene WSO AP | 2 | 3.1 | .9 | .2 | | | | | | | | .2 | 1.7 | 6.1 |
| Portland WSO AP | 2 | 1.8 | .9 | .1 | | | | | | | | .5 | 2.0 | 5.4 |
| Ashland | 3 | 2.7 | 1.2 | 1.0 | .5 | | | | | | | .3 | 2.4 | 8.4 |
| Medford WSO AP | 3 | 3.0 | .8 | .7 | .2 | | | | | | | .4 | 2.3 | 7.5 |
| Roseburg KQEN | 3 | 2.3 | .6 | .1 | | | | | | | | .0 | .7 | 4.0 |
| Belknap Springs | 4 | 24.4 | 15.9 | 13.3 | 2.7 | .2 | | | | | .3 | 6.8 | 22.3 | 88.0 |
| Detroit Dam | 4 | 7.9 | 3.7 | 2.2 | .4 | | | | | | | 1.0 | 3.5 | 18.2 |
| Government Camp | 4 | 61.6 | 44.6 | 49.2 | 29.8 | 7.5 | .2 | | | .3 | 6.4 | 34.1 | 52.7 | 278.2 |
| McKenzie Bridge | 4 | 13.2 | 6.9 | 4.3 | .4 | | | | | | .3 | 2.6 | 8.8 | 40.1 |
| Crater Lake | 5 | 85.3 | 73.2 | 87.5 | 43.0 | 19.3 | 4.0 | .5 | .2 | 4.1 | 21.3 | 69.1 | 84.0 | 495.0 |
| Silver Lake | 5 | 5.0 | 2.7 | 3.1 | 1.4 | .7 | | | | | .3 | 2.2 | 6.4 | 18.6 |
| Hood River Exp Stn | 6 | 14.0 | 6.4 | 1.5 | | | | | | | | 3.4 | 9.9 | 36.5 |
| Moro | 6 | 6.0 | 2.7 | 1.2 | .2 | | | | | | .2 | 2.5 | 6.2 | 19.3 |
| Pendleton WSO AP | 6 | 6.1 | 2.1 | 1.0 | .2 | | | | | | .2 | 2.2 | 5.2 | 17.0 |
| Bend | 7 | 10.0 | 3.9 | 4.1 | 2.0 | .3 | | | | | .2 | 5.6 | 9.5 | 34.8 |
| Burns WSO | 7 | 6.6 | 6.9 | 4.6 | 1.0 | .3 | .1 | | | | .6 | 6.4 | 10.4 | 42.3 |
| Klamath Falls | 7 | 9.3 | 4.7 | 3.7 | .9 | .1 | | | | | .5 | 4.5 | 10.0 | 34.9 |
| Enterprise 2 S | 8 | 12.0 | 8.2 | 8.1 | 5.0 | 1.4 | | | | .2 | 1.3 | 7.6 | 9.4 | 52.6 |
| John Day | 8 | 6.2 | 3.7 | 3.2 | 1.2 | .1 | | | | | .3 | 2.5 | 7.1 | 24.0 |
| LaGrande | 8 | 9.0 | 4.7 | 1.7 | .7 | | | | | | .2 | 3.0 | 7.4 | 28.7 |
| Ontario | 9 | 7.2 | 2.8 | .7 | .1 | | | | | | .1 | 2.2 | 6.7 | 20.3 |
| Rome 2 NW | 9 | 4.4 | .8 | 1.4 | .5 | .2 | | | | | .2 | 1.7 | 3.7 | 13.5 |

Values represent 1961-1990 averages. Blank cells indicate 0 or negligible snow for that month.

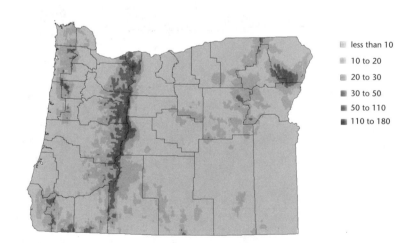

*Figure 10. Average annual snow water equivalent (inches) (1961-90 averages) across Oregon.*

less than 10
10 to 20
20 to 30
30 to 50
50 to 110
110 to 180

# Fronts—A More Detailed Look

In a previous section, the formation of fronts in a mid-latitude system was described. Each type of front has its own characteristics, and its unique influence on weather conditions.

## Warm Front

A warm front is the separation between warm and cold air when the warm air is moving into and replacing the colder air mass. The air behind a warm front is also generally more moist than in the colder air ahead of the front. There is usually a change in wind direction when the front passes.

Warm fronts occur at the leading edge of mid-latitude storms. Not every storm reaching Oregon has an active warm front, since the front may have occluded—been overtaken by a cold front—before arriving here. When they do occur, warm fronts produce characteristic weather conditions at the surface.

Table 10 is a summary of weather conditions before, during, and after passage of a warm front. See Cloud Table at right for keys to cloud types.

| Cloud types | |
| --- | --- |
| As | Altostratus |
| Cb | Cumulonimbus |
| Ci | Cirrus |
| Cs | Cirrostratus |
| Ns | Nimbostratus |
| Sc | Stratocumulus |
| St | Stratus |
| TCU | Towering cumulus |

**Table 10. Characteristics of a warm front**

| Weather element | Before passing | While passing | After passing |
| --- | --- | --- | --- |
| Winds | South-southeast | Variable | South-southwest |
| Temperature | Cool-cold, slow warming | Steady ride | Warmer, then steady |
| Pressure | Usually falling | Leveling off | Slight rise, followed by fall |
| Clouds | In this order: Ci, Cs, As, Ns, St, and fog; occasionally Cb in summer | Stratus-type | Clearing with scattered Sc; occasionally Cb in summer |
| Precipitation | Light-to-moderate rain, snow, sleet, or drizzle | Drizzle or none | Usually none, sometimes light rain or showers |
| Visibility | Poor | Poor, but improving | Fair in haze |
| Dew point | Steady rise | Steady | Rise, then steady |

Reference: Ahrens, C. Donald, "Meteorology Today," Fifth edition.

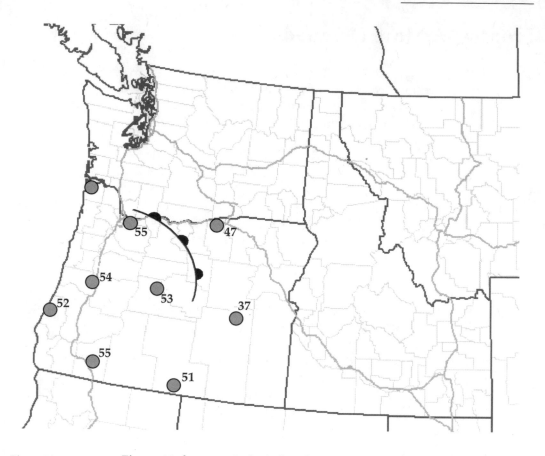

*Figure 11.*
*Typical*
*temperatures*
*ahead of and*
*following passage*
*of a warm front.*
*The front is*
*shown by a*
*curved line with*
*half-circle*
*markers, and is*
*moving from*
*southwest to*
*northeast.*

Figure 11 shows typical wind and temperature conditions in the vicinity of a warm front; the letters correspond to the locations described below. The front is indicated by the thick line with (warm air) semicircles pointing away from the warmer air, in the direction of movement of the front.

*A. Well ahead of the front.* Winds are generally from the southeast, and increasing. Temperatures are cool. High clouds may appear overhead or on the horizon.

*B. Approaching the front.* Winds are still from the southeast, and stronger. Temperatures have changed little. Clouds have lowered, and light rain has begun.

*C. Very near the front.* Winds and temperatures are unchanged. Clouds are lower still, and light rain continues and increases in intensity.

*D. Behind the front.* A wind shift occurred as the front passed over, and winds are now from the south. Temperatures have gone up markedly, as has the humidity.

# Cold Front

A cold front is the separation between warm and cold air where the cold air is moving into and replacing the warm air mass. There is usually a change in wind direction when the front passes.

Cold fronts occur at the trailing edge of mid-latitude storms. Since they move faster than warm fronts, they generally overtake them, producing occluded fronts. Cold fronts are usually associated with the most severe weather in a mid-latitude system.

Figure 12 shows typical wind and temperature conditions in the vicinity of a cold front; the letters correspond to the locations described below. The front is indicated by the thick line with (cold air) arrows pointing away from the cold air, in the direction of movement of the front.

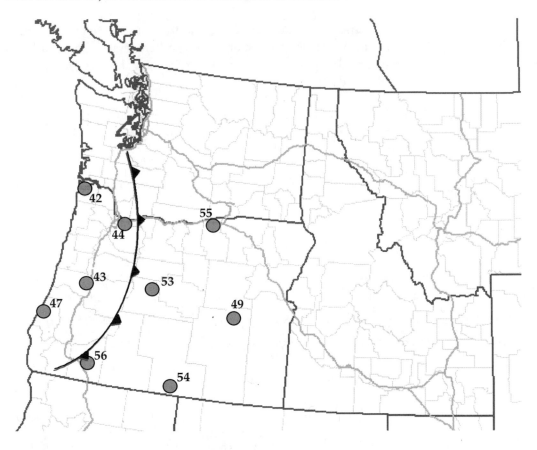

*Figure 12. Typical temperatures ahead of and following passage of a cold front. The curved line denotes the front, which is moving from west to east.*

*A. Well ahead of the front.* This is the same position as D on Figure 10. Temperatures are relatively high; in fact, the highest winter temperatures in Oregon nearly always occur at these pre-frontal locations. Winds are from the south and can be quite strong. Skies are partly cloudy to cloudy. There may be some rain, but it is probably intermittent.

*B. Approaching the front.* Winds are still from the south, and stronger. Temperatures have changed little. Thick clouds have approached from the west. Rain may have begun.

*C. Very near the front.* Winds have continued to strengthen, but temperatures are unchanged. Clouds are thicker and darker. Rain (or snow) has become very intense.

*D. Behind the front.* A wind shift occurred as the front passed over earlier, and winds are now from the west or northwest. Temperatures have dropped markedly, and the air is drier. Intermittent rain/snow showers continue, but sun breaks (in daytime) may occur.

*E. Well behind the front.* Winds continue, but are not as strong. Showers have become less frequent. Sun breaks are more common. Rainbows are often spotted.

Table 11 is a summary of weather conditions before, during, and after passage of a cold front. See Cloud Table on page 25 for keys to cloud types.

## Table 11. Characteristics of a cold front

| Weather element | Before passing | While passing | After passing |
| --- | --- | --- | --- |
| Winds | South-southwest | Gusty; shifting | West-northwest |
| Temperature | Warm | Sudden drop | Steadily dropping |
| Pressure | Falling steadily | Minimum, then sharp ride | Rising steadily |
| Clouds | Increasing Ci, Cs, then Tcu or Cb | Tcu or Cb | Often Cu |
| Precipitation | Short period showers | Heavy showers of rain or snow, sometimes with hail, thunder, and lightning | Showers, then clearing |
| Visibility | Fair to poor in haze | Poor, followed by improving | Good except in showers |
| Dew point | High; remains steady | Sharp drop | Lowering |

Reference: Ahrens, C. Donald, "Meteorology Today," Fifth edition.

# Occluded Front

When a cold front has overtaken a warm front, the warm air is completely displaced from the surface as advancing cold air meets the cold air which previously lay to the east of the warm front. Since the contrast between the air masses across an occluded front is much less than that across either a warm or a cold front, the weather associated with it is less significant. Clouds, precipitation, and wind gusts are common, but they tend to be less intense than in a well-developed cold front.

Table 12 is a summary of weather conditions before, during, and after passage of an occluded front. See Cloud Table on page 25  for keys to cloud types.

**Table 12. Characteristics of occluded front**

| Weather element | Before passing | While passing | After passing |
|---|---|---|---|
| Winds | Southeast-south | Variable | West to northwest |
| Temperature | | | |
|   Cold Type | Cold-cool | Dropping | Colder |
|   Warm Type | Cold | Rising | Milder |
| Pressure | Usually falling | Low point | Usually rising |
| Clouds | In this order: Ci, Cs, As, Ns | Ns, sometimes Tcu and Cb | Ns, As, or scattered Cs |
| Precipitation | Light, moderate, or heavy | Light, moderate, or heavy continuous precipitation or showers | Light-to-moderate precipitation followed by general clearing |
| Visibility | Poor in precipitation | Poor in precipitation | Improving |
| Dew point | Steady | Usually slight drop, especially if cold-occluded | Slight drop, although may rise a bit if warm-occluded |

Reference: Ahrens, C. Donald, "Meteorology Today," Fifth edition.

## Stationary Front

A boundary between warm and cold air masses which moves very slowly, if at all, is known as a stationary front. If there is very little upper-air wind movement, or if winds are parallel to the frontal boundary, the front is often stationary.

Stationary fronts in Oregon are most common in winter, when cold arctic air moving into eastern Oregon meets milder Pacific air. There is a substantial temperature difference between the cold and mild air masses. Clouds usually occur along the front, but they are generally not extensive; precipitation is minimal, since lack of air movement toward the front keeps uplift to a minimum.

Figure 13 illustrates a typical stationary front in Oregon. The front is designated by the thick line, with (cold air) triangles pointing from the cold to warm air and (warm air) semicircles in the opposite direction. Notice the strong contrast in temperatures on either side of the front.

*Figure 13. Typical temperatures on either side of a stationary front.*

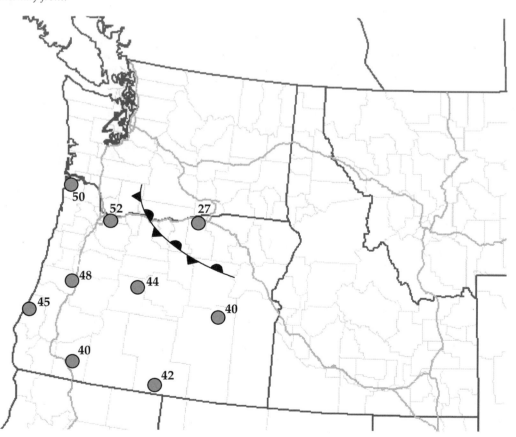

# Local Winds

**W**inds at any location are affected by a number of factors. In general, winds blow from high to low pressure, but rotation of the Earth changes this slightly. Rather than blowing directly away from high pressure or directly in toward low pressure, winds blow at an angle to isobars, which are lines of equal pressure. Figure 14 illustrates typical wind direction in the vicinity of a high (H) and a low (L) pressure area. The circular lines are isobars. Notice how winds blow outward from the high, but at an angle of roughly 60°F, barring other influences such as terrain. They also blow in toward a low, at a similar angle. The greater the difference in pressure in a given area, the closer together are the isobars, and the stronger the winds.

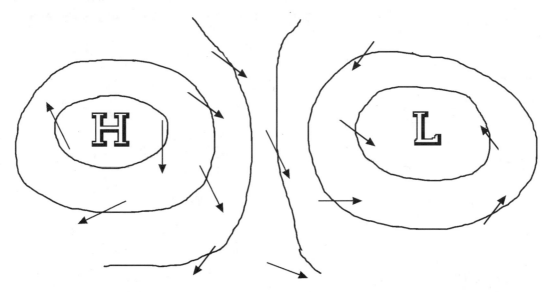

Actual winds can be significantly different from this idealized figure. Winds can vary depending on terrain and other surface obstacles, the presence of a storm system, and temperature differences between nearby areas. Winds can change during the day, from day to day, and seasonally. Below are some of the factors that influence local winds.

*Figure 14. Typical wind direction in the vicinity of areas of high (H) and low (L) pressure.*

# Cyclonic Storms

Mid-latitude storms exert a strong influence on local wind speed and direction. Rising and descending air and horizontal pressure gradients play a key role in determining winds.

Figure 15 shows isobars, frontal positions, and approximate wind vectors (assuming flat terrain) for an idealized cyclonic storm. Locations 1, 2, and 3 show sites in three areas in the storm (or the relative location of one site at three different times, as the storm approaches, arrives, and leaves the area). The vertical cross-section below is along the line connecting the three points.

The cross-sectional diagram shows the generally rising air at the two frontal locations, descending air in the higher pressure behind the cold front, and horizontal winds elsewhere. Notice also that air circulation tends to be closed: air rising at the frontal boundaries connects in a closed circulation with the descending air in higher pressure to the east and west of the storm.

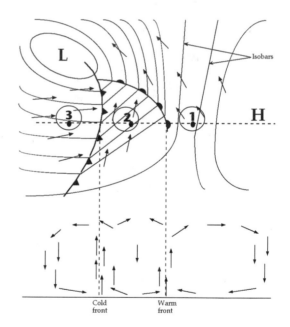

*Figure 15. Isobars and winds in the vicinity of a typical cyclonic storm. Top diagram shows horizontal winds (arrows); bottom diagram shows vertical air flow.*

**Location 1.** *Winds are from the southeast. Pressure is falling. Warm front clouds (cirrus, altostratus, etc.) are observed. Precipitation is likely; it is generally light and steady.*

**Location 2.** *Winds are from the south, generally strong and gusty. Pressure is falling. Precipitation is possible, but less likely than at 1.*

**Location 3.** *Winds from the west or southwest. Pressure is rising rapidly. Precipitation is possible (convective, showery). Temperatures are considerably colder than earlier.*

# Sea Breeze and Land Breeze

Figures 16 and 17 show wind and pressure patterns over Oregon for two idealized cases: high pressure offshore, and high pressure onshore.

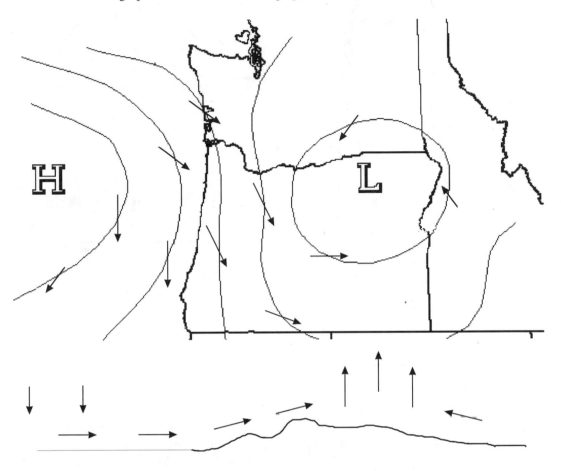

*Figure 16. High pressure offshore ("sea breeze"). High pressure is offshore, low pressure onshore. This occurs day or night during the summer; during the daytime in spring or fall; or the day after a cyclonic storm. This is a common summertime pattern, particularly in the daytime, when high temperatures inland cause lower surface pressure due to convection. Offshore air remains cool due to the rather cold ocean temperatures. General air flow is onshore, but local wind directions vary somewhat. At the coast, winds are from the north due to the orientation of the isobars. Onshore winds are from the west or northwest, but locally can be very different due to terrain influences. Strong winds tend to funnel eastward through the Columbia Gorge.*

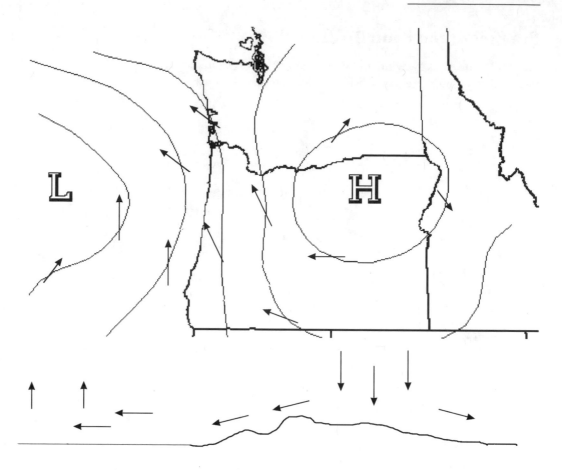

*Figure 17. High pressure onshore ("land breeze"). High pressure is onshore, low pressure offshore. This occurs in the nighttime during fair weather throughout the year; day or night during the cool season; or the day before a cyclonic storm. This is a common cool-season pattern, when colder air over inland areas causes higher surface pressures. The sea surface is now warmer than most inland areas (east of the Cascades). If the storm track is far to the north, cyclonic storms will not disrupt this pattern, and it can persist for many days. Winds are generally easterly over most of the inland areas, and can be locally strong, especially near canyons (the Gorge again serves to funnel air, this time toward the west).*

# Lake Effects

Lakes and other large bodies of water can exert an influence on local winds. Figure 18 shows cross-sections of wind movement during periods when the lake is warmer or cooler than surrounding air.

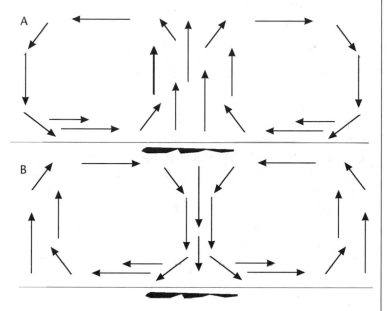

*Figure 18. A. The lake is relatively warm compared with its surroundings; this is most common at night or during the cooler seasons. Warmer air over the lake tends to rise. Air from surrounding areas flows toward the lake to replace the rising air. Closed circulations, with descending air over areas adjacent to the lake, tend to occur, particularly during calm conditions. B. The lake is relatively cool compared with nearby areas.; this is most common during the warm season, especially in the daytime. Air rises over the warmer land areas adjacent to the lake, descends over the lake, and flows at the surface away from the lake.*

## Urban "Heat Island"

The term "heat island" was coined several decades ago when researchers noticed that the atmosphere in and above urban areas was often significantly warmer than surrounding areas due to urban activities, including space heating, industrial activities, and transportation. Much of the early research was done in the St. Louis area, where temperature effects were measured, and where precipitation enhancement was shown to occur.

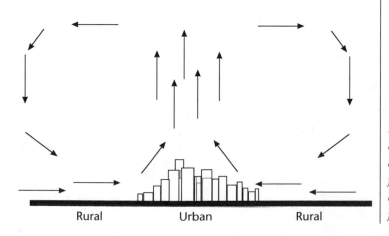

Rural          Urban          Rural

*Figure 19. Typical horizontal and vertical air circulation in and around an urban area. Heat from the city causes air to rise consistently; this pulls in air from surrounding rural areas.*

Figure 19 shows idealized air flow patterns in and around an urban area. Urban areas tend to stay warmer than rural landscapes throughout the year, so this pattern is much more consistent than those described earlier. The warmer air over the urban sections causes rising air and lower surface pressure. This in turn results in air flow into the city from surrounding rural areas. Aloft, there is a closed circulation, which includes descending air over the rural areas.

## Mountain-valley Circulation

Mountain and valley circulations develop in complex topography along mountain slopes. During the daytime (Figure 20a), sunlight warms the valley floor, warming the near-surface air. Due to lower density, this air rises as a gentle upward-moving wind known as an upslope or valley wind. At night (Figure 20b), this trend reverses. Cooler air at high elevations flows downslope into the valley, resulting in a mountain or drainage wind. This cycle is most prevalent during clear, warm weather with light winds.

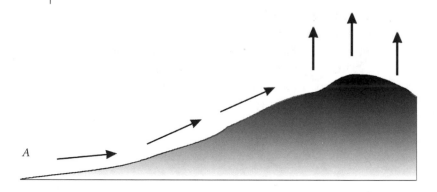

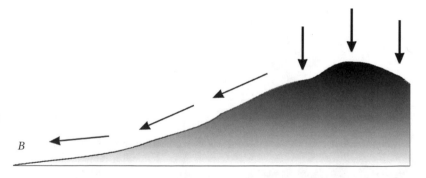

*Figure 20. Mountain-valley wind circulation. (A) daytime (mountain) flow; (B) nighttime (valley) flow.*

# Katabatic Winds

The term "katabatic" refers to downslope winds that are much stronger than typical mountain breezes. Many parts of the world experience katabatic winds, and a number of different local names for these winds exist. The strongest katabatic winds are those with a significant elevation change from high mountain or plateau to low valley or plain; if air is confined to narrow valleys or canyons, speeds can be especially strong.

Figure 21 shows typical pressure patterns and wind vectors during a Santa Ana wind event. The "Coho" wind (see Wind Storm chapter) is a local example of a katabatic wind.

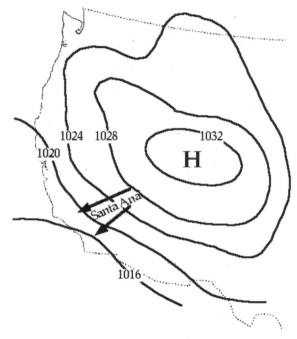

*Figure 21. Typical air pressure patterns during "Santa Ana" wind conditions. Santa Anas funnel through eastern California valleys, often producing high winds in coastal sections.*

*A few examples of katabatic winds are:*

**Santa Ana**—*east winds in Southern California*

**Chinook**—*along eastern slopes of Rockies (westerly wind)*

**Bora**—*northeast wind along the northern Adriatic (Yugoslavia)*

**Mistral**—*east wind in the Rhone Valley of France*

**Sirocco**—*southerly wind along the North African coast*

**Brick fielder**—*westerly wind along the eastern Australian coast*

# PART 3

# Forecasting and Talking about the Weather

# Tips for Amateur Weather Forecasters

**M**any residents of Oregon own and operate weather-recording instruments of various kinds. Others spend time observing winds, clouds, and other parameters. In either case, evidence about weather conditions later in the day or in days to come is often available for those who can "discern the signs."

Folklore abounds with weather-related wisdom, including the famous "red sky in morning, sailor take warning; red sky at night, sailor's delight." That phrase actually originated in the Bible; in Matthew 16, Jesus said,

> *When it is evening, you say, "It will be fair weather, for the sky is red." And in the morning, "There will be a storm today, for the sky is red and threatening." Do you know how to discern the appearance of the sky, but cannot discern the signs of the times?*

Here are some tips on how alert weather-watchers can interpret weather signs without turning on the TV news or the Weather Channel!

## Wind

Wind direction tells a great deal about future weather. Although winds are often affected very strongly by terrain and such surface features as trees and buildings, general wind direction is a useful indicator. Sometimes low-level cloud movement is the best gauge of winds in the lower atmosphere.

The general rule of thumb in the Northern Hemisphere is if one stands with the wind to one's back, low pressure is to the left, slightly forward of one's left side. Thus, strong winds from the south indicate low pressure to the west, and since weather systems generally move from west to east (especially in winter), south winds precede the arrival of a low-pressure storm. Similarly, northwest winds are a sign that the storm center is to the east, and likely moving away from the area.

## Barometers

Many living-room walls are adorned with barometers or barometer-thermometers which serve no purpose other than decoration. A lot of information can be gleaned from barometers, even decorative ones, but only if the observer pays attention to trends.

The simple rule is that an approaching storm causes the barometer to fall sharply, since barometers measure atmospheric pressure and storms have low-pressure centers. As soon as a storm center, or its associated surface front, passes an area the barometer begins to rise. In general, the faster the change, the more powerful the storm system and the stronger the winds.

Pressure change also occurs when temperatures change, so observers should not be fooled by slight changes, which are typical during the day—warmer afternoon temperatures cause pressure to fall, while cooler nighttime conditions are associated with rising pressures. These diurnal changes, however, are small compared with those associated with storm systems.

An interesting exercise is to record the barometer reading every day at the same time for a period of a week or two, plot the values on a chart or graph, and make annotations about the weather conditions each day. It is not necessary to "calibrate" a barometer; merely view the day-to-day trend and see how it compares with the actual weather. In Oregon, do this exercise in the cold season—changes in pressure are much more dramatic then than during summer.

Richard Inwards' classic "Weather Lore," published in 1893, contains thousands of proverbs, sayings, and rules concerning the weather. Table 11 is his Barometer Warning table; compass points are abbreviated (N is north, NE northeast, and so on):

**Table 13. Barometer reading and corresponding weather to be expected**

| Barometer warning | Indicating |
| --- | --- |
| Mercury falls during a high wind from the SW, SSW, W, or S | Increasing storm |
| If the fall be rapid | Violent, but short |
| If the fall be slow | Less violent, but longer continuance |
| If the mercury falls suddenly whilst the wind is due West | A violent storm from the NW or N |
| If the mercury is steady or rising while the temperature falls and the air becomes dryer | NW, N, or NE winds, or less wind, or less rain, or less snow |
| If the mercury falls, while the thermometer rises and the air becomes damp | Wind and rain from the SE, S, or SW |
| If the mercury falls while the temperature is low | Snow |
| When the mercury rises, after having been some time below its average height | Less wind, or a change to N, or less wet |
| With the first rise of mercury after it has been very low | Strong wind or heavy squalls from NW, N, or NE |
| When a gradual, continuous rise of the mercury occurs with a falling thermometer | Improved weather |
| If the mercury suddenly rising, the thermometer also rises | Winds from S or SW |
| Soon after the first rise of mercury from a very low point | Heavy gales from the N |
| With a rapid rise of the mercury | Unsettled weather |
| With a slow rise of the mercury | Settled weather |
| With a continued steadiness of the mercury with dry air | Very fine weather |
| With a rapid and considerable fall of the mercury | Stormy weather with rain or snow |
| With an alternate rising and falling of the mercury | Threatening, unsettled weather |
| When the mercury falls considerably, with low temperatures (for the season) and N winds or high temperatures and S winds | Much wind, rain, hail, or snow, with or without lightning |

Inwards also quotes some well-known (at least at the time) poems regarding barometer trends:

> *When the glass falls low,*
> *Prepare for a blow;*
> *When it rises high,*
> *Let all your kites fly.*
> *First rise after low*
> *Foretells stronger blow.*
> *Long foretold, long last;*
> *Short notice, soon past.*

# Clouds

Alert observers can often get weather messages from the clouds. An approaching storm is often signaled first by high, wispy cirrus clouds, which thicken into a more or less continuous shield. These are followed by mid-level clouds (cirrocumulus and altocumulus), and then even lower, darker clouds. A falling barometer and south winds confirm the storm's approach. Clouds change much more gradually for an approaching warm front than for a cold front; the latter is arranged so vertically that storm clouds often give only a brief warning prior to the arrival of winds and rain.

# Temperature

Prior to the arrival of a storm from the west, winds are generally from the south, bringing relatively warm air into the state. The warmest periods in winter usually occur during these pre-storm conditions. Western Oregon temperatures can rise into the 60s, and eastern locations can get almost as warm. Often the stronger the southerly winds, the warmer the air, and the more intense the storm.

# Animals

Animals may be much better forecasters than humans. For centuries, their behavior has been shown to predict weather with sometimes astonishing accuracy. Inwards lists many ways in which animal behavior is said to forecast the weather, most of them from naturalists, shepherds, and others who are in constant contact with animals. Here are some:

### General
When animals seek sheltered places instead of spreading over their usual range, an unfavorable change is probable.

If animals crowd together, rain will follow.

## Dogs

The unusual howling of dogs portends a storm.

When dogs eat grass, it will be rainy.

If dogs roll on the ground and scratch, or become drowsy and stupid, it is a sign of rain.

If spaniels sleep more than usual, it foretells wet weather.

Dogs making holes in the ground, howling when anyone goes out, eating grass in the morning, or refusing meat, are said to indicate coming rain.

## Cats

When a cat sneezes, it is a sign of rain.

Cats are observed to scratch the wall or a post before wind, and to wash their faces before a thaw; they sit with their backs to the fire before snow.

When the cat scratches the table legs, a change is coming.

When cats wipe their jaws with their feet, it is a sign of rain, and especially when they put their paws over their ears in wiping.

## Horses

Horses sweating in the stable is a sign of rain.

If horses stretch out their necks and sniff the air, rain will ensue.

If horses start more than ordinary and are restless and uneasy, or if they assemble in the corner of a field with heads to leeward, expect rain.

Horses and mules, if very lively without cause, indicate cold.

## Cows

When cows fail their milk, expect stormy and cold weather.

When cows bellow in the evening, expect snow that night.

When cattle remain on hilltops, fine weather to come.

If cows stop and shake their feet, or refuse to go to pasture in the morning, or when they low and gaze at the sky, or lick their forefeet, or lie on the right side, or rub themselves against posts, or lie down early in the day, it indicates rain to come.

*When a cow tries to scratch its ear,*
*It means a shower is very near.*
*When it thumps its ribs with its tail,*
*Look out for thunder, lightning, and hail.*

## Sheep

Before a storm comes sheep become frisky, leap, and butt or "box" each other.

If old sheep turn their backs towards the wind, and remain so for some time, wet and windy weather is approaching.

Old sheep are said to eat greedily before a storm, and sparingly before a thaw. When they leave the high grounds, and bleat much in the evening and during the night, severe weather is expected. In winter, when they feed down the hill, a snowstorm is looked for; when they feed up the burn, wet weather is near.

## Pigs

When pigs carry straw to their sties, bad weather may be expected.

Swine are so terrified and disturbed and discomposed when the wind is getting up, that countrymen say that this animal alone sees the wind, and that it must be frightful to look at.

Hogs rubbing themselves in winter indicates an approaching thaw.

And since this is the *Oregon* weather book, we cannot forget the beavers and ducks!

## Beavers (the only one in Inwards' book)

In early and long winters the beaver cuts his winter supply of wood, and prepares his house one month earlier than in mild, late winters.

## Ducks

If ducks do shake and flutter their wings when they rise, it is a sign of ensuing weather.

*When ducks are driving through the burn,*
*That night the weather takes a turn.*

If ducks and geese fly backwards and forwards, and continually plunge in water and wash themselves incessantly, wet weather will ensue.

# The Mt. Nebo Goats

*The most memorable Oregon example of animal weather forecasting involved a herd of goats residing on Mt. Nebo, near Roseburg. As Mike Thoele reported in the Eugene Register-Guard (May 27, 1986), the goat herd slowly became a legend in Roseburg, but quickly became notorious when a local radio station began a promotional series which pitted the goats' forecasting skill against the National Weather Service—and some claimed that the goats did better.*

*Mt. Nebo is a hogsback ridge west of Roseburg. Goats were introduced to the area in 1885, when Ike Thornton drove two thousand Angora goats from California and sold them to local ranchers to clear brush. Some of the goats escaped from captivity, and their offspring have roamed the mountain ever since. According to goat-watchers, the animals ranged high on the mountain when good weather was approaching, but moved to the lower slopes when rain was in the offing. Said Roseburg veterinarian Don Bailey, "There were women in Roseburg who wouldn't hang out the wash until they looked to see where the goats were on the mountain."*

*In the early 1970s, Tom Worden and his crew at radio station KRSB mounted a light-hearted publicity campaign, keeping records comparing the goats' forecasts with those of the Weather Service. Stories began to run in newspapers around the country. David Brinkley had some fun with the story on his network newscast. Even foreign media picked up the story.*

*Unfortunately, as civilization encroached, the goats began to be a nuisance. Homes were built closer and closer to the mountain, and goats started wandering into gardens, chewing on flowers and landscaping. Then in 1978 Interstate 5 was rerouted, the project carving away a sizable chunk of Mt. Nebo and creating a major hazard for drivers and goats when, every now and then, a goat would walk onto the highway. A fence was built, at a cost of $8,000, but within a month the goats had figured out a way around it. Over the years other attempts were made to remove the goats or fence them in, mostly without success. But recently it was reported that the last of the goats had been removed. If so, Roseburg has lost one of the most unique and interesting groups of "weather folks" anywhere.*

# Historical and Contemporary Perceptions of Oregon's Weather

*Such a wonderful,*
*    wonderful climate*
*Everybody had said.*
*There never was such*
*    another*
*Anywhere to be had.*
*There never was any snow*
*    storms,*
*There never was any cold,*
*People never got sickly*
*And people never got old.*
*So I came to this wonderful*
*    country,*
*And I say as others have*
*    said:*
*No such another climate*
*Is anywhere to be had.*
*It began to rain about*
*    noonday,*
*The very first week I was*
*    here,*
*And it kept raining and*
*    raining*
*For five months long and*
*    drear.*
*For five months long and*
*    lonely,*
*There wasn't a ray of sun.*
*And the oldest inhabitant*
*    told me,*
*"It hadn't just begun."*
*Of the truth of this*
*    assertion,*
*There isn't a shadow of*
*    doubt;*

It was near 11 p.m., closing time for the Knight Library on the University of Oregon campus. Students were spilling out of the library on this late winter night. Greeting one and all on this dark, dreary night was a deluge of rain—the continuation of a rainstorm that had been swamping "duck country" since early morning.

One female student, perhaps exhausted by the demands of school and the late hour could take the weather no longer. In a screeching, ear-splitting voice (loud enough for members of the nearby fraternities and sororities to hear, to say nothing of those exiting the library), the student proclaimed, "God, I hate this rain. I'm tired of this rain. I'm sick of this damn rain . . ."

That evening, no doubt, the Eugene-based television weather forecaster probably predicted the predictable: " . . . another weather front will move across Oregon tomorrow bringing rain to Western Oregon and . . . The long-range forecast calls for more rain on Thursday and Friday . . ."

A number of years ago, while doing research on Oregon's weather and climate, author Hatton solicited newspaper readers' perceptions and thoughts on their local weather. A lady who had moved to Lebanon, Oregon, with her family, from New Hampshire, wrote (in part):

> *Dear Professor Hatton,*
> *I love the rain! The first winter here my daughter, then four, asked, "Mommy, where's my sun?" A few years later, I discovered the winter through a camera lens. Shiny. The rain makes everything shine. The rain makes the colors come out. Pewter skies, silver roads, and glowing 35 shades of green. Nothing so boring as a sunny, summer day . . .*

Perceptions of rain in Oregon were revealed following two statewide polls conducted in the fall of 1978 by Bardsley and Haslacher, Inc., an independent research organization. The results, published in *The Sunday Oregonian*, December 3, 1978, are shown in Table 14. Location made a difference to the responses. Residents of southern Oregon and east of the Cascades found the rain more welcome than depressing by a ratio of seven to one. Those living in the Willamette Valley and Portland, not surprisingly, were less positive towards rainy weather, but, overall, still perceived rains to be "welcome rather than depressing" by a ratio of two to one.

**Table 14. Attitudes of Oregonians to rainy weather**

|  | Recent arrivals (less than 2 yrs) | Oregon residents (2-9 yrs) | (10 yrs +) |
|---|---|---|---|
| Depressed by rain | 22% | 22% | 12% |
| Welcome the rain | 24% | 35% | 33% |
| Doesn't matter | 49% | 41% | 47% |
| Undecided | 5% | 2% | 3% |

Visitors and residents since the early explorers have described Oregon's weather. For example, on June 3, 1578, when his ship reached what is now Oregon's southern border, Sir Francis Drake and his crew, who admittedly had arrived from the tropics, complained about the weather:

> . . . *some of them fearing their health much impaired thereby, neither was it that this chanced in the night alone, but the day following carried with it not only the marks, but the stings and force of the night . . . the very ropes of our ship were stiffe, and the rain which fell was an unnatural congealed and frozen substance, so that we seemed to be rather in the frozen zone, than any where so neere unto the sun, or these hotter climates . . .*

About 140 miles farther north the weather got worse. The journal entry notes, " . . . yet the nearer still we came to it (the coast), the more extremity of cold did cease upon us." On June 5, Drake's comments on the weather of the Oregon coast included mention of extreme wind gusts, followed by a "most vile, thicke and stinking fogges, against which the sea prevailed nothing." Cold temperatures and wind forced Drake to turn southward. By June 17, his ship found a "convenient and fit harborough and sunshine." This harbor, now called Drake's Bay, is north of the present site of San Francisco, California.

Captain Cook, describing his 1778 voyage to the Northwest, spoke in more favorable terms: "When ever it rained with us Snow fell on the Neighboring hills, the Clemate is however infinately milder than on the East coast of America under the same parallel of latitude."

It is well known that the Lewis and Clark expedition was plagued by almost non-stop rains from November 7, 1805, when the explorers reached the Oregon coast, to the day they

*They knew from past experiences,*
*What they were talking about.*
*The healthfulness of the country*
*Is certainly but the truth;*
*With no sun to spoil the complexion*
*In a howling wilderness*
*Give me the land of the tropics;*
*I could stand the North Pole, I insist;*
*I wouldn't mind much about the freckles;*
*But I can't stand the "Oregon Mist."*

—Mollie Earley, in *The Land that Kept its Promise*

# Webfoots

*The wet weather that historically has been (and still is) a trademark of western Oregon is now legendary—with the name "webfoot" part of the legend. Nash (1878), following a visit to Oregon in 1877, wrote:*

I should think that no State is so much scoffed at as Oregon on the score of wet weather. Our neighbors in California call us "Web-feet," and the State is called "The Web-foot State." Emigrants are warned not to come here unless they want to live like frogs, up to their necks in water, and much more to the like effect.

*More precisely, the name "webfoots" was applied to those who endured the precipitation in western Oregon. Settlers who arrived in the Willamette Valley in the mid-1800s, spent only one winter in the valley, and relocated east of the Cascades were called "bunchgrassers."*

*There are different accounts as to how the name "Webfoot" became part of Oregon's folklore. One story is that it was a name derisively applied to*

left, March 23, 1806. The weather when they arrived was a "teaser." A journal entry for that day stated:

*We had not gone far from this village when the fog cleared off, and we enjoyed the delightful prospect of the ocean—that ocean, the object of all our labors, the reward of all our anxieties. This cheering view exhilarated the spirits of all the party, who were still more delighted on hearing the distant roar of the breakers.*

Alas, that night, a soaking rain doused the exploring party. Thereafter, day after day journal entries repeatedly noted the almost daily downpours. Clothing rotted and foods spoiled.

The journal entry by Sergeant Gass for April 8, 1806 (after the expedition had left the Oregon coast) stated:

*Some of the men are complaining of rheumatic pains which are to be expected from the wet and cold we suffered last winter during which from the fourth of November, 1805, to the 25th of March, 1806, there were not more than 12 days in which it did not rain, and of these but six were clear.*

Was the winter of 1805-06 excessively wet? Donald H. Clark in an article titled "Remember the Winter of ?" (*Oregon Historical Quarterly*, June 1853) wrote:

*Many of the hardships suffered by early northwest explorers and settlers were caused by inadequate shelter. If one studies carefully the weather descriptions of the lower Columbia in the Lewis and Clark journals, the winter of 1805-06 will be identified as about average for the vicinity during recent years. Members of the expedition suffered from exposure because they traveled in open canoes and camped with meager equipment. Their winter quarters at Fort Clatsop were rather crudely built and were poorly heated.*

Climate records (mean values for the period 1961-90) indicate that precipitation at Astoria for the November-March period averages 45.27 inches.

In March 1811, one of the parties sent out by John Jacob Astor arrived at the mouth of the Columbia River. The spring weather was delightful and the landscape was green and inviting—and, according to Gabriel Franchere, who described the scene, "The weather was superb."

A. W. Greely submitted a very favorable report on the climate of Oregon and Washington Territory to the U. S. Senate in October 1888. It is quoted in David Laskin's delightful book, *Rains All the Time* (1997):

> *Nearly all of Oregon and Washington Territory experiences very dry Julys and Augusts; the rain-fall, fortunately for these states, being deficient, while clear and sunshiny days are particularly frequent at that season of the year when the staple crops have fully ripened. The alternation of wet and dry seasons renders it possible for crops to be raised, with certainty that the rain-fall will come during certain months, and be followed later by fair weather suitable for harvesting.*
>
> *Oregon and Washington are favored with a climate of unusual mildness and equability; while the immediate coast regions have very heavy rain falls, yet such rain occurs during the winter months of December to February, and in all cases the wet season gives place gradually to the dry season, during July and August. While the preponderating amount of rain falls during the winter, yet the spring, early summer, and late fall are all marked by moderate rains at not infrequent intervals.*

Over the years there have been different perceptions of Oregon's winters and, in particular, the extent and the intensity of the rains on the westside. A description of winter weather in Oregon and the nature of those rains was included in Bancroft's *History of Oregon* (Vol. I) in the chapter titled "Oregon in 1834."

> *The winters of western Oregon are so mild that little ice forms; but they are wet, and cloudy of sky. The rains begin about mid-autumn and continue with greater or less constancy till May, after which fleeting showers occur until the June rise of the Columbia begins to decline . . .*
>
> *Observing this, the early Oregonians call their ordinary rains "mists," and maintain that they do not wet people; and by a further stretch of imagination their descendants may fancy themselves not affected by the December and January mists.*

Once settlers had reached Oregon and land was opened for entry, reports, promotional literature, and personal letters included descriptions and perceptions of Oregon's climates.

*Valley residents by California miners who were traveling through the region during the time of the California gold rushes (1850s). Egbert S. Oliver, Willamette University professor, in a article, "Is Oregon Rain a Myth?" (The Sunday Oregonian, March 1, 1942), discussed his version of the story: Lieutenant George Horatio Derby, U. S. Army, who had been for several years stationed in southern California, was assigned the task—to him a very unpleasant one—of supervising the construction of military roads in Oregon, more specifically between Astoria and Salem, some of the wettest places in the state, in 1855 and 1856. Writing under the pen name of John Phoenix, Lt. Derby wrote of Oregon's rain in humorous essays that were widely read throughout the United States.*

While acknowledging that, in moderation, rains do have their benefits, (causing the grass to grow, blossoms to flourish and are a positive necessity to the umbrella-maker), when you get to the country where it rains incessantly twenty-six hours a day, for 17 months of the year, you cannot resist having the conviction forced upon your minds that the thing is slightly overdone. That's the case in Oregon; it commenced raining pretty heavily on the third of last November, and continued up to the 15th of May, when it set in for a long storm, which isn't fairly over yet. There's moisture for you . . .

*Phoenix went on to add that "dry humor" in Oregon is, of course, a physical impossibility." "John Phoenix" gave Oregon a reputation as a rainy state, a state where people grow mossy backs and webbed feet.*

*In 1974, a folklore student named Jean Campbell interviewed local historian Francis Blair and learned that the origin of the name "webfoot" came about when a traveling salesman stayed overnight at a farmhouse that supposedly was located on the Long Tom River. When the salesman remarked that it was a wonder that children in Oregon didn't have webbed feet like a duck, the lady of the farmhouse picked up*

In a May 4, 1851, letter written to his brother back east, William R. Allen of Oregon City wrote:

*The climate is the most delightful one in the world . . . weather for some time after my arrival in this country was fine. The rains commenced some time in November. Then for about four months it rained every four days out of five—that is to say, it rained some days very little and other days all day. It never rains very hard in this country. As Dick used to say, "It muzzles." When it begins to rain the grass begins to grow and grows all winter. Stock require no feed in this country, summer, or winter . . .*

Contained in the papers of Rev. F. Blaine and his wife Catharine are the following comments about the weather:

*Oregon City, January 4, 1858.*
  *. . . It has been so pleasant some of the time that we did not feel the need of a fire to keep us comfortable . . . New Year's Day was fine, some fog but so mild that in making calls we felt no need of overcoats . . .*

Weather is usually a concern for tourists to any region. Oregon's reputation for rainfall is legendary. Most Chamber of Commerce offices are armed with climatic data to answer the question that both tourists and potential residents are likely to ask. In 1950, the Department of Vocational Education in Salem, in a booklet titled, "One Day More: An Outline for Tourist Host Schools," included some suggested responses to the question "Doesn't it ever stop raining in this country?"

*It's the rain that fills our lakes and rivers.*
*It's the rain (pure rain) that keeps us healthy.*
*It's the rain (fresh rain) that keeps our cities clean.*
*It's the rain (gentle rain) that keeps our lawns and gardens growing.*
*It's the rain (delightful rain) that keeps Oregon so green, so fresh, so beautiful.*

Usually (except in summer and early fall), it is not a problem to find a rainy day in western Oregon. However, the crew of a film about the late Steve Prefontaine (a legendary distance runner who grew up in Coos Bay) had to use a rain-making machine when filming near Florence during August! Indeed, there have been several other instances when artificial rain was needed to make Oregon-made films look more authentic.

While there are many times when western Oregonians get weary of the rains during extended periods of wet weather, even a short bout of of what many other Americans would consider *real* winter weather is more of an inconvenience. An interesting description of the replacement of snow and ice by warmer temperatures and rainfall was included in a weather bulletin for January 29, 1890:

> Summer morning sun, or spring south wind, never imparted hope to the disheartened more effectually than did yesterday's rain, coming down without let or hindrance, annihilating the snow and filling the air with moisture, which the hungry lungs, burdened with bronchitis and pneumonia, eagerly inhaled. The bounteous downpour affected the spirits of the populace. Pedestrians greeted acquaintances with a smile, and gaily piloted their protecting shade through the sea of umbrellas. The true Webfoot, native here and to the manor born, hurried out upon the street, armed cap-a-pie from helmet to top boots, shoulders thrown back, chin well poised, and sniffed the ozone with pardonable zest. Ladies sallied forth on shopping errands bent, and children trotted gaily off to school. The prayer for rain has been answered, and hope and health are restored to Oregon.

Fast forward a little more than a hundred years—more specifically to the extremely wet December of 1996, a month when floods plagued sections of the Willamette Valley including the Portland area. Undoubtedly some regions of the country had their dreams of a white Christmas come true, but many Oregonians were hoping to keep their head above water. *The Oregonian* on Christmas Day 1996 commented on the wet weather in an editorial titled, "In Oregon, Yule be damp."

> Every year, the Christmas pressure becomes harder on Americans who live outside the standard seasonal structure. Each December, a sizable majority of Americans finds itself bombarded by values that have no relation to the meaning of their winter solstice.
>
> So, on behalf of millions of Oregonians—especially those in the Willamette Valley—we say that we're not dreaming of a white Christmas.
>
> We're dreaming of the rain level stopping short of our chimneys.
>
> And, to put it bluntly, we have no idea what fun it is to ride on a one-horse open sleigh.

*her baby from its bed and indeed, the child did have webbed feet.*

*The name "webfoot" was in use in 1862, if not sooner. The Salem Statesman, April 14, 1862, included a letter written from The Dalles, which said,*

I believe the largest crowd of the season came up yesterday evening on the boat. The Wascoans may as well quit abusing the climate of the Willamette, and twitting about web-footed citizens. It rains here whenever it pleases and snows at intervals. It rained here last night and this morning. I notice that the Clickitat (Klickitat) hills across the river are robed in snow. The weather is disagreeable and abominable, and to help the matter the wind has to indulge in a daily frolic around this devoted place.

*Figure 22. In 1895 the Oregon Land Company placed this ad in newspapers throughout the western U.S. in an attempt to entice farmers to move to the Willamette Valley.*

Instead, we drop off to sleep with visions of sugarplums floating merrily in our basements.

Around here, no matter how many magazine advertisements we see, Christmases aren't white. They're wet. And while TV weather people breathlessly raise the possibility of snow on Christmas, they soon stop kidding and resume guessing at how many inches of rain we'll get.

It's not easy living someplace where Santa's sleigh needs not runners but pontoons. Around here in December, people don't wake up, look at the weather and race out to make snowmen; they race out to make sandbags.

And through it all, we're forced to watch TV specials of people singing in the middle of artificial snowdrifts. And there's no comfort in knowing that in the place where the specials are being made—Los Angeles—there's no more snow than there is in Beaverton.

It's time for us to take a stand—at least until we're washed away. In the meadow we won't build a snowman; for one thing, the meadow is now part of a lake. And we won't be walking in a winter wonderland; we'll be wading.

> *The larger society will just have to become more flexible and sensitive to our cultural values. Next Christmas, we want to see the Osmond Family singing carols while standing in two inches of mixed precipitation. And some TV advertising needs to show toddlers leaping from their beds and running for the windows, to see whether Christmas morning has brought showers turning to rain or rain turning to showers.*
>
> *We don't want to interfere with the majority's rituals—or to rain on any one's parade. But it should be remembered that in greetings of this season, Oregon has some bargaining power.*
>
> *If the cultural elite stonewalls Oregon on Christmas, we'll just take our trees and go home.*

While sunrise-to-sunset day-after-day rains get to some Oregonians (especially in the winter season when daylight is greatly reduced), there are those who become a little edgy after being besieged by a seemingly endless procession of clear skies—especially if the cloudless skies are accompanied by searing heat by day and nights that are muggy. There are those who take to task those television forecasters who, day after day, beam the message to their viewers that, "Tomorrow will be sunny all day with highs in the 90s and lows in the 60-69° F. range. The extended forecast calls for more of the same."

In a "First Person Singular" column that was included in *The Oregonian* October 18, 1987, Connie Soth of Beaverton, under the heading, "Nice Day in Oregon Should Include Raindrops, Wind, Umbrellas," wrote:

> *I'm lonesome for the rain. Lonesome for the sounds and the smells and taste and the feel of rain. It's been so long since I heard the friendly drumming of rain on the roof, the gurgle in the gutters, the rattle and splash of wind-blown rain against the windows. One night a rare rainstorm (can this be Oregon?) surprised us. I loved it so much I left the back door open to hear the rain hush-hushing on parched leaves and thirsty ground like a mother soothing her fretful baby. After the shower passed, the dripping from roof and tree drew me again and again to stand at the back screen door just to listen and to revel.*
>
> *And the smell. I can smell rain before it starts. Sometimes when the clouds roll in from the southwest and both temperature and pressure drop, I step outside and draw an anticipatory breath. Centering my whole being, the way dogs and cats do, I close my eyes, flare my nostrils and gently inhale. The smell of rain is elusive, to be sure, but I am patient. Soon, I catch the fresh, cool scent of marine air off the Pacific, 100 miles away as the sea gull flies. The tang of ozone, salt-tinge and just a touch of seaweed brings promise of moisture to come.*
>
> *"It's going to rain," I announce, ignoring skeptical glances.*

*The evening I heard the rain begin I rushed outside, hesitating mere seconds when a voice in my head scolded, "You'll get all wet!"*

*"So what?" I retorted, running out to stand delighted as tiny shocks of cold hit the top of my head and bare arms, and delicious shivers raced up and down my back.*

*I tipped back my head, opened my mouth and tasted the rain as it fell. Eventually, when the rain settled into a serious downpour, I retreated to the house. Toweling my wet hair, I still could taste that special wine of the rain on my tongue.*

*I'm so tired of interminable sunny days. Every day the same. The early morning sky reddens—no clouds again today. The feverish, smoky sun pokes long dry fingers into every exhausted nook and cranny of drying-up life. Sunshine, like the fixed smile of a false friend, promises everything while it sucks out all our juice— rom people, animals, and trees alike.*

*How lovely it would be to curl up beside the fireplace where a good blaze snaps and crackles. How comfort-making to be warm while listening to rain murmuring in the downspout.*

*Why, I've almost forgotten how rain sounds. Could the worst happen? Could we go on so long without rain that we Oregonians might come to a day when the only way we could remember rain would be by listening to one of those audio cassettes called relaxation tapes?*

*And when the TV weatherman announces that tomorrow's weather will be "good" again, I get this rage of longing to rub Aladdin's lamp and wish Mr. Weatherman right out to the middle of the Sahara.*

*One of these evenings, right after the 5:30 news, I swear I'm going to call the station and demand a new definition of "good weather."*

*When the hot, dry winds continue to torment blackened areas of what once were magnificent stands of timber, should we call that "good weather"? I will say. When mile upon mile of apple orchards scorch and slowly burn under relentless sun—is that "good weather"? I will ask. When our Cascade Range metamorphoses from white-mantled majesties to a pitiful huddle of wrinkled cardboard— is that a welcome result of the "good weather"'you bragged on?*

*And the next time a supermarket clerk tells me to "have a good day," I will not snap back something sarcastic. Instead, I will make myself believe she means, by "a good day," a wild, wet, windy, western Oregon day, with leaves flying, umbrellas happily bobbing and traffic shooshing on wet pavement—a symphony of water music fit for a king.*

When it comes to weather in Oregon, we can't please all the people all of the time!

# PART 4

# Oregon: A State of Extremes

# Temperatures

H ere are month-by-month descriptions of some of Oregon's temperature extremes.

*Out-of-state residents have a stereotype of Oregon's weather: it rains a lot and temperatures are mild. In reality, Oregon has some of the most extreme ranges of temperatures and precipitation anywhere in the United States.*

## January

The record low temperature for the month is -52°F at Danner on January 21, 1930 and at Austin on January 8, 1937. The highest temperature was 82°F at Fremont on January 31, 1934.

Temperatures have dropped below 0°F at one Oregon weather station or more every year since 1896 with two exceptions: 1°F in 1934 and 2°F in 1900. But despite so many extremely cold Januarys, there was only one year when no Oregon weather station reported a high of at least 60°F in January; in 1937, the highest temperature in the state was 56°F.

In January 1943, there was a temperature range of 121°F with extremes ranging from a balmy 74°F in Brookings to a frigid -47°F at Meacham.

## February

February's record low temperature—the all-time record for any month—in Oregon is -54°F at Ukiah on February 9, 1933 and at Seneca the next day. The highest temperature was 89°F at Williams on February 22, 1907.

February temperature ranges can exceed those in January. The greatest occurred in 1932 when Seneca reported a minimum of -49°F on the 14th and both Drain and Roseburg experienced maxima of 70°F (128°F higher than the Seneca minimum) on February 26.

In recent years, February maxima in Oregon have included 85°F at Coquille in 1992, 83°F in Brookings in 1988 and Coquille in 1983, and 81°F at Brookings in both 1985 and 1986. Even in February 1993, one of the coldest Februarys of this century, a mild 77°F was recorded in Langlois.

## March

The records for March are -30°F at Fremont in 1922 and 99°F in 1900 at Merlin.

The high temperature for the month has been 70°F or higher every year except 1897, when it was 66°F. Maxima of

80°F or higher have occurred in the state about one year out of two. Subzero temperatures in March can be expected somewhere in Oregon about two years out of three.

# April

The record high temperature for April is 102°F at Marble Creek on April 21, 1906. Meacham's -23°F on April 1, 1936 is the low temperature record.

Oregon's highest temperatures in April are likely to reach or exceed 80°F In recent years, April maxima have included 93°F April 17, 1994, 92°F April 21, 1986, and 91°F April 14, 1990—all at Pelton Dam on the Deschutes River, Jefferson County.

# May

In 1986, Pelton Dam tied the all-time May temperature record with a 108°F reading; Blitzen had previously reached that temperature in 1924. The lowest May temperature in Oregon was 0°F at Juniper Lake (in the Alvord Basin, east of Steens Mountain) on May 2, 1968.

# June

June's high temperature record is 113°F at Blitzen on June 28, 1932. The low record is 11°F at Crater Lake on June 12, 1952.

In only sixteen years since 1896 has the June extreme maximum not reached 100°F in some part of Oregon. All of Oregon's extreme minima in June have been between 11°F and 26°F, most in the Fort Rock Valley.

# July and August

July and August have identical all-time maximum and minimum temperatures. The record high, which is a record for any month, is 119°F at Prineville on July 11, 1898, and at Pendleton on August 10, 1898. The lowest temperature is 14°F at Fremont on July 2, 1955 and August 24, 1925.

Maximum temperatures in Oregon during July and August have exceeded 100°F every year since 1896, except for August in both 1899 and 1900 when the state's highest temperatures were, respectively, 97°F (Pendleton) and 99°F (Arlington).

Except for August 1901, when Oregon's lowest temperature was 33°F (at Beulah), at least one weather station in Oregon has reported a freezing temperature every month of the year since 1896. The lowest July and August minima include 14°F at Fremont (July 2, 1955) and 13°F at Seneca (August 28, 1937).

# September

The September low temperature record is 2°F at Fremont, September 14, 1970, and Harney Branch Experiment Station, September 24, 1926. The all-time high for the month is 111°F at Illahe on September 3, 1955.

By September, marked changes usually occur in Oregon's maximum and minimum temperatures. Most (88%) of the September extreme minima in the state have been under 20°F.

At the other end of the thermometer, some afternoons in September may actually be too warm for comfort with 100°F or higher occurring in about three years in four. Only once (89°F in 1941) has the temperature not reached 90°F somewhere in the state.

# October

Some subzero minima show up in October. The record low is -13°F at Chemult on October 12, 1938 and Seneca the next day. The record high is 104°F at Dora and Lost Creek Dam on October 2, 1980.

Most of Oregon's lowest temperatures in October have been below 12°F.

Even in October, usually during the first week, the mercury has climbed to 90°F or above. It has gone above 100°F in six years, including 103°F at Pelton Dam on October 9, 1996. Extreme maxima in the 90-99°F range have been noted in October in 61 years and between 86-89°F in another 30 years.

# November

The record low temperature for the month is -32°F at Ukiah on November 15, 1955 and November 23, 1985. But despite the occurrences of subzero minima, there have also been some relatively warm daytime temperatures. The record high is 89°F at Mitchell on November 22, 1936. Maxima of 80°F or above have been recorded in November in 24 years and between 70 and 79°F in 63 years. Most of the highest temperatures have been recorded in either Umatilla County (Pendleton, Pilot Rock, or Umatilla, for example) or in southwest Oregon (notably Medford, Grants Pass, and Brookings). Virtually all the state's extreme minima occurred in either Seneca or at stations in the Fort Rock Valley.

# December

Temperature extremes in Oregon during December have ranged from an exceptionally mild 80°F at Port Orford on December 15, 1980 to an arctic -53°F at both Riverside and Drewsey on Christmas Eve 1924. Only once in this century (1950) has there not been a subzero minimum in Oregon during December. Most of the state's extreme maxima during December have been in the 60-69°F or 70-79°F ranges.

Table 15 shows the monthly extreme maximum and minimum temperatures in Oregon, and where and when they have been recorded.

**Table 15. Oregon monthly temperature records**

| Month | Maximum temperatures | | | Minimum temperatures | | |
|---|---|---|---|---|---|---|
| | Temp (F) | Station | Year | Temp (F) | Station | Year |
| Jan. | 82° | Fremont | 1934 | -52° | Austin | 1937 |
| Feb. | 85° | Coquille | 1992 | -54° | Seneca | 1933 |
| | | | | | Ukiah | 1933 |
| Mar. | 99° | Merlin | 1900 | -30° | Fremont | 1922 |
| Apr. | 102° | Marble Creek | 1906 | -23° | Meacham | 1936 |
| May | 108° | Blitzen | 1924 | 0° | Juniper Lake | 1968 |
| | | Pelton Dam | 1986 | | | |
| June | 113° | Blitzen | 1932 | 11° | Fremont | 1952 |
| | | | | | Crater Lake | |
| July | 117° | Umatilla | 1939 | 14° | Fremont | 1955 |
| Aug. | 119° | Pendleton | 1898 | 13° | Seneca | 1937 |
| Sept. | 111° | Illahe | 1955 | 2° | Harney Br. Exp. Stn | 1926 |
| | | | | | Fremont | 1970 |
| Oct. | 104° | Dora | 1980 | -9° | Fremont | 1971 |
| | | | | | Seneca | 1991 |
| Nov. | 89° | Mitchell | 1936 | -32° | Ukiah | 1955, |
| | | | | | Silver Lake | 1896 |
| Dec. | 81° | Dayville | 1897 | -53° | Drewsey | 1924 |
| | | | | | Riverside | |

# Oregon Extreme Temperatures Compared with those of Other States

Nationwide, the state with the greatest differences in temperatures is Montana with a 117°F maximum and -70°F minimum for a range of 187°F. Oregon, with 119°F (Pendleton, August 1898) and -54°F (Ukiah and Seneca in February 1933) ranks equal tenth with Minnesota in temperature extreme with a statewide temperature range of 173°F (see Table 16).

**Table 16. Range of extreme temperatures (°F)**

| State | Extreme maximum | Extreme minimum | Range |
|---|---|---|---|
| Montana | 117 | -70 | 187 |
| North Dakota | 121 | -60 | 181 |
| Alaska | 100 | -80 | 180 |
| California | 134 | -45 | 179 |
| Colorado | 118 | -60 | 178 |
| Idaho | 118 | -60 | 178 |
| South Dakota | 120 | -58 | 178 |
| Wyoming | 114 | -63 | 177 |
| Minnesota | 114 | -59 | 173 |
| **Oregon** | **119** | **-54** | **173** |
| Nevada | 122 | -50 | 172 |
| Wisconsin | 114 | -54 | 168 |
| Arizona | 127 | -40 | 167 |
| New Mexico | 116 | -50 | 166 |
| Utah | 116 | -50 | 166 |
| Washington | 118 | -48 | 166 |

# Wet and Dry Extremes

Oregon has its wet and its dry sides—with remarkable precipitation differences between the two geographical areas. The wettest station in Oregon (on an annual basis) is that at Laurel Mountain (in Polk County) in the Coast Range, where in 1996 the precipitation totaled a whopping 204.12 inches, washing away the previous record of 168.88 inches at Valsetz (1937). By way of contrast, on the dry side of Oregon, at the Warm Springs Reservoir Station (located about ten miles southwest of Juntura, in Malheur County) the annual precipitation total in 1939 was a meager 3.33 inches (3.05 inches below the annual average).

The wettest places in Oregon, as evidenced by data from official rain gauges, are in or close to the Coast Range. For example, a weather station was established at Glenora, Tillamook County, near the upper reaches of the Wilson River, in 1892. For several years, the highest monthly precipitation total in Oregon was frequently reported from Glenora. Selected monthly totals at Glenora are shown in Table 17, along with the station's rank in the state for that month, and the amounts for Oregon's driest station for the same months. "Rank" in this case means where that

**Table 17. Wet months at Glenora, Tillamook County**

| Month/Year | Total (inches) | Rank in state | Least amount | Station |
|------------|----------------|---------------|--------------|---------|
| Jan. 1914 | 42.80 | 2nd | 0.58 | Diamond |
| Mar. 1916 | 29.29 | 2nd | 0.17 | Merrill |
| Nov. 1909 | 57.00 | 1st | 1.08 | Dayville |
| Dec. 1897 | 42.21 | 2nd | 0.95 | Burns |

monthly totals fall in the all-time monthly records. For example, Glenora's 57.00 inches in November 1909 is the highest November total ever recorded in Oregon.

The Glenora weather station closed in 1918. Commencing in 1926, a station was established at Valsetz, Polk County, and for half a century Valsetz was recognized as Oregon's perennial "wet spot." Some of the monthly totals from here still rank among the wettest on record. Table 18 shows selected monthly precipitation totals at Valsetz along with Oregon stations that had the least totals for the same periods as Valsetz. When lumber operations ceased in Valsetz, so did observations of climatological data; indeed, the entire company town was obliterated.

In recent years a rain gauge was established at Laurel Mountain, also located in the Coast Range about 25 miles west of Salem and only seven miles away from where Valsetz was located. Laurel Mountain was in the spotlight during the intense rainstorms that resulted in widespread flooding in 1996 and early 1997; in the February 1996 flood, Laurel Mountain

**Table 18. Wet months at Valsetz, Polk County**

| Month/Year | Total (inches) | Rank in state | Least amount | Station |
|---|---|---|---|---|
| Jan. 1953 | 47.23 | 1st | 0.19 | OO Ranch |
| Feb. 1961 | 34.19 | 1st | 0.19 | Alvord Ranch |
| Mar. 1931 | 29.54 | 1st | 0.50 | Lake |
| Apr. 1937 | 18.54 | 4th | 0.58 | Warm Springs Reservoir |
| Oct. 1956 | 30.62 | 1st | 0.74 | Arlington |
| Nov. 1942 | 34.99 | 8th | 1.16 | Plush |
| Dec. 1937 | 35.96 | 8th | 0.55 | Grizzly |

received over 27 inches of rain in four days. In December 1996, a record total precipitation for that month, 49.57 inches, was measured at Laurel Mountain. By way of contrast, in that same month the rain gauge at Fields, Harney County, measured only 0.78 inches. In April 1997, Laurel Mountain recorded 24.97 inches of precipitation, an amount that narrowly eclipsed the previous record for that month of 24.46 inches near Port Orford in April 1993.

Other weather stations in Oregon that frequently have been contenders for the monthly "Wettest-spot-in-Oregon" award include the following:

—Nehalem 9NE (i.e., the station 9 miles northeast of Nehalem), Oregon Department of Fish & Wildlife

—Port Orford 5E, Elk River Salmon Hatchery, 5 miles east of Port Orford

—Illahe

Table 19 shows monthly precipitation totals in Oregon for the period beginning 1896 and listing (by month) the wettest and the driest stations; the contrast between the wet west and dry east is apparent.

**Table 19. All-time record monthly precipitation totals in Oregon during the months November through February, and the lowest monthly totals in the state during the same month and year when the records were set.**

| Month | Year | Most precipitation Station | Amount (inches) | Least precipitation Station | Amount (inches) |
|---|---|---|---|---|---|
| Nov. | 1909 | Glenora | 57.00 | Dayville | 1.08 |
| | 1973 | Port Orford | 45.45 | Burns Junction | 1.15 |
| Dec. | 1897 | Glenora | 42.21 | Burns | 0.95 |
| | 1981 | Port Orford | 42.07 | Baker | 1.41 |
| | | | | McDermitt | 1.41 |
| | 1996 | Laurel Mtn | 49.57 | Fields | 0.78 |
| Jan. | 1953 | Valsetz | 47.23 | OO Ranch | 0.19 |
| | 1914 | Glenora | 42.80 | Diamond | 0.58 |
| Feb. | 1961 | Valsetz | 34.19 | Alvord Ranch | 0.19 |

# Individual Storm Precipitation Totals

Needless to say, when examining precipitation totals for major storms that sweep across Oregon, there are major differences from west to east. Table 20, for example, is an analysis for three storm systems.

### Table 20A. December 12 - 31, 1961

| Station | Precipitation (inches) |
|---|---|
| Brookings | 6.74 |
| Newport | 7.64 |
| Valsetz | 13.40 |
| McKenzie Bridge | 9.72 |
| Government Camp | 9.85 |
| Bend | 0.58 |
| Brothers | 0.24 |

### Table 20B. January 16 - 25, 1964

| Station | Precipitation (inches) |
|---|---|
| Astoria | 10.36 |
| Corvallis | 6.33 |
| Santiam Pass | 13.26 |
| Sisters | 2.54 |
| Redmond | 0.93 |
| John Day | 0.65 |

### Table 20C. December 24 - 31, 1996

| Station | Precipitation (inches) |
|---|---|
| Tillamook | 11.01 |
| Laurel Mtn | 26.01 |
| Corvallis (OSU) | 7.29 |
| Santiam Junction | 8.85 |
| Bend | 1.48 |
| Burns | 1.01 |
| Nyssa | 1.14 |

# Heat Waves

## August 5-11, 1898

In this week there was record-breaking heat east of the Cascades. At that time there were fewer weather stations in Oregon than there are now, but data from Pendleton and Vale—still perennial hot spots—were available. The August 10, 1898, maximum of 119°F is still recognized as being the all-time record high in Oregon, although, according to the *East Oregonian* ". . . the government thermometer is only calculated to 115°, so that the 4° indicated above that had to be measured (estimated) by an observer." The newspaper added (without elaboration) that a recording of 122°F at Umatilla was mixed in with reports from other towns.

Table 21 shows maximum temperatures for two eastern Oregon stations (Pendleton and Vale) and for two coastal stations (Bandon and Astoria) for the dates of the August 1898 hot spell.

**Table 21. Daily maximum temperatures (°F), August 5-11, 1898**

| Date | Pendleton | Vale | Bandon | Astoria |
|------|-----------|------|--------|---------|
| Aug. 5 | 99 | 90 | 64 | 70 |
| Aug. 6 | 105 | 95 | 70 | 66 |
| Aug. 7 | 110 | 98 | 62 | 65 |
| Aug. 8 | 105 | 100 | 65 | 68 |
| Aug. 9 | 111 | 101 | 64 | 69 |
| Aug. 10 | 119 | 104 | 67 | 68 |
| Aug. 11 | 102 | 105 | 67 | 68 |

## July 21-28, 1928

Many new record high temperatures were established in this period—not only for daily extremes but for continuous heat. The highest temperature in Oregon during this hot spell was 116°F at Pilot Rock on July 25. Exactly a week prior to this date, the month's extreme minimum of 24°F was recorded at Fremont, in the Fort Rock Valley.

Table 22 shows maximum temperatures for three inland and two coastal stations for this period.

One side note: Newport's extreme maximum temperature in July 1928 was 67°F (on three dates); the lowest maximum temperature was 62°F!

**Table 22. Daily maximum temperatures (°F), July 21-28, 1928**

| Date | Eugene | Grants Pass | Pendleton | Newport | Marshfield |
|------|--------|-------------|-----------|---------|------------|
| July 21 | 98 | 105 | 101 | 65 | 73 |
| July 22 | 100 | 109 | 104 | 66 | 69 |
| July 23 | 101 | 114 | 111 | 66 | 71 |
| July 24 | 102 | 109 | 112 | 65 | 74 |
| July 25 | 97 | 110 | 114 | 62 | 75 |
| July 26 | 93 | 109 | 109 | 65 | 71 |
| July 27 | 86 | 106 | 108 | 63 | 66 |
| July 28 | 79 | 104 | 103 | 65 | 61 |
| July avg. maximum | 82.2 | 93.5 | 93.0 | 65.0 | 60.3 |

## August 1967

Except along the coast, the average daily maximum temperatures were (to that time) the highest on record. The temperature at 96 stations reached 100°F—Ontario (23 days), Spray (16), Medford (15) and Pendleton (11).

Table 23 compares average August maximum temperatures for 1967 at selected inland and coastal stations.

On a daily basis, when the maximum temperatures were 97°F and 98°F in Portland on August 14 and 15, along the north Oregon coast at Seaside it was only 68°F and 71°F on the same days. From August 10 to 20, while Medford residents sizzled with readings ranging from 100°F to 107°F, nature's air conditioner was working well at Brookings; between those same dates, the city's highest temperature was 65°F. On three dates (August 14, 18, 19) when Medford's maxima were 107°F, Brookings' high readings were, respectively, 59°F, 60°F, and 61°F.

**Table 23. Average daily maximum temperatures, August 1967**

| Inland stations (°F) | | Coastal stations (°F) | |
|---|---|---|---|
| Portland | 88.1 | Seaside | 69.8 |
| Eugene | 90.4 | Newport | 67.1 |
| Salem | 91.1 | North Bend | 67.7 |
| Medford | 98.7 | Bandon | 68.0 |
| Spray | 100.3 | Cape Blanco | 58.7 |
| Ontario | 102.4 | Brookings | 66.3 |

## July, August 1971

The first half of July was cool, but the weather changed suddenly in the middle of the month, and temperatures remained high in eastern Oregon for the next four weeks. Ontario set an all-time record for Oregon stations with 32 consecutive days of 100°F or more (July 20 - August 20). For that period, Ontario's average high was 105°F, and the heat wave included two days at 110°F and two at 109°F. Spray had 26 consecutive 100°F days during the same period, and Huntington had 20.

Pilot Rock topped all stations at 111°F on August 1. And there were consecutive days over 100°F even in western Oregon. Hillsboro and McMinnville had four in a row during early August, and Portland Airport had three. Lost Creek Dam in the southwest got up to 110°F, and Medford and Toketee Falls reached 109°F. The only place in Oregon spared the intense heat was the coast. For example, North Bend's high for the entire two-month period was only 76°F.

---

The heat waves (1898, 1928 and 1967) were selected from the nine identified in "Hot Spells: Outstanding Occurrences of Record," p. 431, The Climatological Handbook. Columbia Basin States. Vol 1, Part B. 1969.

## July 1994

As Portlanders wilted with consecutive temperatures of 102°F, 103°F, 101°F, 97°F, and 96°F, from July 19 to 23, the heat wave made headlines on page 1 of *The Oregonian* on the 20th, 21st, and 22nd. On the 21st the headlines were "103° and Sweating It." Stuart Tomlinson wrote: "It's not the heat, it's heat, heat, heat. Triple digits. Misery times three. A century mark and more. Portland's high of 103° Wednesday vaporized a record for the date of 102° set back in 1946, and pushed water and electricity use to record levels. . . ."

As is often the case, when it's hot in the Willamette Valley, an hour's drive to the coast usually provides immediate relief. For the dates in discussion here (July 19-12) Seaside's maxima were 68°F, 70°F, 67°F, 67°F and 65°F. Most likely a light sweater was a useful garment there.

# Cold Spells

Every few years, arctic air slides west of the Rockies and makes its way into eastern Oregon. On occasion the modified air mass extends its icy fingers into western Oregon, even reaching the Oregon Coast. Below are three of the twenty or so spells of bitterly cold weather that have occurred in the state (the ones that had some of the lowest temperatures on record) with inland and coastal temperatures compared for the same periods.

## December 16-26, 1924

The U. S. Department of Agriculture, Weather Bureau general summary in Climatological Data for December 1924 stated,

> The month was the coldest December of record for Oregon, the record going back to 1890, and the cold period which began the 15th and continued for almost two weeks was one of the longest and most severe ever experienced in Oregon since the coming of the white man. At some interior stations the temperature fell below the lowest point indicated on the thermometers.

The cold spell commenced December 16. Just a few days earlier, all sections of Oregon had experienced (and probably enjoyed) some exceptionally mild temperatures with, for example, 63°F at Port Orford, 64°F at Bend, 68°F at Pendleton, and warmest of all, 71°F at Pilot Rock (Umatilla County), all on December 13. Then the mercury tumbled—and tumbled. On December 17 the maximum temperature in Baker City was -1°F! From there, things only got worse. Madras minimum temperatures for the next week included -16°F (18th), -20°F (22nd), -38°F (23rd), -40°F (24th), -34°F (25th) and -29°F (26th).

**Table 24. Daily temperatures (°F), December 22-26, 1924**

| Date | Central/Eastern Oregon | | | | | | Western Oregon | | | |
| | Hermiston | | Madras | | Riverside | | Grants Pass | | Port Orford | |
| (Dec.) | Max | Min | Max | Min | Max | Min | Max | Min | Max | Min |
|---|---|---|---|---|---|---|---|---|---|---|
| 22 | 10 | -15 | 11 | -20 | 12 | 4 | 42 | 26 | 48 | 31 |
| 23 | 13 | -8 | 4 | -38 | 6 | -31 | 43 | 27 | 47 | 28 |
| 24 | 5 | -26 | 4 | -40 | -17 | -53 | 47 | 20 | 55 | 28 |
| 25 | 4 | -24 | 13 | -34 | -15 | -54 | 50 | 14 | 52 | 30 |
| 26 | 7 | -15 | 17 | -29 | -8 | 40 | 50 | 12 | 54 | 40 |

Table 24 shows maximum and minimum temperatures for December 22-26 (the peak of the cold spell) at selected stations both east of the Cascades and in western Oregon.

On Christmas Day 1924, there was 104°F difference in temperature between Riverside's minimum of -54°F and the maximum at Grants Pass, 50°F.

## January 25-31, 1957

**Table 25. Daily temperatures (°F), January 25-31, 1957**

| Date | Central/Eastern Oregon | | | | Oregon Coast | | | |
|---|---|---|---|---|---|---|---|---|
| | Bend | | Seneca | | Brookings | | Bandon | |
| (Jan.) | Max | Min | Max | Min | Max | Min | Max | Min |
| 25 | 5 | -5 | 18 | -14 | 44 | 33 | 40 | 32 |
| 26 | 8 | -23 | 16 | -43 | 47 | 29 | 35 | 23 |
| 27 | 20 | -22 | 12 | -40 | 40 | 30 | 38 | 21 |
| 28 | 12 | -13 | 18 | -37 | 51 | 31 | 38 | 29 |
| 29 | 25 | -16 | 5 | -33 | 49 | 33 | 44 | 26 |
| 30 | 36 | -12 | 30 | -29 | 50 | 31 | 48 | 30 |
| 31 | 40 | -3 | 34 | -26 | 48 | 40 | 50 | 40 |

This cold spell followed what had already been a chilly January. Most extreme low temperatures occurred in the state on January 26 and 27.

Comparisons between temperatures of two stations located east of the Cascades and two situated on the southern Oregon coast for the period are shown in Table 25.

## February 2-9, 1989

Late January had been exceptionally mild and sunny through parts of Oregon. Indeed, with, for example, the mercury reaching 63°F in Bend (29th), 64°F at Cottage Grove (29th), 65°F at Heppner (30th and 31st) and 73°F at Brookings (29th), it felt as if spring had arrived. However, with good reason, meteorologists had been warily eyeing arctic air that had caused temperatures to plunge to -60°F and lower in Alaska at about the same time that Oregonians were enjoying their readings of 60°F or higher. Alas, within a week, the arctic air had moved into Canada—and then took aim at Oregon. It even had the audacity to visit the coast—and cause a rash of burst pipes at coastal vacation homes!

Table 26 shows maximum and minimum temperatures for selected stations in Oregon for the period.

**Table 26. Daily temperatures (°F), February 2-9, 1989**

| Dates | Central/Eastern Oregon | | | | | | Southern Oregon Coast | | | |
| | Baker City | | Seneca | | Bend | | Brookings | | Gold Beach | |
| (Feb.) | Max | Min | Max | Min | Max | Min | Max | Min | Max | Min |
|---|---|---|---|---|---|---|---|---|---|---|
| 2 | 2 | -19 | 14 | 3 | -1 | -6 | 39 | 31 | 38 | 32 |
| 3 | -2 | -11 | 0 | -12 | -6 | -12 | 35 | 30 | 39 | 32 |
| 4 | 2 | -25 | -1 | -45 | 0 | -12 | 39 | 31 | 39 | 28 |
| 5 | 6 | -25 | 1 | -42 | 10 | -17 | 46 | 24 | 40 | 21 |
| 6 | 2 | -25 | 6 | -48 | 19 | -15 | 50 | 32 | 51 | 26 |
| 7 | 3 | -28 | 18 | -32 | 23 | -14 | 50 | 30 | 48 | 27 |
| 8 | 5 | -27 | 32 | -29 | 23 | -11 | 53 | 30 | 48 | 26 |
| 9 | 17 | -22 | 32 | -18 | 29 | -10 | 55 | 35 | 60 | 32 |

A couple of notes:

—The maximum (!) temperature of -6°F in Bend on February 5 was and is (as of 1998), the lowest maximum on record in Bend (since 1901).

—On February 6 there was a 99°F difference between Seneca's minimum (-48°F) and the maximum (51°F) at Gold Beach!

Not only are there likely to be wide temperature differences across the state, especially in the winter and summer seasons, but in late spring, late summer, and early fall there have been wide daily temperature ranges at certain High Desert stations.

Table 27 shows three stations that experienced large diurnal temperature ranges on the dates shown.

In late August and early September it is quite common for Central Oregonians to experience minima that are in the low to mid 20s by night followed by maxima that reach well into the 80-89°F range. In other words, one freezes by night and roasts by day.

**Table 27. Daily temperatures and diurnal range (°F)**

**A. Riverside (Malheur County), August 1916**

| Dates | Max. | Min. | Range |
|---|---|---|---|
| Aug. 21, 1916 | 90 | 28 | 62 |
| Aug. 22 | 92 | 24 | 68 |
| Aug. 23 | 95 | 25 | 70 |
| Aug. 24 | 98 | 28 | 70 |

**B. Crescent (Klamath County), August 1917**

| Dates | Max. | Min. | Range |
|---|---|---|---|
| Aug. 11, 1917 | 93 | 22 | 71 |
| Aug. 12 | 98 | 26 | 72 |

**C. Juniper Lake (Harney County), May 1968**

| Dates | Max. | Min. | Range |
|---|---|---|---|
| May 2, 1968 | 81 | 0 | 81 |
| May 3 | 80 | 10 | 70 |
| May 4 | 81 | 9 | 72 |

# PART 5

## Weather Events

# Ice Storms

Ice storms are among the most damaging and potentially deadly of all winter weather events. Heavy accumulations of ice can coat roadways, turning them into the equivalent of long, narrow skating rinks. Ice can also bring down trees, electrical wires, telephone poles and lines, and communication towers. Power and phone service can be disrupted for days while utility companies work to repair damage.

Ice storms require the same ingredients that are needed for a snow storm: cold temperatures and moisture. But although the ingredients are identical, subtle changes in moisture and temperature have profound effects upon what happens on the ground. Let's begin by defining the kinds of ice formation that can occur.

**Sleet (ice pellets).** Rain drops that freeze into small pieces of ice before reaching the ground. Sleet usually bounces when hitting a surface and does not stick to objects, but it can accumulate like snow and cause a hazard to motorists.

**Freezing Rain.** Rain that falls onto a surface that is freezing. This causes the rain to freeze to surfaces such as trees, cars, and roads, forming a coating or glaze of ice. Even small accumulations of ice can cause a significant hazard. Freezing rain is also known as freezing drizzle (if the rain drops are very small), glaze, or silver thaw.

**Graupel.** Small pieces of ice, actually just small hail. Like sleet, ice pellets usually bounce when hitting a hard surface, and do not stick, but they can accumulate like snow.

The character of the precipitation is determined by the temperature of the layer of air between the cloud (where condensation occurs, creating precipitation) and the ground (see sidebar).

Freezing rain is the most dreaded and damaging of these, because it causes dangerous conditions for motorists and pedestrians and can bring down trees, communication towers, and wires due to the sheer weight of ice buildup. Freezing rain can occur anywhere in Oregon, if a period of very cold temperatures is interrupted by a mild rainstorm. Eventually, temperatures usually warm enough to change the freezing rain to rain, but this may take hours or even days.

The most common freezing rain problems occur in the proximity of the Columbia Gorge. As is noted several times in this book, the Gorge is the most significant east-west air passage through the Cascades. In winter, cold air from the interior commonly flows westward through the Gorge, bringing very cold air to the Portland area. Rain arriving from the west falls on frozen streets and cars and other sub-freezing surfaces, creating severe problems. As one moves away from the Gorge, temperatures moderate as the marine influence becomes greater, and cold interior air mixes with milder westside air. Thus freezing rain is often confined to areas in the immediate vicinity of the Gorge: Corbett, Troutdale, perhaps as far west as Portland Airport. Downtown Portland and the western and southern suburbs often escape with no ice accumulation.

## What conditions cause these ice formations?

*Freezing rain*
Temperatures above freezing above the ground, with a shallow layer of below-freezing air near the ground.

*Snow*
Termperature below freezing from cloud to ground

*Sleet*
Temperatures above freezing above the ground, with a deep layer of below-freezing air near the ground.

*Graupel*
Temperatures below freezing in the cloud, with a shallow layer of above-freezing air below the cloud and a layer of below-freezing air just above the ground.

# Significant Ice Storms in Oregon

*Northwestern counties*  Feb. 1-2, 1916
Electric light, telephone, and telegraph companies, and fruit and ornamental trees suffered severe damage from this ice storm.

*Northwestern counties and Willamette Valley*  Jan. 5 - 7, 1942
Moist, warm air from the south and southwest met cold air coming through the Columbia River Gorge. In some areas there was considerable sleet, followed by freezing rain, but throughout the middle and upper portions of the Willamette Valley the precipitation was mostly freezing rain, which resulted in heavy accumulations of ice on all exposed surfaces. Roads and streets became dangerous for travel, orchard and shade trees were damaged, and telephone, telegraph, and power wires and poles were broken down.

*Across the state*  mid Jan.-Feb., 1950
Extremely low temperatures plagued Oregon for nearly two months, injuring a large number of orchard and ornamental trees and shrubs and harming many power and telephone lines and outdoor structures, costing thousands in damages. Severe blizzard conditions on January 13th and a heavy sleet and ice storm on January 18th and 19th together caused several hundred thousand dollars' worth of damage and virtually halted traffic for two to three days. The Columbia River Highway was closed between Troutdale and The Dalles leaving large numbers of motorists stranded; they were moved to safety by railway.

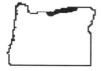

*Columbia Basin, East of Cascades*  Dec. 5-7, 1950
A very severe ice storm began as light freezing rain on the evening of December 5 over the Columbia Basin, east of the Cascades. As this weather continued intermittently on the 6th and 7th, fairly heavy ice accretions formed on trees, highways, and power and telephone lines, causing broken limbs from slippery pavements and downed power lines.  Scattered areas across Oregon also suffered from heavy snowfall. Crater Lake, for example, received 93 inches of snow for the month. Property damage was estimated at $40,000.

*Northern Columbia Basin*  Jan. 18, 1956
Freezing rain mixed with snow coated trees, highways, and utility lines with ice. Traffic accidents were common because of the slick surfaces. Trees were so heavy with ice that many broke, sometimes on top of houses.

*Western and Central Oregon*  Jan. 11-12, 1960
Light to moderate snows accompained in some areas by freezing rain produced dangerous highway conditions. A considerable number of automobile accidents, with four known injuries, but no known fatalities. Accidents blocked arterial highways creating serious traffic jams in some cases.

*Most of northern half of state*  Jan. 30-31, 1963
Substantial snowfall amplified by moderate to severe icing conditions produced hazardous highways. Large numbers of power lines were downed. Many injuries, one reported death, and statewide school closures were due to the icy streets and highways.

*Hood River County and Columbia Gorge* Jan. 17-19, 1970
Stagnant and cold air in the Columbia River Basin area east of the Cascades kept surface temperatures well below freezing for a week. Ice accumulated on tree branches up to $1^1/_2$ inches thick. Damage was done to both orchards and utilities.

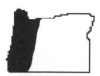

*Western half of state* Nov. 22-23, 1970
Freezing rain caused severe glazing across western Oregon, especially in Corvallis, Albany, Salem, Independence, and Dallas. Ice accumulations up to .half an inch thick broke thousands of tree limbs and telephone lines. Hazardous traffic conditions, power and phone outages, and felled trees were common. Temperatures warmed quickly late on the 23rd.

*Northwestern Oregon* Feb. 4-6, 1972
Several days of sub-freezing temperatures across Oregon were followed by an influx of warm moist air aloft across the northwestern part of the state. Glazed roads were very hazardous and a check of eleven Portland metropolitan area hospitals showed at least 140 persons had been treated for sprains, fractures, or head injuries resulting from falls on the ice. Some ambulance services did twice their normal business.

*Willamette Valley and Columbia Gorge* Jan. 11-12, 1973
Rains beginning in the Willamette Valley soon glazed streets and highways in the immediate Portland area and into the Gorge, where travel conditions became treacherous by 7:00 p.m., contributing to numerous auto, bus, and truck accidents and persons injured in falls. Most hospitals reported "full house" conditions. Glaze of $^1/_4$ to $^1/_2$ inch thick was common in Portland with up to $^3/_4$ inch of ice covering all surfaces in the West Hills of Portland.

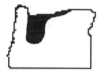

*Columbia Gorge, Willamette Valley, Portland/Vancouver* Jan. 1978
Very cold temperatures occurred in late December and early January. A moist storm system from the west brought rain that froze as it hit the ground and, by the night of January 9, over an inch of rain had covered everything with ice. There were power outages (some for more than 10 days) for many, but the area hit the hardest was east of Portland.

*Portland, Multnomah County* Jan. 9–10, 1979
A severe ice storm occurred in the Portland area as a very active and wet Pacific storm moved across the state. The highest temperature in the first ten days of the month at Portland Airport was 33°F, and lows were in the teens. The half-inch of rain that fell on the 9th and 10th mostly turned to ice. Five people died in the storm.

*North-central Oregon* Jan. 5, 1986
This ice storm covered the roads with ice and caused power outages to several thousand houses.

*All of eastern Oregon* Jan. 6-7, 1991
There was constant precipitation all over Oregon. The Willamette Valley had freezing rain, which made transportation difficult. A woman was killed when her car slid off a frozen rain-covered highway and another died when she was struck after abandoning her disabled car. The higher lands of eastern Oregon accumulated between 1 and 6 inches of new snow and the Columbia Gorge received 12 inches.

*Columbia Gorge, Willamette Valley, Portland/Vancouver*  Jan. 16-18, 1996
Cold air funneling through the Columbia River Gorge with overrunning moisture created freezing rain with heavy accumulations of glaze ice in the Gorge, Northern Cascades, and extreme eastern Portland metropolitan area. Scattered power outages resulted, as well as numerous minor traffic accidents. Light amounts of freezing rain were reported in the Willamette Valley as far south as Eugene.

*Columbia Gorge, Willamette Valley, Portland/Vancouver*  Feb. 2-4, 1996
A warm front overrunning cold air trapped in western Oregon valleys and the Columbia Gorge produced an ice storm that caused widespread disruption of traffic and power outages in the Willamette Valley and Coast Range valleys. Freezing rain began over the Willamette Valley during the afternoon of February 3 and continued throughout the night and into the next day. Numerous traffic accidents were reported including a 100-car minor damage pileup near Salem. One fatality occurred when a car lost control on the ice, slid off the road, and flipped over near Lincoln City.

# Floods

Floods are among the most frequent and costly natural disasters in the United States in terms of human hardship and economic loss. Between 1985 and 1994, the cost of floods in the United States averaged $3.1 billion per year. An average of 95 lives are lost every year to floods.

*East of Willamette River Bridge, Corvallis, 1916 flood. (OSU Archives P95:114g)*

Oregon is no stranger to floods. Most of Oregon's most destructive natural disasters have been floods. Loss of life, property damage, and economic consequences have been severe.

Floods can occur in Oregon at various times of year and in nearly every county. Of course, they have one thing in common: excessive amounts of water. But the causes of flooding are many and varied, due to Oregon's very diverse physical setting and climate. In the interests of simplicity, however, four general categories of floods in Oregon can be identified:

**Flash floods.** Severe local thunderstorms occasionally produce high-intensity precipitation which can lead to flash flooding. Floods of this type are common during warmer months, and in eastern Oregon.

**Rain-on-snow floods.** Heavy rains falling on a deep snowpack can produce flooding due to the cumulative runoff from rainwater and snowmelt. These are most common during winter months.

**Spring snowmelt floods.** Warm weather in spring or early summer melts the high-elevation snowpack. If the snowpack is extensive and temperatures rise very quickly, the resulting snowmelt can produce significant flooding.

**Debris flows.** Logs, ice, or other debris can temporarily dam a river or stream, creating a backlog of water; when this "dam" breaks, flooding can result from the sudden release of water.

# Flash Floods

*The town of Heppner before the 1903 flood, looking south. Willow Creek enters Heppner from the left rear and flows through the center of town. (Oregon Historical Society, negative number OrHi 25194)*

Western Oregon's annual precipitation is dominated by large winter storms that affect extensive areas over a period of several days. A typical winter storm might cause rain all the way from British Columbia into northern California and last one to three days. Although storm total rainfalls can be quite high, precipitation intensities are usually light to moderate (less than one half inch per hour, for the most part). In general, western Oregon locations receive about 75% of their annual precipitation between October and March.

East of the Cascades, however, things are very different. In crossing the Cascades, winter storms lose much of their available water, and consequently produce significantly less precipitation on the eastside. Mild marine air has much less influence to the east of the Cascades than to the west, so summer temperatures are often higher in eastern Oregon. As a result, summer thunderstorms (and potentially high amounts of precipitation) are fairly common during the summer months. Many eastern locations, in fact, receive more precipitation during summer than winter, while others are more or less uniform throughout the year.

Thunderstorms result from a process called "convection," in which air near the ground is heated by the warm surface and rises in the atmosphere. As the air rises, it cools, eventually condensing to form clouds or produce precipitation. If the surface is very warm, heating occurs quickly and the air rises rapidly; the warmer the surface, the faster the air will rise. In turn, the faster the air rises, the more intense will be the condensation and precipitation which result. Thunder, lightning, and hail are additional products of these extremely strong storms.

Topography plays an important role in thunderstorm formation. Terrain discontinuities (such as ridges and valleys) produce uneven surface heating, which can concentrate convection in certain areas. Mountain and hill slopes can direct moving air upward, often triggering the upward air flow that can result in a thunderstorm.

Nearly all of eastern Oregon is susceptible to thunderstorms (western Oregon is susceptible as well, but the storms are much less frequent). The most common areas for storm formation are over mountains (such as the Cascades, the Blues, and the Wallowas). Occasionally a thunderstorm will produce such intense precipitation that local flooding occurs.

Dr. John Merriam, a University of California paleontologist, experienced just such a flash flood during a fossil hunt in 1900. On June 23, Merriam and a companion were digging near Bridge Creek, 6 miles downstream from Mitchell in central Oregon. They were working in the shade of a low cliff under a partly cloudy sky. Suddenly,

> . . . there began to fall what might best be called balls of water. Thinking the shower would soon pass, we kept at work, but heavy clouds swung across the sky. During the next hour, as we made our way out of the area, we were exposed to one of the hardest rain storms I have ever seen.

That storm devastated a large area in Wheeler County. Crops were destroyed, mud- and rockslides were common, and farm buildings were ruined. Eyewitnesses reported hailstones up to 6 inches in diameter. Fortunately, no lives were lost (*The Oregonian*, 1976).

Not far away from the site of that storm, in a secluded graveyard, are buried Nancy Wilson and three of her children. They died on June 2, 1884, when an intense thunderstorm sent a "wild torrent of muddy boulder-laden water over the flatlands of what is now Painted Hills State Park" (*The Oregonian*, 1976).

The same area was also the scene of one of the largest flash floods in the United States. On July 13, 1956, intense thunderstorms and heavy rain occurred near Mitchell between 5 and 6 p.m., with the greatest intensities near Bridge Creek. The creek rose from its usual depth of about 1 foot to a rapidly moving torrent; more than twenty buildings were destroyed (including houses, businesses, a garage, and a post office). A highway was blocked by washouts and mud and rock slides. People who had accidentally left two open containers out during the 50-minute storm calculated that the rainfall was $3^1/_2$ inches in Mitchell and 4 inches in Girds Creek—more than 25% of the area's annual average rainfall!

Two other eastern Oregon towns that appear to receive more than their share of flash floods are Heppner and Ashwood. Heppner, in Umatilla

County, north-central Oregon, was the scene of the greatest natural disaster in Oregon's history (see below) as well as several smaller floods. Ashwood, on Trout Creek about 30 miles east of Madras, has seen several large flash floods. In August 1976, over 2 inches of rain fell during a short period of time, resulting in a wild flood of water carrying logs, boulders, and debris through the little town.

Recent years have proven that flash floods remain a danger, even with better weather-forecasting tools. On July 24, 1991, tremendous rainfall occurred in Deschutes County; more than $4^1/2$ inches fell in an hour at LaPine. Mudslides washed out part of a highway. Hail from the storm broke windows and windshields, and damaged cars, roofs, and satellite dishes. Snow plows were needed to remove hail from the roads. On Century Drive the hail was 6 to 8 inches deep. Two weeks later, on August 5, 1991, Newsome Creek Canyon in Crook County was the scene of a wall of water 200 feet wide and 50 feet high that rushed into the Aspen Valley Ranch. A man died while holding onto a fence that was swept up by the water. There were reports of farm equipment, cars, and animals that had been swept up to 6 miles downstream.

New technologies now in use by the National Weather Service (particularly the NEXRAD Doppler radar) greatly improve our knowledge of the atmosphere and our ability to identify the locations of severe thunderstorms. Flash floods will continue to occur on occasion, but early warning and good communications should reduce the danger of loss of life from such floods and insure that an event such as the 1903 Heppner flood will never again occur in Oregon.

## Heppner, 1903

Many farmers in Oregon east of the Cascades were worried about water conditions during the late spring of 1903. Very low precipitation totals in April and May had left the soil dry and began to threaten crops. The agricultural report for May 25 stated: "Ranges drying up, and more rain needed in eastern and southern Oregon. Wheat backward and becoming weedy . . . corn, sugar beets, field onions, and gardens making very slow growth." Dry and warm weather continued, although local showers brought some relief. The June 8 report included a single sentence about water conditions: "Spring wheat and forage plants deteriorating on account of the drought." Little wonder, then, that gathering clouds on the afternoon of June 14 were welcomed by the residents, many of them dry-land farmers whose economic survival depended on summer rains.

Heppner is the county seat of Morrow County, and had a population in 1903 of about 1,400. Willow Creek, which originates in the Blue Mountains only a few miles southeast of Heppner and flows northwestward toward the Columbia, had created an alluvial valley 500 to 1,500 feet wide, a fertile strip of cropland on which Heppner was built.

As storm clouds gathered over the Columbia Plateau on the afternoon of June 14, they seemed to congregate near the slopes of the Blue Mountains

*Destruction in downtown Heppner following the 1903 flood. (Photo used with permission of Portland District, U.S. Army Corps of Engineers)*

just south of Heppner. They grew darker and darker. Thunder was heard. Abruptly, a massive and deadly hailstorm began. John T. Whistler, a U.S. Geological Survey agent, later reported:

> *Some of the hail stones are said to have measured $1^1/4$ inches in diameter . . . A grim evidence of the amount of hail that fell is that, while most of the bodies being recovered on the fifth day were already badly decomposed, one was occasionally found almost perfectly preserved in a large drift of hail. Nearly all the hail was of clear ice and, unlike the usual hail stones, which are of a more opaque ice, being built up from a nucleus in successive layers.*

As bad as the hail storm was, things quickly grew worse. Heavy rain, appropriately called "cloudbursts" by residents, inundated the slopes of the Blues and the upper parts of the valley. Most of the rain fell in areas beyond any measurement gauges, but later reports estimated that an average of $1^1/2$ inches fell over an area of 20 square miles, most of it in a short period of time.

Unfortunately for Heppner, most of this 20-square-mile area funneled into Willow Creek and its tributaries. A wall of water surged downstream; in many places, the first surge of water coincided with the peak depth. Eyewitness reports of the height of the "wave" at the head of the floodwaters ranged from 15 to 50 feet high, but many of these appear to have been exaggerated. Nonetheless, the water was very deep, and arrived so suddenly that residents were taken almost completely by surprise. The first notice that the people in the business district had of the flood was when T.W. Ayers' large two-story residence left its foundation, floated across the street, and crashed into some wooden buildings. Poplar trees over 2 feet in diameter were "snapped off like cornstalks." Julian Keithley, age 70, stayed in

*View of central Heppner following the 1903 flood. (Photo used with permission of Portland District, U.S. Army Corps of Engineers)*

his home until everything was gone but the roof. He rode the current atop the roof for almost 2 miles, saving the life of another resident by pulling him onto the roof as he floated by.

About one-third of Heppner was completely destroyed, and more than two hundred people died (about one-fourth of the total population). About 150 residences were destroyed. Whistler speculated that the destructiveness of the flood "is due more to the rugged character of the topography and the almost utter absence of vegetation than to the unusual rainfall." If this statement is true, it suggests that the biggest reason for the disaster was the location of Heppner in a very exposed and potentially dangerous location.

In the days following the flood, many remarkable stories were told as residents began to clean up, bury the dead, and rebuild their town. The heroic story of a Paul Revere-like ride by two horsemen became a legend. Leslie Matlock and Bruce Kelley, expert horsemen, secured horses from a livery stable and, armed with pruning shears, set out to warn ranchers and residents of Lexington (9 miles away) and Ione (18 miles away), both on lower Willow Creek. Below Heppner, Willow Creek meanders considerably, so the two riders cut across country, cutting fences as they went. Said Matlock in recalling the ride later, "We (Kelley and I) didn't talk much, except to call warnings at homes along the way. The flood waters had already beat us to Lexington, but we felt we could make it to Ione before the water hit." In Lexington the flood waters had swept through the community at about 7:00 p.m., destroying several buildings and forcing residents to evacuate to the hills nearby. Matlock and Kelly secured fresh horses and continued on to Ione, beating the crest of the flood.

# Rain-on-Snow Floods

Oregon's water supply is very dependent on snowfall, due to a fundamental fact of Oregon climatology: water demand is greatest in summer, at low elevations, while most of the precipitation occurs in winter, and at high elevations. Snow serves the same function as a reservoir—it holds water in reserve through the low-demand months, making it available when it is needed during the warmer months. Ideally, the snowpack melts slowly during spring and summer, providing a steady supply of water to the soil, streams, and rivers. Occasionally, however, a dramatic change in weather conditions causes a rapid melting of the snowpack, bringing with it the possibility of flooding. Spring snowmelt floods discussed in the next section are an example. Another occurs when warm rain falls on a deep snowpack, producing the feared and often destructive "rain-on-snow."

During winter, Oregon is affected primarily by air flowing across the Pacific from the west. The cool, wet storms associated with this air flow produce the wet winters so characteristic in the state, west of the Cascades. But, at times, the direction of movement of the air masses changes somewhat. Air coming from the northwest tends to be somewhat cooler; from the north, cooler still. Often, though, winds in the upper atmosphere blow from the southwest. Air reaching Oregon from that direction is always

*Looking west (downstream) along the Walla Walla River near Milton-Freewater during the December 1964 flood. The river has broken out of its constructed channel and begun to meander in a very consistent manner. (OSU Archives, P20:607)*

83

mild, and often wet. And in some cases a deep, wide, humid mass of air, almost literally a "river" of moist air, makes a beeline from the tropical Pacific directly for the Northwest. Known as a "subtropical jet stream," this wet air mass generally passes near the Hawaiian Islands on its way to Oregon. For that reason, many locals have begun calling this the "Pineapple Express," a misnomer since it actually is birthed much farther southwest, above the western Pacific near the equator. To be more accurate, perhaps we should call this the "Sumatra Sponge" or the "Java Jet."

The effect of this weather event in Oregon is often dramatic: mild and wet, generally producing Oregon's wettest winter weather. When the moist tropical air reaches the land and is forced to rise, abundant quantities of water are liberated (this is known as "orographic precipitation"). West-facing slopes of the Coast Range and Cascades in particular will receive large amounts of precipitation, but all of western Oregon, and often much of the area east of the Cascades, is affected. These air masses are warm; it is not unusual for temperatures to rise 20° following the arrival of tropical air. Above-freezing temperatures extend very high, sometimes well above pass level in the Cascades (4,000-5,000 feet). The combination of warm air and rain can cause significant melting of the snowpack.

Most tropical air masses linger over Oregon for only a day or so, but on rare occasions they remain overhead for several days, pumping warm, moist air into the region. Such occurrences, especially if they happen when snow is abundant, can result in huge quantities of runoff—a combination of snowmelt and rain. In February 1996, just such a situation occurred, and it was the largest flood in western Oregon in more than thirty years.

### The Flood of February 1996

A series of intense surges of subtropical moisture inundated western Oregon during the period February 5-9. The combination of record-breaking rain, warm temperatures, and a deep snowpack led to severe flooding throughout northern sections of the state. River flood stages were comparable to the December 1964 flood, the largest in Oregon since flood-control reservoirs were built in the 1940s and 1950s. The first precursor to the flooding was an unusually wet winter, saturating soils and filling streams and reservoirs to high levels. Most of northwest Oregon received at least 125% of normal precipitation for the first four months of the Water Year (October-January). There was very little snowfall in fall and early winter; in mid-January, the snow water average for high-elevation sites in the Willamette drainage was only 29% of average. Beginning in mid-January, however, unusually high amounts of snow fell in the middle and high elevations of the Cascades and Coast Range; in many locations, several feet per day were reported for many days. By January 31, the average snowpack for the Willamette drainage had risen to 112% of average.

Then on February 6th a strong subtropical jet stream reached Oregon. This warm, very humid air mass, which originated near the equator in the western Pacific (near the Date Line), brought record rainfall amounts to northern sections of the state over the next four days. Although such subtropical storms are by no means rare, it is unusual for them to persist with such intensity for such a long period of time. Table 28 shows four-day total precipitation for northwestern Oregon locations, as well as the all-time four-day records (some of them now surpassed—new records are in bold). The most spectacular total was at Laurel Mountain in the Coast Range. Nearly 30 inches of precipitation fell in the 4-day period!

Temperatures were also unusually mild. In the Willamette Valley, daily minimum temperatures were higher than normal maximum values for early February. Nighttime lows in the mid-50s were quite common. The freezing level quickly moved upward, to 7,000-8,000 feet. Rain fell even at mountain pass level.

The warm rain and air temperatures quickly began to erode the snowpack. Streams rose quickly on the 6th and 7th, reaching flood stage in many locations. At Vida on the McKenzie River, the flow jumped from 4,000 cublic feet per

**Table 28. Four-day precipitation totals at Oregon locations, February 1996 flood event, and four-day records. New record values indicated in bold.**

| Site | 4-day total | Previous record | |
|---|---|---|---|
| | inches | inches | year |
| **Astoria** | **8.88** | **8.24** | **1975** |
| **Corvallis** | **8.10** | **7.84** | **1974** |
| Eugene | 9.14 | 10.30 | 1964 |
| Govt. Camp | 11.30 | 13.84 | 1964 |
| **Hillsboro** | **6.70** | **5.91** | **1974** |
| Hood River | 7.50 | 8.67 | 1964 |
| Newport | 9.81 | 10.17 | 1965 |
| **Oregon City** | **7.51** | **7.29** | **1964** |
| **Portland Airport** | **7.00** | **5.10** | **1994** |
| Salem | 8.18 | 8.69 | 1937 |

*Flooded street in Corvallis, 1916 flood. (OSU Archives, P95:114b)*

**Table 29. River flood stage and February 1996 crest during February 1996 flood. New records are shown in bold.**

| River/site | Stage (feet) | Crest (feet) | Previous record (feet) | Previous record (year) |
|---|---|---|---|---|
| Columbia at Vancouver | 16.0 | 27.2 | 31.0 | 1948 |
| Willamette at Portland | 18.0 | 28.6 | 33.0 | 1894 |
| Willamette at Salem | 28.0 | 35.1 | 47.0 | 1891 |
| Willamette at Corvallis | 20.0 | 23.5 | 32.4 | 1891 |
| Sandy near Sandy | 22.6 | 22.3 | | 1964 |
| Clackamas at Estacada | 10.0 | 17.4 | 18.4 | 1964 |
| Johnson Cr. at Sycamore | 11.0 | 13.8 | 14.7 | 1964 |
| **Tualatin at Farmington** | **32.0** | **37.2** | **37.0** | **1933** |
| Molalla at Canby | 13.0 | 14.6 | 16.8 | 1964 |
| **Pudding at Aurora** | **22.0** | **30.5** | **30.0** | **1923** |
| **S. Yamhill at Whiteson** | **38.0** | **47.5** | **47.2** | **1964** |
| N. Santiam at Mehama | 11.0 | 13.4 | 17.5 | 1923 |
| Santiam at Jefferson | 15.0 | 23.2 | 24.2 | 1964 |
| Luckiamute at Suver | 27.0 | 33.0 | 34.5 | 1964 |
| **Nehalem at Foss** | **14.0** | **27.4** | **24.9** | **1990** |
| Wilson at Tillamook | 13.0 | 18.1 | n.a. | n.a. |
| Nestucca at Beaver | 18.0 | 18.2 | n.a. | n.a. |
| Siletz at Siletz | 16.0 | 24.5 | 31.6 | 1921 |

second (cfs) on the 5th to over 20,000 cfs on the 6th. Major and minor tributaries throughout western Oregon jumped their banks. Gradually the levels in the major tributaries and the main stem rivers increased as well. Several set all-time flood stage records. Table 29 is a summary of 1996 crests, as well as all-time records, for rivers throughout northern Oregon; new record levels are in bold.

The 1996 flood was the most recent rain-on-snow event, and easily the most documented: television crews were everywhere, and the live and film coverage was almost continuous. Similar stories, albeit with less documentation, are told about other such events. Probably the best comparison with the 1996 flood occurred in 1964.

## The "Christmas Flood" of 1964

In general, weather in the Northwest is more reliable and predictable than in many other parts of the country. The Southwest, for example, can have year-to-year variations in total precipitation of as much as 400%, far exceeding what is observed in the Northwest. Nonetheless, there are times when the severity of weather change over a short period of time almost defies description. 1964 was one such year.

The first half of December 1964 was wet and mild. Temperatures were slightly above normal in Oregon, and precipitation totals were above normal as well. Then on the 14th and 15th, a strong surge of arctic air entered Oregon, and temperatures quickly approached record low levels in many parts of the state. West of the Cascades, the nighttime lows dropped to 5° to 15°F, while east of the mountains they ranged to as low as -38°F. Statewide, this was the coldest winter period since 1919.

*View eastward from Corvallis during the December 1964 flood, with the Willamette River in foreground. (OSU Archives R6:131. Photo by Western Ways, Inc.)*

*Southwest Corvallis during the December 1964 flood, with Marys River in the foreground. (OSU Archives R6:131. Photo by Western Ways, Inc.)*

On the 18th, a powerful storm moved into Oregon, bringing heavy snow to virtually all of the state. In the next 24 to 36 hours, near-record snow depths accumulated through the northern half of the state. Hundreds of motorists were trapped in their cars, unable to drive because of snow and ice conditions; most were rescued, forced to abandon their cars. Portland Airport reported 11 inches of snow on the ground on the morning of the 19th. Residents began to expect that this would be a rare "White Christmas," an event that occurs in the Willamette Valley only a handful of times per century.

But this was not to be. December 19th brought a tremendous record-breaking rainstorm, accompanied by unusually warm temperatures. In retrospect, this storm almost certainly originated in the subtropics, as did the 1996 storm. Temperatures were so mild that rain was reported nearly to the crest of the Cascades.

At Government Camp, in the Cascades (elevation 3,900 feet), the situation was typical of much of the state. The 55 inches of snow on the frozen ground on the 20th contained almost 5$^1$/$_2$ inches of water. Twenty-four hours later, rain had compacted the snow to a depth of 45 inches with an additional 1$^1$/$_2$ inches of water. Most people did not worry; rain had fallen on snowpacks before. But this time the rain did not stop. In the next 48 hours another 9 inches of rain fell at Government Camp, melting all but 6 inches of the snow.

This pattern of snow followed by heavy rains was occurring throughout the state. New December record three- and four-day precipitation totals were established at many locations, some of them at stations with 75-100 years of record. Many places reported two to three times the December monthly normal precipitation in a five-day period.

Eventually the snowpack collapsed. Immediately, the mass of rainwater mixed with melting snow began to move into drainage streams. This, in combination with the ceaseless rains, greatly increased the water level in streams and rivers, with some of them 50% higher than any levels measured before. The next day, Dorena Dam could no longer hold back the water, which surged over the dam at a depth of 8 feet. Water flowed over the Cottage Grove Dam so forcefully that people living below had to be evacuated and moved to homes and shelters. In one case, eighteen children were all brought to a single house; the family living there was not aware that this

*Flooded meadows below Dayville, Grant County, December 1964 flood. (OSU Archives, P20:1927)*

was happening until they woke up the next morning. Thousands of people had to evacuate their homes.

Just when it seemed that the situation could not get worse, the storm reintensified. Even more heavy rains fell on the 25th through the 29th. The already densely saturated ground could hold no more water; the result was mud and debris slides and even more flooding of streams. Many highways and roads were closed and streams were dammed. In Mapleton, a mudslide buried several buildings and as many as thirty cars as well as much of the town. On the lower Umpqua, the town of Reedsport was almost completely covered with 10 feet of water. Homes were flooded, bridges, wood piles, and lawn furniture were carried away, trees were uprooted, and roads were destroyed all over Oregon, southern Washington, most of Idaho, and northern California. Interestingly, many old bridges remained intact during the storm, even when struck by logs and other debris, yet many of the newer ones broke quickly.

At the end of December, temperatures once again dropped, slowing the rescue and reconstruction process. According to Gilbert L. Sternes, the Weather Bureau State Climatologist,

> *Destruction in Oregon due to weather was greater in this December than in any previous month or storm in this state's recorded history. Practically every facet of the state's economy was seriously affected.*

Many families had instantly become homeless and helpless. Regionally, the damage totals came to $430 million ($34 million in Oregon). In the four states affected, 47 people died, 17 of those in Oregon. It was not a very merry Christmas for most area residents.

# Spring Snowmelt Floods

Strictly speaking, floods occur every spring in Oregon and the Northwest, as high-elevation snowfields melt as temperatures rise. The U.S. Army Corps of Engineers for many years published annual summaries describing each year's event, with titles like "The Flood of 1953." Many of these "floods" were not particularly damaging nor unusual.

The dams on the Columbia River have greatly reduced the intensity and danger of spring floods. The Army Corps of Engineers and other dam operators can now draw down the reservoir levels in the spring prior to onset of snowmelt and prevent flooding by retaining much of the snowmelt behind the dams. The Northwest River Forecast Center (the National Weather Service office with primary responsibility for river forecasts) has improved its forecasts due to better observational data (such as remote sensing platforms and high-elevation automated stations such as NRCS SNOTEL sites).

Although spring floods are no longer the danger that they once were in most low-elevation areas in Oregon, they remain an important aspect of Oregon's weather history. Among the state's most significant weather-related disasters, several were spring snowmelt floods. Probably the most notable was the one that inundated the town of Vanport in 1948 (see story below).

Dams have nearly eliminated snowmelt floods in the Willamette Valley and other "regulated" areas, but floods can still occur in areas that are not downstream from dams, as the last two examples show. Fortunately, such floods are far less damaging than the huge floods that once affected nearly all low-lying areas in the state.

On the other hand, those same flood-control strategies that have been so successful in reducing the impacts of spring snowmelt flooding may be contributing to increases in the frequency of cool-season rain-on-snow floods. By keeping winter river levels higher than during pre-dam periods, the dams may make it more likely that winter flooding will occur.

*Examples of snowmelt floods include:*

**1894.** *There was flooding along the entire lower Columbia. Much of the Umatilla River valley was under water. Flow rate at The Dalles was 1,200,000 cfs, the highest ever observed on the Columbia River. The Willamette River was 33 feet deep in Portland. Photographers caught people boating and fishing in downtown Portland.*

**1989.** *Warm rains and warm temperatures in eastern Oregon caused extensive melting of snowpacks over a short period of time. Many rivers and creeks overflowed their banks.*

**1993.** *Rain and warm temperatures helped to melt a deep snowpack. The Owyhee River had been nearly dry in February, but the snowmelt produced a record flow of 42,000 cfs on the 18th. Owyhee Reservoir, the largest in the state, was nearly empty in February, but by the end of March it had filled and was spilling. Flooding also occurred in Harney, Grant, and Wheeler counties.*

## Vanport

*Floodwaters inundating Vanport, 1948. (Oregon Historical Society, negative number OrHi 100769)*

Oregon's major industries—forest products, agriculture, and tourism—were deeply affected by the Great Depression of the 1930s. Although agriculture was helped somewhat by New Deal programs of the Roosevelt administration, the tourism industry was virtually destroyed. World War II changed things dramatically. New industries developed almost overnight, the population quickly became more diverse, and the federal government began to play an important role in the lives of the state's citizens. Oregon's role in the war effort was primarily production of ships, food, fiber, and aluminum; however, its relatively small population required an influx of additional workers.

By 1942, Portland had become a major shipbuilding center, primarily because of three very large shipyards built by Henry Kaiser. Nearly 100,000 people were employed in the shipyards, many of them recent arrivals to the area; Portland's population grew from 340,000 to 500,000 in the first years of the war, creating a monumental housing shortage. Kaiser attempted to satisfy the need for housing by purchasing 650 acres of lowland along the Columbia River, not far from the shipyards, planning what would become "the most spectacular of all" wartime housing projects and the major project of the largest local housing authority in the nation. The city of Vanport was completed in 1943. It comprised a patterned arrangement of two-story buildings 38 by 108 feet, each with 14 apartments. A total of 9,942 dwelling units was built, housing a population of about 40,000. Post-war layoffs reduced the population significantly; by 1948, about 18,500 residents called Vanport home.

Despite Vanport's location on a flood plain near the largest river in the western U.S., there was very little concern about its safety. A Kaiser publication stated that "the entire project is surrounded by an impervious dike." Because of that confidence, the exceptionally heavy winter snowfall in the upper Columbia Basin during the winter of 1947-48 produced little concern. But warm temperatures and heavy rains in May 1948 caused snowmelt to occur very quickly. Tributaries overflowed their banks, and the biggest flood since 1894 filled the Columbia to overflowing.

In Vanport, the initial reaction was minimal. Routine patrols of the dikes surrounding the city began on May 25. Sandbags were procured, as well as quantities of baled straw, canvas tarpaulins, and dump trucks. Assistance was sought from the U.S. Army Corps of Engineers, who had built the dikes and had extensive flood-control experience. The Engineers informed Kaiser that there was no need for worry.

On Sunday, May 30, Portland residents were enjoying a warm, sunny Memorial Day weekend. Meanwhile, river levels continued to rise. At Vancouver the level was 28.3 feet, 15 feet above flood stage. Since Vanport was almost exactly at flood-stage elevation, river levels were 15 feet above the Vanport apartments' lower floors. At 4:17 p.m., the railroad fill along the west boundary of the development gave way. A seaplane flying over the tracks at that time reported that a sudden 6-foot break in the dike quickly increased to 60, then 500 feet wide. Water poured into Vanport. In the next two hours, the entire development was flooded.

The following day, the dike on the east side of Vanport also collapsed. The town was completely destroyed, with damage to government property totaling over $21 million. The number of lives lost is uncertain, but most estimates now place the total at about twenty-five. In addition, so little warning was given that most residents lost nearly all their personal belongings. Cars and trucks choked the single exit road from Vanport; many cars were abandoned to the rising flood waters. Scores of young children watched, terrified, as their homes were destroyed; their parents had repeatedly assured them that nothing would happen, as the officials had said. Those assurances, almost up to the time the flood began, were the reason many residents left their homes with almost none of their belongings.

Later analyses indicated that the railroad fill was poorly built, despite its massive and strong appearance. At one time the railroad ran along a trestle over the lowlands. In about 1918, the fill was made by simply dumping aggregate around the trestle. Over the years, the timbers rotted, weakening the roadbed at those points.

Blame for the disaster was an ongoing and hotly debated issue. Many lawsuits were filed. Eventually a federal court decision was made regarding damage claims by Vanport residents. In 1951, Judge James Alger Fee agreed with the defense (the U.S. government) that Title 33 of the judicial code applied: the government shall not, he concluded, be held responsible for flood damage. Thus the Vanport residents were able to collect nothing other than their personal insurance payments.

Could the Vanport disaster reoccur? According to the Corps of Engineers, the answer is no. There are now fourteen major dams on the Columbia system, and peak river levels are now much more controllable. Nonetheless, the Vanport area was never rebuilt for housing; an auto race track, golf course, and parks cover the flood plain. The viewer can behold "a sense of peace and tranquillity that was never present in Vanport City."

*The flooded street at 3rd and Washington, in Portland, during the 1894 flood. (Oregon Historical Society, negative number OrHi 3644)*

# Debris Flow Floods

Debris flow floods occur when ice, mud, logs, or other material creates a temporary dam. Water backing up behind this dam continues to increase in depth and pressure; eventually the dam collapses, and the resulting flow of water can be comparable to a large flash flood.

Debris flow floods are rather rare in Oregon, and usually quite localized. The 1980 Polallie Creek event was by far the biggest and most significant one of its kind in Oregon's recorded history.

## Polallie Creek

Christmas 1980 was not white in northern Oregon, but was one of the mildest ever. Pendleton, Eugene, and Salem all had record-breaking high temperatures, and Portland set its all-time high of 64°F for the month of December. Earlier rains had saturated the ground, and when warm heavy rains began on Christmas Day, the headwall near Polallie Creek, on the northeast flank of Mount Hood, began to slump and form a landslide. In almost no time the landslide became a large debris flow, depositing more than 100,000 cubic yards of creek material at the confluence of Polallie Creek and the east fork of the Hood River. The debris formed a dam that blocked the flow of water and formed a lake behind it. As water behind the dam deepened, the pressure increased, until the dam collapsed, causing a massive flood wave. The wave destroyed everything in its path, including roads, a bridge, and a campground; it left only boulders, river sand, and pieces of demolished trees. The wave flowed across Highway 35 and forced the closure of 10 miles of highway.

**Eastern Oregon, 1985-86**
*Several weeks of freezing temperatures caused over 40 miles of ice jams on the Snake River between Farewell Bend (northwest of Weiser, Idaho) and Ontario on December 30, 1985, and January 1, 1986. The ice jams forced water outside the normal channels and caused flooding. In one case, the water went around the state information center east of Ontario and moved into a K-Mart parking lot. At least 35 people were forced to evacuate their homes.*

# Significant Floods in Oregon

*Willamette River basin*  1813 (type of flood unknown)
Little is known about this flood, but it was probably as great as the 1861 and 1890 floods. This may have been the flood described by Indians to survivors of the 1861 flood.

*Willamette River basin, Oregon coastal rivers*  Dec. 12, 1861 (type of flood: R-on-S, SM)
Known as "the great flood," this was the largest flood of known magnitude on the Willamette and Rogue rivers. It came after two weeks of heavy rain and snow melt. Every town on the Willamette was flooded or washed away. Oregon City was 4 feet deep in water and had 57 feet of water above the mean low. Mills and breakwaters were carried away. Below Willamette Falls the water rose 75 feet, while in Albany the river was 19 feet over its banks. Portland had a flow of 635,000 cfs, the highest ever recorded there. 353,000 acres were flooded. Champoeg, Orleans, and Syracuse were all completely destroyed. The only house spared from the flooding in Champoeg was the first meeting place of the Provisional Government on the upper Willamette River. Scottsburg, farther south, was completely wiped out. By moving up and down the streams, Indians saved the lives of many settlers who had lost everything. They talked of a flood "many moons ago" that was much larger than this one and proved it with water marks that even today have not been reached.

*Willamette River*  Dec. 1-3, 1862 (type of flood: R-on-S)
In late November strong warm rains fell on top of the snow from previous weeks. The Willamette River flooded and reached its peak on December 3 at 55 feet above the low-water mark. That same day the water in Portland took over Front Street. Buildings were chained down in an effort to protect them from being taken away by the rushing water. Champoeg was demolished and West Linn had only two houses remaining. Onward, a steamer, embarked on December 1 from Oregon City on a trip to Salem. Along the way it served as a relief system, picking up 40 people from their houses, rafts, and even tree tops.

*Bridge Creek, near Mitchell*  Jun. 2, 1884 (type of flood: FF)
In a thunderstorm-induced flood of Bridge Creek, a woman and three of her children died. A vicious torrent flowed over the flatlands of the area (now part of Painted Hills State Park).

*Willamette River, Oregon coastal rivers*  Feb. 5, 1890 (type of flood: R-on-S)
This was the second largest flood of known magnitude on the Willamette and Rogue rivers. At least five people were killed. Almost every large bridge in the Willamette Valley washed downstream; it was rarer to see a bridge that was not destroyed than one that was. Millions of feet of saw logs were lost when the flood created a new channel for the Willamette. In Champoeg the water was within 2 inches of the 1861 flood, and in Portland water levels reached 22.3 feet. Oregon City had 35 feet of water over its low-water mark. Rivers in southern Oregon also flooded; much of Gold Hill was destroyed. After a slide of rocks, trees, and dirt on the Siuslaw (at Mapleton), a dam was formed. Before the dam broke, the water level went below the lowest tide. When the dam broke a wall of water rushed down the river taking houses, barns, and livestock with it. Some elderly people at Myrtle Point claimed that there was so much debris on the river that one could have walked across it.

*Main-stem Columbia River* Jun. 4, 1894 (type of flood: SM)
This flood, which inundated Umatilla, flowed past The Dalles at a rate of 1,200,000 cfs and was the largest flood ever observed on the Columbia River. The Willamette River backed up and rose a record of 33 feet in Portland. A line on the inner side of the most northern arch of the Haseltine Building (133 SE Second Avenue) marks the level of the flood; it is 12 feet above the street level east of the Skidmore Fountain. The current was small and caused unusually little damage. Photographers caught people boating through the streets.

*Willow Creek* Jun. 14, 1903 (type of flood: FF)
The Heppner flood was caused by a cloudburst that created a 40-foot wall of water, mud, and debris which flowed down Willow Creek for one hour. It continued on to Ione but people there were given a warning and had sufficient time to evacuate. Most of the town and 2 miles of railroad were destroyed by the stream discharge of 36,000 cfs from a drainage area of less than 100 square miles. Bodies of some of the 247 people killed were found as far as 10 miles away from Heppner and it is thought that some may have even been carried all the way to the Columbia river (45 miles away). In the city alone, damage was estimated at $500,000; 141 houses were destroyed.

*Willamette, lower Columbia and middle Columbia rivers* Jan. 1-8, 1923 (type of flood: R-on-S)
1923 began with large amounts of rain and mild weather, and the temperatures were unusually high. The combination of these factors caused the most serious flood of the Willamette River since 1890; it damaged railroads, highways, bridges, and crops, as well as killing livestock.

*Cottage Grove* Feb. 1927 (type of flood: R-on-S)
Flooding swamped houses and businesses as water flowed down 6th Street in Cottage Grove. A little boat gave people rides from the train station to the hotel. Since there was no system of flood control, flooding in this area was common.

*Western and northeastern Oregon* Mar. 31-Apr. 1, 1931 (type of flood: R-on-S)
The last several days of March were extremely wet and quite mild. Parkdale received over 41/2 inches of rain on the 31st, while Headworks reported more than 7 inches in a two-day period. The abundant rains falling on already wet soil caused rivers to rise very quickly, washing out bridges and destroying crops in some places. The flood waters subsided quickly in early April.

*Northern Oregon, Washington, Idaho, British Columbia* Dec. 21-24, 1933 (type of flood: R-on-S)
This flood began because of intense warm rains and a collapsing lake on a lava field. Heavy snows had accumulated in the mountains early in winter and a huge storm from the Pacific brought massive quantities of warm rain and winds. In Pendleton temperatures reached 65°F and in Portland they were at 58°F. Various bridges were washed out and many dikes were broken. Several farms were completely covered with water. On the 22nd the Willamette River rose 2.2 feet, to a height of 18.4 feet, in a 24-hour period; the Columbia rose 1.2 feet. The Clatskanie River set a record for its height. Big Creek, in Kellogg, rose 30 feet in one night because of a dam that formed during a slide; on Thurman Street between 50 and 60 yards of dirt were left due to a slide. Conditions such as this closed many highways. At one time two hundred families were without food and shelter. Many people considered this the worst flood in several years, as fourteen people died and fifteen cities were partially or completely submerged.

*Cottage Grove*   Jan. 1936 (type of flood: R-on-S)
There was so much water that in the Pioneer Hardware Store the nail bins were submerged 13 inches deep; for a long time after this flood people in Cottage Grove used rusty nails. A man caught a trout swimming down the street in a bucket and later freed it in Silk Creek.

*Northwest Oregon*   Dec. 26-30, 1937 (type of flood: R-on-S)
Heavy rains caused flooding along the coast and in the Willamette Valley. Traffic problems occurred because of highway flooding and slides.

*Northwest Oregon*   Dec. 26-29, 1945 (type of flood: R-on-S)
Heavy rains, accompanied by very warm temperatures, produced a major rain-on-snow flood event. Damages were greatest in the Willamette drainage, where they totaled in the millions of dollars.

*Main-stem Columbia River*   May-Jun. 1948 (type of flood: SM)
Vanport, a community of 19,000 near Portland, was completely destroyed by the largest flood on the Columbia River since 1894. The flood resulted from cold, wet weather occurring until mid-May and a snowpack greater that average in April and early May. The temperature rose above normal beginning in mid-May, producing a large snowmelt runoff. The waters of the Columbia River crested at 30 feet on June 1. Most of the floodwaters originated in southeast British Columbia, western Montana, Idaho, and eastern Washington. The peak discharge of the Columbia River near Portland was more than 1,000,000 cfs for almost 3 weeks. This was the most destructive flood in the Columbia River Basin in 180 years. In less than one hour the entire town was completely destroyed. At least 50,000 people evacuated their homes. If the major flooding had occurred at night many times more than the 25 that were killed would have died.

*Northwest California and southwest Oregon*   Oct. 1950 (type of flood: R-on-S)
This flood resulted from rains during mid-October, which raised stream levels before the heavy rains of October 27-29 pushed them above flood stage. The peaks on most streams occurred on October 29. Six lives were lost and 2,000 people evacuated, losing many belongings. Most of the damage was to roads, bridges, and transportation and communication systems; the road damage was the worst in the history of the state up to that time.

*Western Oregon*   Jan. 8-10, 1953 (type of flood: R-on-S)
Heavy rains accompanying a major wind storm produced flooding along coastal streams and in some inland rivers. Ships were prevented from entering the Columbia for several days because of high water and large numbers of logs in the river.

*Snake and Columbia Rivers, Willamette River basin, Oregon coastal rivers*   Dec. 1955-Jan. 1956 (type of flood: R-on-S)
After a strong rainfall in December, which saturated the ground, several strong storms hit northern Oregon. Gusts of 50-65 mph in western Oregon were accompanied by intense rains and wet, heavy snow. Five people were killed, and power and telephone poles, windows, roofs, and trees were damaged. The rains increased water levels in western streams but low temperatures stopped the water barely below flood stage. Hundreds of roads around the state were closed. Five cars on a freight train were derailed and many houses were damaged. Car accidents occurred in the heavy snow in the Cascade and Coast Range passes as well as the Willamette and Umpqua valleys. There was general flooding in the far western states.

*Meyers Canyon*   Jul. 13, 1956 (type of flood: FF)
One of the largest flash floods in the United States. Bridge Creek (northeast of Mitchell) became a rapidly moving torrent taking twenty buildings with it. A highway was blocked by washouts and mud and rock slides. It was calculated that the rainfall was 3$^{1/2}$ inches in Mitchell and 4 inches in Girds Creek within 50 minutes.

*Southwestern Oregon*   Dec. 2, 1962 (type of flood: R-on-S)
Heavy rains, totaling 3-4 inches at many locations, caused severe flooding, especially in the Rogue Valley. 84 families living near the river had to be evacuated, and some homes were destroyed. The biggest economic loss was from erosion in prime farm land.

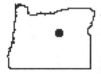

*Pacific Northwest and northern California*   Dec. 1964-Jan. 1965 (type of flood: R-on-S)
This flood was the result of two storms, the larger on December 19, 1964, and the other on January 31, 1965. On the first date intense rain topped frozen, snow-covered ground. Near-record early-season snow depths had occurred in Oregon, and these were followed by record-breaking December rainfall. On December 23, 8.44 feet of water flowed over the Dorena Dam and 3.2 feet over the Cottage Grove Dam. Hundreds of large slides were reported. Many bridges and roads were washed out and homes were destroyed and damaged. Thousands of people were evacuated. There were record river levels on December 22, 1964, at the Willamette, Rogue, Umpqua and Coquille rivers. Dams on tributaries of the Willamette were calculated to have reduced flood levels at Eugene from 39 to 24.2 feet, Salem by 7.5 feet, and Portland by 4.5 feet. This was the largest flood in Oregon since flood control reservoirs were built in the 1940s and 1950s. On the lower Umpqua the town of Reedsport was almost completely covered with 10 feet of water. There were a total of 47 deaths in the four states affected, 17 in Oregon. The damage in those same states was $430 million, $34 million in Oregon.

*Lane Canyon*   Jul. 26, 1965 (type of flood: F)
This was one of the largest flash floods in the United States. It occurred when heavy rains in the upper and middle drainage of Spears Canyon formed a wall of water an estimated 200 feet across and 8-10 feet high that crashed into one house and destroyed much farmland as well as destroying some areas of a highway and burying others under mounds of rock, mud, and debris. One person was killed and 4 or 5 were injured.

*Lower Willamette and Sandy rivers and northern Oregon coastal area*   Jan. 11 1972 (type of flood: R-on-S)

This flood, which caused at least two deaths and at least three injuries, was limited to drainages on the west side of the Cascade range. Tillamook evacuated 104 of its 3,900 citizens before mud slides and high waters trapped the remaining residents by closing all highways surrounding the community. Many bridges were demolished or damaged by flooding on the Trask, Wilson, Nehalem, and Nestucca rivers. Six million coho salmon may have died at the Klaskanine State Fish Hatchery because muddy water contaminated their holding ponds. Corvallis received over 3 inches of rain on the 11th and 12th. This flood exceeded the December 1964 to January 1965 flood in many northern Oregon coastal rivers. It was followed by several smaller floods which occurred within the next two weeks.

*Western Oregon*   Jan. 13-17, 1974 (type of flood: R-on-S)

Following heavy snow and freezing rain, a series of mild storms with intense rainfall caused large snowmelt and rapid runoff. Nine counties in Oregon were declared disaster areas. Thirteen people were injured. Port Orford 5E (the station 5 miles east of the town) received 9.01 inches of rain in one day and 19.97 inches in four days.

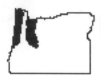

*Willamette River, northern Oregon coastal drainages*   Dec. 10-12, 1978 (type of flood: R-on-S)

An intense rain, some snowmelt, and previously wet soils contributed to the overflow of all the coastal streams and some of the streams on the western side of the Willamette Valley. Two adults drowned on the 11th while attempting to drive through a flooded section of the Yaquina River on Nashville Road (6 miles northeast of Eddyville). A 65-year-old man died on the 12th in a effort to reach dry land from his flooded car on Oakville Road (5 miles southeast of Corvallis).

*Polallie Creek*   Dec. 25, 1980 (type of flood: DF)

Very heavy warm rains on an already water-saturated headwall of Polallie Creek (on the northeast flanks of Mount Hood, 38 miles south of Hood River) created this flood in which one person died. The headwall slumped and a resulting landslide quickly became a debris flow depositing about 100,000 cubic yards of debris at the confluence of Polallie Creek and the East Fork Hood River forming a debris dam across the East Fork Hood River. A lake formed behind the blockage and breached the natural dam within minutes. Ten miles of highway were closed. A bridge was washed out and a campground was destroyed. Mapleton (east of Florence, on the coast) received 5.3 inches of rain in 24 hours. Johnson Creek near Portland had between 2 and 3 feet of water over its banks. Hood River County was declared a disaster area.

*Klamath River*   Feb. 1982 (type of flood: R-on-S)

This flood was the result of very heavy rain. Keno reported nearly 2 inches in a two-day period on the 21st and 22nd. Temperatures were in the 50s and 60s during that period, causing significant snowmelt in addition.

*Eastern Oregon (Pendleton)*   Feb. 11-12, 1985 (type of flood: SM)

Melting snow caused flooding in eastern Oregon that blocked U.S. Highway 397. Snow slides covered Highway 35 and Highway 20 with 10 to 15 feet of snow but it was cleared in two hours. Some rural roads were also blocked. Wind gusts were up to 78 mph.

*Ontario*   Dec. 30, 1985-Jan 1, 1986 (type of flood: DF)
After several weeks of freezing temperatures there were over 40 miles of ice jams on the Snake River between Farewell Bend (northwest of Weiser, Idaho) and Ontario. The ice jams forced water outside its normal channel and caused flooding. At least 35 people evacuated their homes.

*All of Oregon*   Feb. 22-23, 1986 (type of flood: SM)
Powerful rains and melting snows combined to push rivers to flood stage. West of the Cascades 4 to 6 inches of rain fell in the 48-hour period from the 22nd to the 24th. Flood warnings were issued for the lower Columbia River, the Willamette River from Albany to Portland, the lower Coquille River, the Umatilla River in western Umatilla County, and the Luckiamute, Pudding, Nehalem and Wilson rivers. Numerous homes had to be evacuated and many roads were closed because of high water, mudslides, and washed-out portions of road.

*Wallowa County*   Jun. 5, 1986 (1530 PST) (type of flood: FF)
A forceful thunderstorm brought $5^{1/2}$ inches of rain and 3 inches of hail and resulted in flash flooding in Enterprise. Roads washed out and mud slides occurred in some locations.

*Western Oregon*   Feb. 1-4, 1987 (type of flood: R-on-S)
The flooding of the Willamette River, its tributaries, and the central and northern coastal rivers was the result of heavy rains from the storms of January 31 and February 1. One man was killed while trying to save his boat on the Yamhill River. Mud slides, flooded highways, and damaged homes resulted from the flooding.

*South-central and northeast Oregon, the east end of the Columbia Basin*   Mar. 9-11, 1989 (1600-1700 PST) (type of flood: SM)
Warm rains combined with sudden increases in temperatures in eastern Oregon caused extensive snowpacks to melt quickly. Many rivers and creeks overflowed their banks. Rain fell even at high elevations; Crater Lake received nearly 2 inches of rain on the 9th and 10th, causing a significant reduction in the snow depth. Most low-elevation sites received 1 to 2 inches of rain during that same period.

*Malheur County*   Jun. 15, 1989 (1700 PST) (type of flood: FF)
A flash flood occurred due to thunderstorms that began in southeast Oregon and moved north. In Nyssa there were $1^{1/4}$ inches of rain in only 30 minutes. Crops were damaged by hail up to one-half inch in diameter. Large trees were pulled from the ground by high winds.

*Clatsop, Tillamook, Lincoln, Marion counties*   Dec. 3-4, 1989 (type of flood: R-on-S)
The most northwestern portions of Oregon were affected by a warm Pacific storm system that brought heavy rain and high wind. Following 24 hours of rainfall (generally 2 to 3 inch totals), flood warnings were issued for the Wilson, Nehalem, and Siletz rivers. Woodburn and Keizer also flooded. Two highways were closed because of mud slides. Near Newport, a 42-foot-long fishing vessel capsized and caused the death of one person before two other passengers were rescued.

*Western Oregon*   Jan. 6-10, 1990 (type of flood: R-on-S)
The damage from this flood was worst in Tillamook County, along the Nehalem River, which was 11.9 feet above flood stage. The water was 5 feet deep in the town of Nehalem. On a nearby farm, 51 cattle were drowned. Throughout Western Oregon, ten rivers in eight counties flooded in a five-day period. Many bridges were washed away.

*Wilson River, Tillamook County*   Apr. 4-6, 1991 (type of flood: R-on-S)
Flooding was caused by a 48-hour rainstorm. that raised the Wilson River to 5 feet above its flood stage. A mudslide 600 feet wide and 700 feet tall covered the Wilson River Highway, which had to be closed for months for repairs. In 48 hours, Lee's Camp (in the coastal mountains) received 12 inches of rain. Thirty businesses were affected in Tillamook due to 3 feet of water in the city's downtown.

*Union County, Baker County*   May 19-20, 1991 (type of flood: R-on-S)
This normally dry area received between 2 and 4 inches of rain in two days, with the greatest amounts in the mountain canyons. This caused an outpouring of water into the Umatilla and Grande Ronde rivers. Farms at low elevations and highways flooded when rivers and creeks rose 3.5 feet above their flood stages. A piece of highway 35 feet wide, 35 feet long, and 20 feet deep was washed away. Umatilla County lost at least fourteen bridges and 14 miles of fencing, while in Union County 15,000 acres of wheat farms were flooded and in Baker County twenty irrigation dams were damaged.

*South-central Oregon*   Jul. 24, 1991 (type of flood: FF)
This flash flood was caused by tremendous rain— 4.8 inches fell in one hour at LaPine. Mud slides washed out part of a highway and bales of hay. Hail from the storm was so deep that snow plows were used to get it off the roads.

*Crook County*   Aug. 5, 1991 (1445-1600PST) (type of flood: FF)
Newsome Creek formed a wall of water 200 feet wide and 50 feet high that rushed into the Aspen Valley Ranch. A man died because he was holding onto a fence that was swept up by the water. There were reports of farm equipment, cars, and animals that had been swept as far as 6 miles downstream.

*Malheur County*   Mar. 18-21, 1993 (type of flood: R-on-S)
The snowpack for this cold, wet winter was far above normal in the river basins of Harney County. On the 17th and 18th freezing levels were high and an inch of rain fell, melting the snowpack into the rivers. The Owyhee River had almost dried up the previous fall, but reached its record flow of 42,000 cfs on the 18th. Owyhee Reservoir, the largest in the state, was nearly empty in February, but by the end of March it had filled and was spilling. Because of the remote locations involved, only a few roads and farmhouses were damaged. Highways 20 and 95 were closed for two days because of the excessive water. Flooding also occurred in Harney, Grant, and Wheeler counties at the same time.

*Northwestern Oregon*   Feb. 5-9, 1996 (type of flood: R-on-S)
This flood was caused by a combination of deep snowpack, warm
temperatures, and record-breaking rains that saturated the soil. Rain (over 20
inches in four days at some high-elevation sites) caused streams to rise on the
6th and the 7th, reaching flood stage and setting all-time flood records in some
locations. The South Yamhill River (near Whiteson), Pudding River, Tualatin
River, Sandy River, Nehalem River, Grande Ronde River (at Troy—2 feet higher
than previous record), and the Deschutes River (at Moody) all had water levels
equal to more than a 75-year occurrence. This flood was comparable in
magnitude to the flood of December 1964.

*Northern California and Oregon*   Nov. 18-20, 1996 (type of flood: R-on-S)
Record-breaking precipitation throughout much of Oregon caused local
flooding, landslides, and power outages over much of the state during
November 18-20. The rain resulted from a broad upper-air weather system of
moist subtropical air from the tropical Pacific. The air reached southwestern
Oregon on the 17th and spread to the remainder of the state the following day.
Several locations in Oregon set their all-time 24 hour precipitation records; the
all-time one-day record for any NOAA site in Oregon, 11.65 inches, was
recorded at the Elk River Fish Hatchery on the 19th. Landslides in Douglas
County killed 5 people.

*Northwest*   Dec. 30, 1996 to Jan. 5, 1997 (type of flood: R-on-S)
Mild subtropical moisture persisted over the entire Northwest for several days,
causing heavy rain and rapid snowmelt. This flood affected a large region from
California to Idaho with a total of seventy counties declaring disasters and
estimated damage totaling in the hundreds of millions of dollars. Washington
Governor Mike Lowry declared nineteen counties disaster areas and more than
a dozen storm-related deaths were reported. In Oregon eight counties were
declared disaster areas. Hardest hit was Ashland in southern Oregon where
21,000 residents tried to cope with a river running through the middle of town.

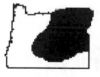

*Central and eastern Oregon*   May 1998 (type of flood: R-on-S)
Persistent rains throughout May set numerous records for monthly precipitation
and caused widespread flooding. Prineville was declared a disaster area due to
flooding when Ochoco Dam filled and began to spill. Mudslides caused
problems in Malheur, Wheeler, Crook and Wallowa counties.

# Snowstorms

The recipe for creating a snowstorm is quite simple: start with cold air, add moisture, and stir. In high elevations in the Cascades, and in central and eastern Oregon, snow is a common winter occurrence; the air is generally cold enough for snow, so the mere addition of sufficient moisture (generally from Pacific storms) is all that's needed. In western Oregon, however, snow is a rare commodity (at least at low elevations). Most of the time, moisture is abundant, but cold air is not. The Cascades form a natural barrier that keeps the cold air from the interior from reaching western valleys and the coast. The Cascades essentially partition Oregon in winter into two different air masses: mild and moist to the west and cold and dry to the east. While precipitation in the west is primarily in the form of rain, a significant percentage to the east is in the form of snow.

Snow is relatively rare along the immediate coastline throughout the study area. As one moves inland or upward, the amount of snowfall reported per year increases steadily. For example, Laurel Mountain, in the Coast Range at 3590 feet above sea level, averages 110 inches of snow per year. Assuming a ratio of snow to water of 10:1, this represents about 10% of Laurel Mountain's average annual precipitation of 116 inches. Newport, at sea level, averages 1.57 inches of snowfall, which would represent only 0.2% of its annual average of 72.04 inches.

*Oregon State Capitol, Salem, January 1950. (OSU Archives P218)*

In the Willamette Valley, Portland Airport averages 36.12 inches of precipitation and 5.44 inches of snow, so the water in the snow represents 1.5% of the annual average. Government Camp, near Mt. Hood (at about 4,000 feet in elevation), gets an average of 86.03 inches of precipitation and 278 inches of snow, so the snowfall there makes up about 32% of the total precipitation.

The one break in the natural Cascades barrier is the Columbia Gorge, the only low-level passage through the mountains. Cold air which lies east of the Cascades often moves westward, funneling cold air into the Portland area. If a wet Pacific storm happens to reach the area at the same time, big snow events may result. In fact, Oregon's greatest one-day snowstorm occurred in just such a situation.

## The Biggest Single Day Storm: January, 1980

A series of strong storms, accompanied by snow, ice, wind, and freezing rain, hit Oregon very hard over a three-day period. On January 9, high snowfall and extreme winds caused travel problems, injuries, and power outages. Hood River received 30 inches of snow, while Cascades Locks had 20 and The Dalles 15. At Bonneville Dam, however, the one-day total was 39 inches, the all-time record for any location in Oregon. How unlikely that in a state with many high mountains, the record snowfall occurred at only 60 feet above sea level!

Avalanche warnings were issued in the Cascades above 4,000 feet, but snow extended all the way to the coast; Astoria reported 2 inches of snow on the 9th. Six deaths occurred during the storm:

—Kenneth Connolly, 29, of Baker was killed when his tractor-trailer truck collided with another truck on US 730.

—Louis Lang, 64, of Parkdale, collapsed while plowing snow with a tractor.

—In Portland, a falling tree killed Pamela McClean.

—Elma Grace Gabrielson, 79, was found buried under several inches of snow near her Woodland, Washington, home; she had apparently slipped while attempting to check her mail.

—A 24-year-old Bothell, Washington, man was trapped beneath a moving automobile and dragged more than 500 feet.

—A four-year-old boy was missing in Hermiston after an unsucessful two-day search of nearby woods and ponds was called off.

Portland mayor Connie McCready declared a limited state of emergency on January 10, as 200,000 Portland area customers were without power or phone for several days. Emergency road crews, shelters, and other services were created to alleviate the effects of the storm. Amtrak trains following Union Pacific Railway snowplows rescued stranded motorists, including secretary of state Norma Paulus, who took the train back to Salem, leaving her car in The Dalles where she was scheduled to speak at the Chamber of Commerce. An estimated 125 boats, with a combined value of over $3 million, sank in the Gorge and Portland. Sporting events, including a high adventure seminar in snowshoeing, were cancelled. A Union Pacific train struck two vehicles in snow-related incidents. In the first, a motorist in Portland was seriously injured after running a stop sign and driving into the path of the train; authorities said that poor visibility caused by the snowfall had contributed to the accident. Later the same day, at The Dalles, a pickup became stuck in packed snow at a crossing and was hit by the same train and hurled about 20 feet. The driver was treated for multiple fractures and other injuries.

## Crater Lake

Although Bonneville Dam holds the one-day record, Oregon's true "snow champion" is Crater Lake. Located at 6,480 feet elevation at the Park headquarters, the Crater Lake measurement site has seen more snow more often than any other long-term weather station in the state. Although Crater Lake is south of the typical path of the main winter storm track, it still receives significant snow during most winter storms. In addition, it often picks up abundant moisture from subtropical systems arriving from the southwest, often receiving more snow than at Cascade peaks farther north.

Winter comes early at Crater Lake. In 50% of all years, the first snow comes prior to September 29, and by the end of the snow season (generally some time in June), an average of 98 days will have had measurable snowfall.

Table 30 lists the top ten occurrences of snowfall at Crater Lake.

**Table 30. Crater Lake snowfall records**

| 1-day total | | Monthly total | | Season (July-June) | | Calendar year | |
|---|---|---|---|---|---|---|---|
| (inches) | Date | (inches) | Month | (inches) | Season | (inches) | Year |
| 37 | Jan. 27 37 | 313 | Jan. 1950 | 836 | 1951-52 | 903 | 1950 |
| 37 | Jan. 17 51 | 248.5 | Feb. 1949 | 830 | 1932-33 | 819 | 1948 |
| 37 | Feb. 28 71 | 241.6 | Jan. 1933 | 824 | 1949-50 | 766 | 1933 |
| 34 | Nov. 17 94 | 216 | Jan. 1904 | 822 | 1948-49 | 740 | 1932 |
| 31.5 | Jan. 13 47 | 213.4 | Jan. 1937 | 789 | 1931-32 | 735 | 1964 |
| 31.5 | Oct. 30 56 | 198.7 | Feb. 1938 | 677 | 1937-38 | 732 | 1951 |
| 31 | Jan. 2 33 | 196 | Dec. 1948 | 677 | 1936-37 | 726 | 1937 |
| 31 | Jan. 26 54 | 195.5 | Dec. 1996 | 672 | 1970-71 | 717 | 1996 |
| 31 | Jan. 20 64 | 194.1 | Mar. 1938 | 660 | 1955-56 | 703 | 1952 |
| 30 | Dec. 25 31 | 194 | Jan. 1952 | 651 | 1947-48 | 698 | 1971 |

# Notable Snowstorms

### The "Big Snow"—December 1919
In December 1919, Oregon was blitzed by prodigious snows, chilled by a record-setting arctic air mass—and blessed by 60°F temperatures and sunshine.

Many of the all-time minimum temperatures and deepest snowfalls that were recorded in that month for Central Oregon still stand in 1999. In Bend, snow, which started to fall about 1:00 a.m. Tuesday, December 9, totaled 5 inches by 8:00 a.m., and had doubled in depth by noon. That night, Bend's minimum temperature was -7°F, At Fort Rock the mercury plummeted to -24°F. The most immediately noticeable effect of the low temperatures in Bend was when the flow of water into the Bend Water, Light and Power Co. plant on the Deschutes River was diminished, sharply reducing the supply of electricity to city residents.

Heavy snow continued to fall nonstop in Bend all day Tuesday and throughout most of Wednesday, December 10. By that time, a total of 47 inches of snow had fallen in two days, in addition to the 8 inches that was already on the ground when the storm started. The deep snow brought all motorized traffic to a halt; horse-drawn snowplows were put into operation and endeavored to clear streets in the downtown area—at that time, the only business district in Bend. Train service into Bend from all directions was delayed due to tracks being blockaded with snow.

*Oregon State University campus following 1940 snow storm. (OSU Archives #40)*

Both the Brooks-Scanlon and the Shevlin-Hixon Company, Bend's two giant lumber companies, suspended all operations at their mills and their logging camps in the nearby forests. As a result, two thousand men were temporarily without their usual work. However, the two lumber companies employed crews of men to shovel snow from the roofs of buildings as a precaution against the weight of snow causing them to collapse.

As is often the case during severe weather events, comparisons were made with previous severe winter weather, namely, the historic winter of 1884-85. Pioneer stockman C. J. Allen recollected (*Bend Bulletin*, December 11, 1919) that in the winter of 1884-85 hundreds of cattle and horses died from lack of food, and he lost a thousand sheep out of an original band of 3,500. Ranchers attempting to save their stock had had to battle deep drifts piled up by high winds. While the snowstorm raged some thermometers registered temperatures between 25°F and 30°F below zero. Other thermometers were said to have "frozen."

Back to 1919! Once the snow had ceased, work commenced in earnest to move the snow blockades in the city and on the rural roads. Men with six-horse teams worked to open the streets for travel. Pedestrians floundered through the deep drifts or stayed at home.

By Friday, December 12, the depth of snow combined with the lack of empty railroad cars caused by the railroad blockade forced Brooks-Scanlon and Shevlin-Hixon companies to remain closed. (Even when they opened the following week, the ice on the log pond had to be broken at the Shevlin-Hixon plant.) Men continued shoveling snow from the roof of the shop buildings at the two mills. To keep the boiler fires going at both plants, approximately a hundred cords of wood a day were used. As of Friday, December 12, Brooks-Scanlon had approximately eight hundred cords of wood on hand. Shevlin-Hixon had exhausted its reserves and wood was hauled from the Bend brickyard west of town. Not surprisingly, this large daily consumption of firewood resulted in a shortage of firewood generally available to Bend residents. This became a critical concern. In many homes the supply of firewood was entirely exhausted and several families left their homes and took up residence in local hotels.

On cessation of the snowfall the principal occupation in Bend was removing snow from the roofs of homes and garages. Some property owners had delayed the snow removal until it was too late and there were reports of several collapsed roofs.

Record cold followed the snowstorm. In Bend on December 12 the mercury dropped to -25°F, an official record for the city. To the north, in Madras, there were conflicting reports as to how cold it was. A Madras correspondent to *The Oregonian* reported a temperature of 57°F below zero. *The Oregonian*, with a December 13, 1919, dateline from Madras stated: "The thermometer managed to record the 57 degrees F below mark but committed suicide by bursting."

By Saturday, December 13, the worst of the cold wave had passed. In Bend, where the minimum temperature had been -23°F on December 12, the mercury dropped to "only" -6°F. Train service to and from Portland was nearly back to normal. Snow removal continued in town and in the rural areas. On Monday, December 15, both Brooks-Scanlon and the Shevlin-Hixon Co. plants started partial operations, though a shortage of logs affected the milling operations at the Shevlin-Hixon Company plant.

On Tuesday, December 16, with a warm wind blowing, Bend's maximum temperature reached 42°F—not a heat wave, but 67°F higher than the extreme minimum that had been recorded only four days earlier. Statewide, while December minimums included readings as low as -41°F at Austin, Grant County, and -47°F at Blitzen, Harney County, two weeks later there were several maximums—both east and west of the Cascades—over 60°F. Oregon's extreme December maximum included 67°F at both Brookings and (surprisingly) at Government Camp (December 28), 66°F at Eugene and 62°F at Blitzen—the same weather station that had registered -47°F only two weeks earlier.

## The 1969 Eugene Snowstorm

Usually, even the prospect of snowflakes in Eugene creates quite a stir. Radios and newspapers send out the warning: "chance of snow flurries tonight." Though conditioned for any type of rain, Eugene is generally unprepared for large accumulations of snow.

It was early January, 1969. After a bout of relatively cold weather (13°F in the previous month), on January 4 and 5, Eugene basked in consecutive days of 60°F-plus temperatures. However, as the month progressed, weather forecasters eyed an advancing arctic air mass. On January 22, the heaviest snowfall of the season to date, 2 to 6 inches, covered the Willamette Valley and the coastal areas, restricted traffic, caused school closures, and disrupted air travel at Eugene's Mahlon Sweet Airport. Nonetheless, the official forecast for Thursday, January 23, was for "Improved conditions— decreasing chance of precipitation."

Thursday was cold and every reporting station throughout Oregon reported freezing temperatures. In Eugene, bright sunshine glittered off the snowy landscape. Camera enthusiasts were out shooting Christmas postcard scenes. By afternoon, clouds moved in and forecasters revised their forecasts to a chance of more snow that evening, occasional snow Friday before turning to rain Friday evening. But the snow held off until early Saturday morning (the 25th). A little before 6:00 a.m. large fluffy flakes started falling. By afternoon, Eugeneans were remarking, "It's still snowing." It was, at a rate of an inch an hour. By midnight, there was a whopping 14 inches, double Eugene's previous 24-hour maximum (set in January 1950).

Snow lovers had a field day. Ten sledding hills were set up in Eugene and every night sledding took place at the Laurelwood Golf Course, with the city providing the lights (and wood for warming bonfires). By Sunday, different people reacted in their own way to the continued snowfall. Chamber of Commerce Manager Fred Brenne stated, "It just proves that Eugene has something for everybody!" Other residents felt that they had

*Street near State Capitol, Salem, January 1950. (Photo by Wanda Gifford. OSU Archives, P218, 571F)*

had enough of some of his "everything." Meetings were cancelled. People bundled up close to the warm glow of the fireplace or to the TV set, or both. Old-timers ranked the winter of 1969 in the "Among-the-Worst" category, along with those of 1919, 1924, the "mid-30s" and 1957.

Some residents took to the streets of Eugene on skis. Hardy joggers did their utmost to get in their daily ritual. South of town, 30th Avenue became the city's version of the Willamette Pass, with sledding, skiing, and tubing. The manager of a downtown department store pondered the reasons for a run on swimsuits—buyers were either planning a trip to a warmer climate or were simply morale-building. State police were logging 130 calls an hour for requests for current road conditions. A *Register-Guard* photographer spotted a snowman shouldering a sign saying, "Snow makes me sick!" All high school athletic events scheduled for Saturday were cancelled, except that a "snow-is-nothing-new" Gilchrist team journeyed to Creswell for a basketball game. Taxi companies in Eugene were swamped with calls.

Later Saturday night, winds picked up to 15-18 mph and caused drifting of the snow. By Sunday the streets of Eugene and Springfield were clogged, since neither city owned snowplows. Eugene pressed two graders into service. Still the snow kept coming. Nearly 14 additional inches were added by Sunday morning. Sunday church services were sparsely attended. People with flat roofs worried . . . and shoveled. The almost continuous 70-hour snowfall ended at 3:30 a.m. Monday morning with 29 inches on the ground at the Eugene Airport. However, more intermittent snow was yet to fall. By now, forecasters were put to the test of explaining, "What happened?"

In a nutshell, the prodigious snowfalls were the result of a low-pressure system that forecasters had thought was destined for California, which caused over-running moisture (warm wet air moving at the upper levels over cold surface air in the Valley). As the moisture from the "warm" damp air mass descended through the cold air, it turned to snow. Then another low off the coast of Washington pumped in more moisture.

Police discouraged all except emergency traffic. Public schools were closed throughout most of western Lane County. Lane Community College and, for the first time in memory, the University of Oregon, cancelled classes. Few businesses in Eugene were open—employees could not report to work. In brief, Eugene became a ghost town.

Logging in Lane County came to a halt, and mills were silent. Hotel and motel managers reported a brisk business as registered guests could not leave and those stranded in Eugene sought refuge from the prolonged storm. Virtually all Eugene area meetings were cancelled Monday and Tuesday. The Eugene police noted that the most serious reported "crime" was snowball throwing.

Americans have always been known for their creativity and adaptability; Eugeneans were no exception. People made available four-wheel drive vehicles for police patrols. Children used not only conventional sleds but ironing boards and metal and plastic discs. Residents who were unable to buy snow shovels (one firm sold more snow shovels in two days that it normally sold all winter) attempted to clear snow using pieces of plywood, dustpans and buckets, and garden spades. Snowmen popped up everywhere—including one inside a phone booth on Alder Street. Horses were put to work doing deliveries. KEZI technician, Merl Smith, marooned at the TV station's transmitter in the Coburg Hills, kept the station on the air despite the raging storm. KVAL weatherman Michael Hartfield, snowbound at home, phoned in the weather reports for television viewers.

North Eugene High School's ski team met at Skinner's Butte (at the south end of town) for practice. A hospital x-ray technician was driven to work in a snowmobile. For a time, the National Guard provided transportation for nurses. Four-wheelers chauffeured telephone operators to their jobs.

By midnight Monday, January 27, another 10 inches of snow had fallen and by that time the January total of 43.6 inches far exceeded the previous January record of 36.2 inches set in 1960. Weather bureau employees checked past data to compare snowfalls in Eugene. The verdict? Never before had it snowed so much in Eugene. In the 38 years since weather data were first taken at the Eugene Airport, Eugene winters had averaged 5.4 inches of snow. Total snowfall for *all* of the Januarys between 1951 and 1968 was 42.0 inches—still under the snowfall for January 1969.

Other winters with substantial snows included 1964-65 (15.1 inches in December and January): 1942-43 (14 inches including 12 inches in two days); 1948-49 (13.1 inches); 1956-57 (13.1 inches). In December 1884, Eugene was blitzed by 3 feet of snow and recorded temperatures as low as 6°F. That December chickens froze to their roosts. Store roofs collapsed or leaked. Travel was impaired and one train from Portland to Eugene took 51 hours. Hundreds of fruit trees were splintered by the weight of the snow and ice.

*Snow and ice on water tower in Willamette Valley, 1919. (OSU Archives, P216)*

On Tuesday morning (January 28, 1969) with 34 inches of snow on the ground, the mercury plunged to 1°F. Forecasters warned of possible new snow. The *Register Guard*, in its editorial praised telephone, power, and highway crews for keeping communications and power lines open and some major streets passable. The editor added, "If there is to be a lesson learned from the storm, it was the old Boy Scout motto, 'Be Prepared,'" Reference was made to having some adequate winter clothing, minimum food supplies for a snowy day, and . . . a snow shovel!

By Wednesday, Eugene was slowly returning to normal. The University of Oregon opened for classes, but Lane Community College and the public schools remained closed. Downtown stores reopened but most parking lots were still deep in snow. There were still no flights from Mahlon Sweet Airport. One Air West DC 9 was still stranded at the airport after six days. During the day (Wednesday) another 3 inches of snow fell but the mercury climbed to 38°F. Several Eugene structures collapsed under the weight of the accumulated snow. People dug into snowdrifts checking to see if the white mound was indeed their car. Others, some on skis, ventured to the supermarket. The State Motor Vehicles Division requested that motorists with expired operator or auto licenses renew them by mail.

The heaviest snows of that 1969 storm were largely confined to the southern Willamette Valley and other parts of Lane County. Salem received

11 inches; Portland 8 inches; Florence, normally snow-free most winters, was covered by 14 inches.

Meanwhile, an army of public employees was engaged in the gigantic and costly task of clearing the snow from city, county, and state highways. By Thursday, if not well before, cabin fever had set in and even snow lovers began to grumble. Children were all played out. Motorists, often unavoidably, splashed slush on curbside pedestrians, who, in turn, shook their fists at horn-blaring motorists. Residents of the hilly residential areas of Eugene complained about the lack of snow removal in their areas.

By Thursday, downtown business picked up. However, that was not the case with garbage. There had been no curbside collection since the previous Saturday. The next morning (Friday), Eugene's minimum was a mild 36°F. The snow depth at the airport had shrunk to 10 inches and the main runway had been cleared for flights. Rain, 1.62 inches of it, further reduced the soggy snowpack, but the added weight collapsed the roofs of buildings and barns in Junction City (including the American Can Planing Mill) and elsewhere. Nuisance flooding followed the snow. By Monday, February 2, most children were back in school but highway travel and off-street parking were still impeded by mounds of snow. Lumber operations in Lane County struggled back to production on the Tuesday. The State Employment Office in Eugene processed over seven thousand claims for unemployment compensation (maximum $49 per week) for work lost due to the snowstorm. The storm had cost the City of Eugene over $50,000 in snow-removal expenses.

Wednesday, February 5, snow again appeared in the forecast for the Eugene area. However, the forecasters added, "We have an entirely different (weather) situation. We're not going to have that type of system for another 100 years."

*The 1969 snowstorm affected areas throughout the state. Gilbert Sternes, State Climatologist, was quoted in a news story discussing the significance of the storm. The story (published in* The Oregonian, *February 13, 1969) included the following information:*

*—***Astoria** *set a new record of 25 inches of total snowfall during January, double the previous January record of 10.7 inches. The 18 inches of snow on the ground also beat the previous record of 14 inches on the ground.*

*—***Eugene***'s total of 47.1 inches of snowfall and 34 inches on the ground beat the previous record of 36.1 inches of snowfall and nearly tripled the previous record of 11 inches of snow on the ground at any one time.*

*—***Government Camp***'s 138 inches of total snow depth beat the previous January record of 137 inches.*

*—***Grants Pass***'s 19.1 inches of total snowfall beat the precious January record of 18.8 inches.*

—**Oakridge** *set a new total snowfall record of 40.7 inches, well above the previous record of 34.5 inches.*

—**Roseburg**'s *35.2 inches of snowfall and 27 inches on the ground beat the previous record of 28 inches total and 8 inches of snow depth.*

—**Seaside** *smashed all previous records with 26 inches total, compared to 6 inches, and 12 inches snow depth, compared to the previous record of 6 inches.*

## Strange Brown Snow in Central Oregon

As we all know, snow is normally white. Bacteria and lichens can create interesting color patterns, and we're warned not to eat snow that has a yellow tint. The story of the brown snow is unique, however. *The Oregonian* published the following story by Phil Brogan, a legendary weather writer and Northwest Director of the American Meteorological Society, on March 25, 1956.

It occurred just fifty years ago, in March 1906. Not long after the colored snow appeared, a brown film was visible in parts of Oregon east of the Cascades.

March of 1906 apparently came in like a meek lamb. New lawns in the village of Bend, then on the Oregon frontier, started to green. Flamboyant sunsets formed backgrounds for the Three Sisters, Jefferson, and Hood.

Then came a blizzard, around March 10. Temperature dropped from spring brackets to chilling zero, and lower. In the Deschutes basin a low of -13°F was recorded, and that mark still stands as an all-time low for the month in that area.

Eight inches of snow blanketed much of the interior plateau, south of the Columbia. The snow fell at night. Next morning when residents of the rangelands looked out over the eastern Oregon hills they found the earth covered with brown snow.

At first it was believed that the snow was merely tinted with a brown film. But it was soon found that the pack was brown from top to bottom. Residents of the region were a bit alarmed. There were rumors of volcanic action in the area. The stuff that colored the snow was not confined to the drifts. It permeated buildings. It sifted under shingles. Goods on store shelves were discolored.

What was the source of that mysterious brown snow of half a century ago? Travelers from the north, their trip inland from the Shaniko railhead of that day delayed by storm, had a possible answer.

About the time the March storm broke over interior Oregon, a fierce wind was whipping sand and dust into dunes between Wallulah, Washington, and The Dalles. Six passenger trains in that area had been stalled, not by snow but by drifting sands and dust. The drifting was caused by a stiff downstream wind along the Columbia. Fine dust from the storm apparently was carried aloft, then intermingled with the snow that was falling over the interior country.

Soon the brown snow disappeared from the rangelands. But the dust remained.

## Tragedy on Mt. Hood

Snow gives life to much of Oregon. Occasionally it brings tragedy as well. One of Oregon's saddest weather-related disasters involved snow, winds, and Oregon's highest peak, Mt. Hood.

May 1986 had been exceptionally cool—and wet. Rain had fallen throughout western Oregon every day from May 1 through 7. At higher elevations in the Cascades the precipitation fell as snow. On Friday, May 9, there was a break in the weather. However, the forecast for the coming weekend from *The Oregonian* was not encouraging: "Although Oregon will experience some drying and warming Friday, the spring-like respite will be short-lasting. Another weather system from Alaska should bring clouds and showers to the state for the weekend."

The next two days, Saturday (May 10) and Sunday (May 11), the forecasts were for showers in all areas with cooler temperatures. Snow levels were forecasted at 3,000 feet in the northern Oregon Cascades on Sunday and 3,500 feet on Monday. A more ominous weather forecast was issued for Monday: "A strong weather system off the coast of Alaska will bring heavy rainfall for NW Oregon on Monday." Freezing levels were forecast to be at 3,500 feet.

Early (2:30 a.m.) on Monday morning, with relatively good climbing conditions prevailing, three adults and fifteen teenagers from the Oregon Episcopal School in Portland set out from Timberline Lodge (5,960 feet) to climb Mt. Hood. Ralph Summers, 30, of Welches was the group's professional guide; the students were participating in the school's four-year Basecamp program. The sophomores in the group had previously had extensive training; the experienced seniors went along to offer encouragement to their younger classmates. The two faculty members from the school were Marion Horwell, dean of the upper school students, and the Rev. Thomas Goman.

The climb, which had been completed by 34 previous groups from the school, was expected to take ten hours. Students were expected back at Timberline Lodge between 4:00 and 6:00 p.m. Monday.

Soon after the climb had begun, five students dropped out. Another student got altitude sickness after about six hours of climbing and he, too, returned to Timberline Lodge. The remainder of the climbing party continued. At about 3:45 p.m. the weather suddenly worsened and, despite being within 100 feet of the summit, the group turned back. By then, blinding snow and ferocious winds, estimated to have been 60 m.p.h. or more, cut visibility to practically zero. The wind chill was about 50°F below zero. By then, one of the students was showing signs of hypothermia and the group was forced to take a slower pace.

At 5:15 p.m. near the 8,300 foot level, in knee-deep snow, it was decided to discontinue the descent. Using ice axes and their hands, the climbers dug a small snow cave and breathing hole. Here the group, "packed in like sardines," hoped to wait out the storm. But there were problems. The climbers, having expected to be back at Timberline Lodge by evening, had not packed extra food and drink and, in any case, their backpacks were outside of the cave buried by snow or had blown away. In addition, the cave entrance and the breathing holes were continuously being covered by drifting snow.

That evening, in Portland, the school phoned parents to say that students had not returned from the climb. At 9:30 p.m. the bus driver who had driven the group to Timberline Lodge reported to the Clackamas County Sheriff's office that the climbers were missing.

At first light the next morning (Tuesday, May 13), despite blizzard conditions, the group's leader, Ralph Summers, and Molly Schula, considered to be one of the strongest of the school's climbers, set off down the mountain, hoping to reach Timberline Lodge—and help. However, the couple got lost and ended up at Mount Hood Meadows, 2 miles east of Timberline, at 9:00 a.m.

*An old rotary snowplow clearing the roads near Mt. Hood below Government Camp. (Photo by Ralph I. Gifford, OSU Archives, P218, 0750)*

Meanwhile, that same morning, a full-scale rescue team that included 150 rescuers from several different agencies was launched. However, inclement weather hampered the search and grounded helicopters that were on standby. One of the helicopters (from the U. S. Air Force Reserve's 304th Air Rescue and Recovery Squadron) encountered winds of over 120 m.p.h. at the 10,000 foot level. Plans for Group 2 of the Oregon Episcopal School's Basecamp program, scheduled to attempt the Mt. Hood climb that day, were postponed. That evening family members and friends of the missing climbers drove to Timberline Lodge, where they anxiously awaited word of their children or loved ones.

Tuesday night the weather cleared and at 5:30 a.m. Wednesday a helicopter with Ralph Summers, the leader of the climbing group, on board lifted off. Shortly thereafter another helicopter joined in the search. At 5:55 a.m. one of the helicopters landed at a spot where Summers believed the snow cave was located. Word came by radio communication that "survivors had been found." However, the joy quickly turned to dismay. Search crews had found three bodies, which were flown to Portland's Emanuel Hospital. Efforts by doctors to revive the three climbers, Erin O'Leary, Alison Litzenberger, and Erik Sandvik, failed.

Despite a search that lasted all day Wednesday, air and ground crews, the latter using dogs, were unable to locate the snow cave.

The painstaking section-by-section search resumed at 4:00 a.m. on Thursday (May 15). Toward late afternoon, Ralph Summers, again scrutinizing the landscape from a helicopter, spotted a place that looked familiar. The ground search intensified. At 5:40 p.m., only 20 minutes before the search was scheduled to be called off, a searcher probed the snow and felt something soft. There, buried under 4 feet of snow, were a green backpack and a yellow tarp. More digging revealed the mouth of the 4- by 6-foot cave and packed inside were the missing climbers—six students and two adults.

After emergency first aid treatment was given, the climbers, still alive but suffering from hypothermia, were flown by helicopter to Portland area hospitals. Despite the efforts of a corps of doctors, nurses, and medical technicians using sophisticated life-saving equipment, six of the climbers— the two adults (Marion Horwell and Rev. Thomas Goman) and four students (Tasha Amy, Susan McClave, Patrick Mcginness and Richard Haeder)—died. Surviving the ordeal, but initially in critical condition, were students Brinton Clark and Giles Thompson.

The tragedy stunned the private church-related Oregon Episcopal School community as well as relatives of the victims. Expressions of sorrow came in from round the world.

The week after the tragedy, clear skies and warm temperatures prevailed throughout much of Oregon. On May 18, 19, and 20—a week after the ill-fated climb—temperatures in many parts of Oregon reached into the 70s or 80s and even into the upper 60s at Government Camp.

# Significant Snowstorms in Oregon

*Pacific Northwest*   Dec. 22, 1861
The first snow of this year covered all of the Pacific Northwest with between 1 and 3 feet of snow. The snow did not disappear from the valleys and the lower foothills until late February and mid-March.

*Portland*   Feb. 18, 1862
Portland had between 15 and 18 inches of snow on the ground. "Aggregate winter weather for the past 13 seasons would not be more than that of the past 2 months," according to *Weather History*.

*Portland*   Jan. 1866
Nine inches of snow accumulated in Portland on the 12th, 14th, and 16th. The 17th brought 8 inches, the 18th another 5 inches, the 19th one foot, and the 20th 18 inches of snow. Because of the great amounts of snow, the river rose 18 inches on January 24 alone.

*Columbia River Basin and Willamette Valley*   Dec. 16-18, 1884
Heavy snowfall occurred over the Columbia River Basin and along the Cascade foothills in the Willamette Valley. The Dalles received 29.5 inches in one day and Albany had 16 inches the same day. Portland ended up with a total of 22.3 inches for the 3 days.

*Wasco County*   Dec. 8-28, 1885
This was the most snow that the community of The Dalles had seen since it was settled. The snow began on December 8 and rarely stopped until the 28th of the month. Because of snow between 6 and 10 feet deep, trains were stuck at Viento (7 miles west of Hood River). The trains finally reached Portland on January 10; they had been stuck for three weeks.

*Portland*   Jan. 1890
This was a record-breaking month for Portland, with 35.4 inches of snow in 31 days.

*North and Northwestern Oregon*   Dec. 20-23, 1892
The highest snowfall amounts were reported over northwestern Oregon, with storm totals ranging from 15 to 30 inches. Portland accumulated 27.5 inches, with 14 inches falling in one day.

*Portland*   Jan. 3, 1895
By January 3, the several storms that had hit Portland had left an accumulation of 22 inches of snow, 15 inches on January 2.

*Statewide*   Jan. 11-15, 1916
Two storms affected the entire state. On the 6th through the 10th, the mountains received heavy snow; Siskiyou Summit received 15 inches in one day and 34.5 inches for the storm. Cascade Locks received 7 inches in one day and 24 inches for the storm. Then on January 11 through 15 all of western Oregon, except for the southwestern interior and the coastal areas, recorded storm totals of 5 inches or more. McMinnville recorded the most snow in one day, with 11 inches falling on the 12th. Siskiyou Summit added another 24 inches to the 34 inches already on the ground from the previous storm.

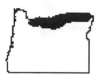

*Northern Oregon border*   Jan. 30-Feb. 3, 1916
The northern Oregon border was affected the most, with heaviest snowfall recorded at Parkdale: 29.5 inches in one day (February 2) and a storm total of 81.5 inches. Heavy snow also fell in the higher Cascades where Government Camp had a one-day snowfall of nearly 40 inches and a storm total of 85.7 inches.

*Portland, Vancouver*   Dec. 9-11, 1919
This was the third heaviest snowfall-producing storm on record in Oregon and occurred in the coldest December since records began in 1890. The Columbia River froze over, closing navigation from the confluence with the Willamette River upstream. Every part of the state experienced heavy snow, with the heaviest falling on the 10th when Portland received 13.5 inches.

*Corvallis*   Dec. 21, 1919
Corvallis received 22 inches of snow and set an all-time temperature record of -14. Oregon State University was closed for the first time ever because of the tremendous snow.

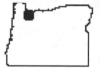

*Portland*   Jan. 24, 1927
On January 24 Portland received 10.5 inches of snow.

*Crater Lake*   Jan. 1932
Crater Lake had the greatest amount of snow, in a year: 879 inches.

*Crater Lake*   Jan. 1933
This January Crater Lake received the greatest amount of snow in one calendar month: 256 inches.

*Portland*   Apr. 1, 1936
An unusually late snowstorm, Portland accumulating 5.2 inches of snow in less than 24 hours.

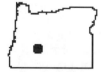

*Crater Lake*   Jan. 27, 1937
Crater Lake set a record for the greatest snowfall in 24 hours (since broken). The area received 37 inches of snow.

*Statewide*   Jan. 31-Feb. 4, 1937
This storm had widespread effects over the state, but the heavy snowfalls were more prominent on the western slopes of the Cascades and the Willamette Valley. For several days, deep snow drifts blocked most roads in northern Oregon and the Cascades. Dallas recorded a one-day total of 24 inches of snow and Salem had 25 inches.

*Portland*   Jan. 24, 1943
Portland accumulated 14 inches of snow.

*Portland* Feb. 1949
The Portland International Airport received 13.2 inches of snow during the month.

*Statewide* Jan. 9-18, 1950
January had the heaviest snowfall since the beginning of weather recordkeeping (1890). For most locations, the period of January 9-18 brought the heaviest snows. All highways west of the Cascades and through the Columbia River Gorge were closed due to large snow drifts. The weather caused hundreds of thousands of dollars' worth of property damage.

*Crater Lake* Jan. 15, 1951
A record was set at Crater Lake when 57 inches of snow fell in the course of a single storm.

*Western Oregon* Jan. 26-27, 1956
This snowstorm started in northwestern Oregon and moved around northern Oregon. Portland received 10.5 inches, forcing the closure of many schools. Many traffic accidents occurred because of the snow that packed down into ice. Portland had 390 accidents during the 26th through the 28th. Hood River County estimated that a hundred accidents occurred in that area during the same time period.

*All of Oregon* Mar. 1-2, 1960
Snow began on the afternoon of the 1st and spread throughout Oregon, producing 3-12 inches in lower elevation and up to 30 inches in the mountains. In Marion County alone there were more than a hundred snow-related car accidents, and two men were killed. Schools were closed for several days.

*Portland* Feb. 1962
The Portland office of the National Weather Service reported that over 3 inches of snow fell in Portland in only 24 hours.

*Statewide* Jan. 25-30, 1969
Lane, Douglas, and Coos counties surpassed their old snowfall records and 2 to 3 feet of snow fell on the valley floors, with much heavier amounts in the higher elevations. Eugene had a snow depth of 34 inches on the 30th, and a total snowfall for January of 47 inches. Roseburg recorded 27 inches and a monthly snowfall of 35.2 inches. Monthly snowfall totals ranged from 2 to 3 feet along the coast. The weight of the heavy wet snow collapsed hundreds of farm buildings and several large industrial buildings, causing $3-4 million in property damage. There were heavy losses in livestock. Many communities were completely isolated for close to a week

*All of Oregon* Jan. 9-11, 1980
A series of strong storms, accompanied by snow, ice, wind, and freezing rain, hit Oregon very hard over a 3-day period. On January 9, high snowfall and extreme winds caused travel problems, injuries, and power outages. Bonneville Dam received 39 inches on the 9th, the all-time record for any location in Oregon. Snow extended all the way to the coast with Astoria reporting 2 inches of snow on the 9th. Six people died as a result of the storms.

*All of Oregon*   Feb. 7-8, 1985
Western valleys of Oregon received between 2 and 4 inches of snow: there was 4 to 7 inches in several eastern basins, and up to 2 feet in the Cascade and northeast mountains. Six thousand people were without power in the Willamette Valley and Klamath Basin because heavy wet snow weighed down tree limbs and caused them to break into power lines. Two people died in car accidents and many others had minor injuries because of the slick snow on the roads.

*Willamette Valley*   Dec. 3, 1985
Snow was heavy throughout the Willamette Valley. Oregon State University closed for only the second time in 117 years because of weather.

*Cascades and Northeast Oregon*   Feb. 11, 1986
The Cascades and the Deschutes Basin received up to 2 feet of snow during this evening storm. Generally there was 6 to 12 inches of snow in the basins and valleys of northeastern Oregon. As a result, schools were closed and there were traffic accidents and power outages.

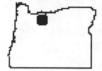

*Mt. Hood*   May 13, 1986
Due to a snowstorm, climbers were stranded on Mt. Hood, 8000 feet up. Ten people died from exposure to the cold, and three were injured.

*Pacific Northwest*   Mar. 23, 1988
All over the Northwest, winds were strong and snow was heavy while the rest of the U.S. sat in the sun. In the Oregon Cascades, Stevens Pass accumulated 18 inches of snow in one night. The wind gusted up to 89 mph.

*Northeastern Oregon*   Dec. 26, 1988-Jan. 22, 1989
Summerville (population 150) was hit hardest by three blizzards during a 4-week period. The snow was 5 feet deep but winds over 60 mph created some 15-feet-deep drifts. People could only move by snowmobile or ski.

*All of Oregon*   Feb. 1-8, 1989
Heavy snowfall (6-12 inches in some coastal areas), record low temperatures, and strong winds were widespread. The Cascades received over a foot of snow and Salem accumulated 9 inches. Wind chill was between 30 and 60°F below zero. Extensive damage occurred in homes and businesses (because of frozen pipes), there were numerous power outages, and several boats sank on the Columbia River (because of ice). Three of the five deaths were due to car accidents and the remaining two people froze to death.

*The Cascades, Siskiyou Mountains, South-Central Oregon*   Nov. 23-25, 1989
Heavy orographic snowfall occurred at high elevations. Santiam Pass in the Cascades received 23 inches of snow.

*All of Oregon*   Feb. 11-16, 1990
Snow fell in large quantities all over Oregon. Bennett Pass had 29 inches, the north Coast Range had up to 28 inches, the north Cascades had 20 to 35 inches, and the Columbia Gorge cities of Cascade Locks and Hood River had 24 and 35 inches, respectively. The Willamette Valley averaged about 4 inches, although the higher hills around Portland received up to 1 foot.

*Western Oregon*   Dec. 16-17, 1992
Snow fell everywhere in Oregon except the southern and central coast.
Between 1 and 2 feet fell at the highest elevations and between 1 and 2 inches
at the lowest. Roads and interstate highways were temporarily closed. This was
the snowiest December in Klamath Falls since 1949, with more than 39 inches.

*Northwestern Oregon*   Feb. 18-19, 1993
This storm began with freezing rain in the southern Willamette Valley. A wet
Pacific weather system moved to the Oregon coast from California. When it hit
the cold air, heavy snow fell. The Portland and Salem airports had record snowfall for a 24-hour period in February (6.4 and 11.9 inches, respectively); 6 to 12
inches of snow fell in the Willamette Valley and Cascades, 3 to 7 inches in
north-central Oregon, and 6 to 10 inches in the eastern section of the Gorge.

*Oregon Cascades*   Apr. 3-4, 1993
Icy cold weather gave the southern Cascades between 1 and 2 feet of snow
during this storm. Crater Lake had about 2 feet of new snow in those two days.

*Oregon Cascades*   Apr. 9-11, 1993
A snowstorm brought the Oregon Cascades 3 new feet of snow at Crater Lake
in three days and Timberline Lodge 2 feet during the same period.

*Northern Oregon Cascades*   Nov. 21-22, 1993
Timberline Lodge received 21 inches of snow, Mt. Hood Meadows 18 inches,
and Government Camp 12 inches during the first major snowstorm of the
winter of 1993. In the foothills of Western Oregon between 1 and 3 inches of
snow fell.

*Cascade and northeastern mountains*   Jan. 4-5, 1994 (2100-1000PST)
On January 4 a frontal system moved across Oregon and brought heavy snow.
The northern Cascades accumulated between 10 and 20 inches of snow while
Tollgate (in the northeast mountains) received 7 inches.

*Southern Oregon Cascades, southeastern Oregon*   Feb. 10, 1994
This was the first major winter storm of 1994. Diamond Lake received 17 inches
of new snow, Crater Lake had 14 inches, Silver Lake 9 inches, and Basque and
Jordan received 8 inches.

*Northern Oregon, Cascade Mountains*   Mar. 20-21, 1994
At Timberline Lodge (6000 feet high) on Mt. Hood, 23 inches of snow fell in
the two days the storm lasted. Santiam Pass had 16 inches of snow.

*Northern Oregon*   Jan. 9-12, 1998
Arctic air brought snow and freezing rain from southeast Washington into
eastern Oregon on the 9th, reaching Portland late on the 10th. Many locations
in eastern Oregon had over 12 inches of snow. Austin had 12 inches in one day
and 36 inches for the storm. Portland Airport received 5 inches of snow.

*All of Oregon*   Winter 1998-99
Not a "snow storm," but a series of storms throughout the winter made this
one of the snowiest winters in Oregon's history. Timberline ski area on Mt.
Hood had snow depths exceeding 300 inches. Crater Lake's snowfall total from
October through March was 586 inches.

# Tornadoes

Tornadoes are the most concentrated and violent storms produced by the earth's atmosphere. A tornado—the name comes from the Latin word *toronae* ("to turn")—is a vortex of rotating winds and strong vertical motion which possesses remarkable strength and can cause almost unbelievable damage. Wind speeds in excess of 300 mph have been observed within tornadoes, and it is suspected that some tornado winds exceed 400 mph. In addition, the low pressure at the center of a tornado can literally explode buildings and other structures that it passes over.

Tornadoes have been observed throughout the United States, but are especially common in the Midwest, which has more tornadoes than any other place on earth. West of the Rockies, tornadoes are infrequent and generally small compared with their midwestern counterparts. But Oregon and other western states have experienced tornadoes on occasion, many of them producing significant damage and occasionally causing injury or death.

While tornadoes in Oregon are sometimes formed in association with large Pacific storms arriving from the west, most are caused by intense local thunderstorms. These storms, which usually also produce thunder, lightning, hail, and heavy rain, are more common during the warm season (April-October). Because of Oregon's relatively low population, many tornadoes probably go unreported. Not surprisingly, most of the tornadoes identified here occurred near populated areas. In a few cases, tornadoes were identified by the damage they caused rather than by eyewitness.

Figure 23 shows a cross-section of a large cumulonimbus (thunderstorm) cloud as it produces a tornado. Air is moving up into the cloud, and the more rapidly this inflow is drawn up, the more quickly it rotates, eventually causing a tornado. The air is released in outflow both at the top and the base of the cloud. The very strong

*Figure 23. Idealized diagram of a severe thunderstorm which has spawned a tornado. Inflow and outflow arrows show typical locations were air is entrained into and flows out of the storm.*

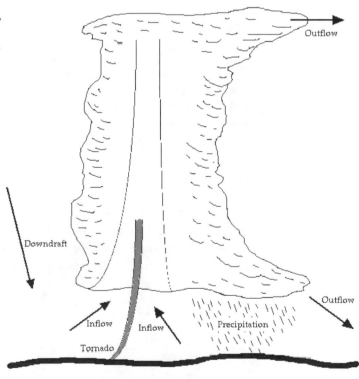

downward motion at the rear of the cloud is called the downdraft; in some cases this descending air is concentrated in a small area and very intense. Such situations produce the dreaded "downburst" or "microburst," which appear to have caused a number of aircraft crashes in the central and eastern U.S.

Considering how often the word "tornado" is heard in the media or read in newspapers, it is interesting to note that at one time it was a forbidden word. A ban on using the word was issued in 1886 and lifted in 1952. In the 1880s John P. Finley of the U.S. Army Signal Corps, which then handled weather forecasting for the U.S.A., developed generalized forecasts for the likelihood of tornadoes on a given day. In 1886 the Army ended Finley's program and banned the word "tornado" from forecasts because "the harm done by a (tornado) prediction would eventually be greater than that which results from the tornado itself." The reasoning was that widespread panic would occur when the tornado prediction became known. The ban stayed in place after the Weather Bureau, now the National Weather Service, took over forecasting from the Army. A tornado that destroyed 52 aircraft at Tinker Air Force Base, Oklahoma, on March 20, 1948, caused Air Force meteorologists to begin working on ways to forecast tornadoes. The Weather Bureau also began looking for ways to improve tornado forecasts and established the Severe Local Storm Warning Center, which is now the Storm Prediction Center in Norman, Oklahoma. The ban on the word "tornado" fell on March 17, 1952 when the new center issued its first "tornado watch."

## Tornadoes in Oregon

Over sixty significant tornadoes have been reported in Oregon between 1887 and 1996. The generally minimal damage that has accompanied most of these tornadoes proves that such storms are not significant threats to people or property. Even the strongest Oregon tornadoes would be considered relatively insignificant in the midwestern U.S., where the truly devastating storms are observed.

### Greatest loss of life

A tornado which formed near Jordan Butte, northwest of Lexington (Morrow County), on the afternoon of June 14, 1888, swept through Lexington, Sand Hollow, and Pine City, and destroyed thirty buildings, including two schools. Six people, including two children at the school, were killed; four others were injured.

## Most memorable day

In April 1957 a very strong storm system brought heavy rains and high winds to northern Oregon from the 12th through the 14th, with wind gusts reaching 70 mph on the 14th. At about noon on the 12th, a very dark storm cloud appeared near the city of Sandy, about 25 miles southeast of Portland. Heavy rain began to fall, and then small hail. The hailstones grew larger, reaching diameters of one-quarter to one-half inch. As the storm moved east from Sandy, a funnel cloud emerged and reached downward, eventually touching the ground and becoming a 50-yard-wide tornado. The tornado churned through the farmland of Sandy heading toward the Cascades. Large fir trees, 18 to 36 inches in diameter, were twisted off or snapped 30 to 40 feet above the ground. A large barn under construction was lifted off its foundation, carried several hundred feet in the air, and then dropped back to the ground, shattering it to pieces. Roofs of houses and barns were torn off and some farm outbuildings were carried a considerable distance before being destroyed.

Shortly thereafter, west of the small farm town of Ione in Gilliam County, a long thin funnel cloud was observed descending from a similar dark storm cloud. This tornado was much larger than the one in Sandy (it was 100-400 yards wide) and had a much longer path (15-20 miles). Fortunately, this area comprises largely rangeland and large wheat farms, and no buildings were in the path of the tornado. Several telephone poles were pulled out of the ground and some damage, mostly minor, was done to fields, much of it caused by the large amounts of hail that accompanied the tornado. In the Heppner area, a few hailstones exceeding one inch in diameter were found.

## Most damaging

The most damaging (and probably the most mysterious) tornado in Oregon occurred during the late afternoon on June 11, 1968. A very strong thunderstorm formed over Wallowa County in extreme northeastern Oregon. The tornado spawned by this storm touched down in mountainous, forested areas that were mostly uninhabited. There were virtually no eyewitnesses to this tornado, but its status as a tornado seems certain; it caused significant destruction along a path one-half to 2 miles wide and 8 to 10 miles long. About 1,800 acres of prime timber were destroyed and another 1,200 acres were badly damaged. Over 40 million board feet of lumber were blown down. Some of the hailstones that accompanied the tornado were reportedly of golfball size.

### First reported tornado in Oregon

*In a letter (dated January 19, 1887) to the January 22, 1887, edition of the Eugene City Guard, a Cottage Grove resident described a "genuine cyclone of small proportions" in the vicinity of Cottage Grove. The tornado twisted a 4-foot diameter fir tree from its roots, picked up a couple of sheep and carried them for 200 yards, and tore down fences. The observer reported that the width of the stormtrack was only 30 yards. The tornado, described as being "funnel-shaped," damaged no homes.*

## Coastal tornado

*Oregon tornadoes are reported chiefly in the Willamette Valley and in the flatlands of eastern Oregon; only rarely do they affect the Oregon coast. In January 1996, an apparent tornado struck the coast near Lincoln City. Police reported a number of windows exploded outward, a trailer overturned, and a number of fish deposited on the land, apparently lifted out of the water by the tornado.*

*In Morrow County the same day, a tornado formed on the McElligott Ranch property southwest of Ione and traveled eastwards 20 miles before disappearing on the outskirts of Lexington. The twister was accompanied by heavy rains and hail, some of which, near Heppner, was golfball size. Two ranches near Lexington measured half an inch of rain in less than 10 minutes and in Sand Hollow another rancher reported 1.20 inches in less than 30 minutes. The tornado passed over rangeland, dairyland, and wheat farms and caused no structural damage.*

## When is a tornado not a tornado?

It is apparent that tornadoes occur in Oregon more frequently than many may imagine. Undoubtedly, because of the sparse population in many parts of Oregon, many tornadoes are not seen. Damage from tornadoes may be written off as being due to a freak wind. On the other hand, there are situations in which damage is attributed to a tornado that in reality was caused by other atmospheric phenomena. These may include wind shear, turbulence, or downbursts. The following story describes such a situation.

In early December 1996, an intense storm caused significant damage to areas east and northeast of Eugene. It was widely reported that a tornado had touched down and caused the damage; several Weather Service representatives were among those who made this assessment. Roger Cunningham, a climatologist from Florence, was there and sent the following report:

*Yesterday (Thursday, 5 December) I was in the middle of some weather excitement without knowing the full extent of it until later. On Thursday morning my mother and I drove over to Eugene-Springfield. We got to Eugene at about 10:00 and stopped at one store on the north side of town. The sky was very black from NW around to NE, but it was mostly sunny where we were. We proceeded across I-5 to the Gateway Mall in Springfield. My mother went into the mall to Christmas shop. I stayed in the '96 Chrysler minivan (with temperature sensor) and read the New York Times.*

*After 30 minutes or so a rain shower began and continued for 15-20 minutes lightly, with a S wind about 5-10 mph. Our parking space faced NW. I could see three flags to my right. At about 11:45, the rain suddenly got heavy and the S wind picked up to (my guess) 30-40 mph, or hard enough to rock the minivan a bit, for a minute; the wind then abruptly shifted to W, 20-30 mph, and quickly dropped to under 10 mph. The whole incident took about 3 minutes. The temperature dropped from 46°F to 41°F. The rain shower stopped by 12:10. My mother returned at 12:00, and said that an air conditioner on the roof of the mall had momentarily lifted up and fallen back, sending debris to the floor. The mall security staff had to get people out of the area. We drove around Eugene to other places in few light showers, and left for home at 14:00. The return trip was mostly dry. . . .*

*Now what I didn't know until I saw the Eugene TV news at 17:00, and the newspaper this morning, was that I had been right in the middle of a thunderstorm DOWNBURST. Some people erroneously thought it was a small tornado. This downburst, which followed a SW-NE path, right past the mall parking lot I was sitting in, did quite a bit of damage in residential areas just over I-5 to my SW and also in Springfield to my NE. The strong winds knocked down several trees, which fell onto power lines and onto one house. A few other things blew around as well. This was the top local story on Thursday, and I serendipitously was in it.*

It is easy to understand why observers would assume that they had experienced a tornado. After all, tornadoes are well known, are frequently in the news, and have even been the subject of several recent motion pictures. Downbursts are much less notorious. Furthermore, they are *invisible*, so even if they occurred in Oregon much more often than tornadoes their presence would go largely undetected.

In the long run, placing the blame on either tornadoes or downbursts may be a pointless exercise, since both phenomena share a common origin: they are small areas of strong winds in association with a severe thunderstorm. And while Oregon will continue to enjoy a near immunity to truly severe thunderstorms, the state will continue to be affected by periodic visits from these interesting and destructive intruders.

## Umatilla County, June 1903

On June 15, the day after the disastrous Heppner Flood, a tornado touched down between Meacham and Huron. The *East Oregonian* for June 17, 1903, stated that the tornado twisted hundreds of trees, including some large pines 3 feet in diameter, and uprooted telegraph poles for many miles.

## East Portland, February 1904

On February 26, 1904, a tornado struck the vicinity of Mount Tabor on Portland's east side. Four houses were destroyed and others were moved off their foundations. Damage totaled $5,000. *The Oregonian*, February 27, 1904, reported that the tornado, spotted at 10:42 a.m., was "not unlike a giant express train." Its width was 50 to 100 feet and its height several times that. In its short 1¹/₂ mile path, it uprooted fir trees and tore

### Grant County, June 1895

*The Long Creek tornado killed three people, injured several, and did considerable damage in Grant County on June 14, 1895. The town of Long Creek, in particular, was struck by the tornado with such violence that not a trace of the buildings in its path remained after the storm. One resident, L.W. Solawn, was picked up by the wind and carried over the top of a store, but fortunately landed safely on a pile of hay. Long Creek lost its school, its mill, and several residences. Damage totaled $5,000.*

down fences. Although there were no deaths, several injuries occurred. *The Oregonian* included a photo of the Starbuck residence, virtually wrecked by the tornado. It also stated that the escape of Mrs. T.H. Starbuck and her daughter, Edith, was little short of miraculous. "My mother and I were in the kitchen at the time of the storm," said the pretty young woman who had so nearly escaped a tragic death.

> *I saw the storm coming and called my mother, and when she came to the window and saw the debris in the air she thought it was a cyclone and cried for me to hurry to the basement. We crossed the room to the basement door, but before we could get through the door, the house shook and we were thrown to the floor and went crashing down with the wreckage. The upper part of the house came down upon us, but was supported by the cook stove, which saved us from being crushed to death. My mother managed to make her escape from the wreckage before I did, although her clothes were nearly all torn from her. My father was in the bathroom putting up a shelf when the storm struck the house. He had a like escape, the bathtub and heavy iron bed frame supporting the wreckage and saving him from great injury.*

### Baker County, June 1937

On June 16, 1937, a tornado formed in Pine Valley (eastern part of Baker County). The cooperative weather observer near Halfway, W.C. MacManiman, reported:

> *One funnel was distinctly seen by many people; some report having seen three funnels. The view of the storm was obscured in some directions by sheets of hail, the stones ranging from one-fourth inch to one inch in diameter. When the storm struck, darkness prevailed. The first damage was done to a barn in the southwestern portion of Halfway; the barn was entirely wrecked. A house 150 feet from the barn was untouched. The storm seemed to jump about 300 yards, then came down again, wrecking buildings and fences and blowing down trees. It again jumped, missing the main part of town, coming down in the part where it tore everything down. The damage done by wind, rain, and hail was serious, covering an area of several square miles. Gardens were ruined, chickens killed, and windows broken. One beneficial result of the storm was the destruction of large numbers of crickets. This was the first tornado ever known in the region affected.*

Property damage attributed to the tornado was estimated at $8,000.

## Lane County, December 1951

U.S. Weather Bureau observers at Eugene Airport on December 6, 1951, were witnesses to a small twister that moved along just above the ground, lifted back into the parent cloud, then touched the ground for a distance of 500 yards. It lifted a 30-by-32-foot barn 300 feet into the air, spreading timbers over a half-mile area. The tornado sucked the water from ditches, leaving them as "dry as dust." Ice pellets $^3/_4$-inch thick accompanied the storm.

## Clackamas County, August 1979

Sandy experienced its second reported tornado when a twister cut a path over 2 miles long through the area on August 20, 1979. An observer to the storm, Robert Lee, described it as "a black roll cloud like a vertical cliff approaching, spitting lightning in a brilliant barrage." It rained so hard that he could not see "4 feet in front." Harold Butler, of Sandy, stated that he saw a funnel snake down out of the cloud touching the ground here and there. A house under construction was flattened, and others were hit by falling trees. A storage building full of machinery was blown apart. Power service through the Sandy area was temporarily knocked out.

## Marion County, October 1984

On October 26, 1984, a "mini-tornado" occurred in the north Marion-south Clackamas County area, destroying the 30-by-80-foot barn of Leighton Whitsett of Aurora. The barn was lifted off its foundation and sent crashing into a clover field where it disintegrated. In addition, the twister lifted two 500-pound blocks from the barn's concrete foundation and uprooted large fir trees, but it missed Whitsett's home by 100 feet. At the same time, 7 miles away, a lightning bolt struck and killed a Woodburn nursery worker who was seeking shelter from the storm.

## Marion County, December 1993

An F2 tornado! (See the legend to the table at the end of the chapter for a description of the categories used to describe tornadoes.) This was the most powerful tornado in Oregon in many years. It started as a cold front that came with a deep surface low along the coast then moved across the Willamette Valley. Six veal calves were killed, a dairy farm was damaged, roofs were blown off some small buildings, and many trees were broken. People reported that the funnel was sucking water from the Willamette River as it moved northeast, where it greatly damaged a mobile home park. A tree at least 2 feet in diameter was snapped off 6 feet above the ground and hit a two-story house. Remarkably, no one was injured.

# Significant Tornadoes in Oregon

*Cottage Grove*   Jan. 19, 1887 (scale unknown)
In a letter (dated January 19, 1887) to the *Eugene City Guard*, a Cottage Grove resident described a "genuine cyclone of small proportions" in the vicinity of Cottage Grove. The tornado twisted a 4-foot-diameter fir tree from its roots, picked up a couple of sheep and carried them for 200 yards, and tore down fences. The storm track was only 30 yards. The "funnel-shaped" tornado damaged no homes.

*Lexington, Long Creek*   Jun. 14, 1888 (scale unknown)
A tornado swept through Lexington, Sand Hollow and Pine City, and destroyed thirty buildings including two schools. Six people, including two children at the school, were killed; four others were injured. A second tornado supposedly struck the Long Creek area at about the same time, tearing up considerable timber in the Monument area.

*Long Creek*   Jun. 14, 1895 (scale unknown)
One of the most noted of all Oregon tornadoes was the Long Creek tornado, which killed three people, injured three, and did considerable damage in Grant County. Long Creek lost its school and its mill, in addition to several residences; of the buildings in the path of the tornado, not a trace remained after the storm. One resident was picked up by the wind and carried over the top of a store, but fortunately landed safely on a pile of hay. Damage in Long Creek totaled $5,000.

*Bay City (near Tillamook)*   Jun. 14, 1897 (scale unknown)
The June 1897 issue of *Oregon Climatological Data* included a report by Captain John J. Dawson, cooperative weather observer at Bay City (near Tillamook), that, "On June 14, 1897 a tornado about 40 rods wide, passed over this station . . ."

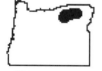

*Between Meacham and Huron*   Jun. 15, 1903  (scale unknown)
The day after the disastrous Heppner Flood a tornado touched down between Meacham and Huron. It twisted hundreds of trees, including some large pines 3 feet in diameter, and uprooted telegraph poles for a distance of 8 miles.

*Mount Tabor (East Portland)*   Feb. 26, 1904 (scale unknown)
On February 26, 1904, a tornado struck the vicinity of Mount Tabor on Portland's east side. Four houses were destroyed and three people were injured. Damage totaled $5,000. *The Oregonian*, February 27, 1904, reported that the tornado, spotted at 10:42 a.m., was "not unlike a giant express train . . . Its width was 50 to 100 feet and its height several times that." *The Oregonian* included a photo of the Starbuck residence which was virtually wrecked by the tornado.

*East Portland*   Mar. 19, 1904 (scale unknown)
What was described as a "cyclonic storm" (Oregonian, March 21, 1904) hit part of east Portland, destroying several shacks, doing considerable damage to the Lewis and Clark fairgrounds, and demolishing a large warehouse.

*See page 137 for tables of damage and scales.*

*Condon*   Apr. 15, 1925 (scale unknown)
What was tabbed as a "baby cyclone" by the Condon *Globe and Times* (April 17, 1925), swept through Condon, wrecking the county machinery warehouse, tearing down the Washington Lumber Company Warehouse, and taking the tops off autos. Altogether, the tornado did $10,000 damage during its 6-mile path.

*SW of Salem, Polk County*   Nov. 11, 1925 (scale unknown)
The tornado, which was estimated to have been 150 feet wide, passed north of Independence, then moved over the Liberty district of Salem. Witnesses (*Capital Journal*, November 12, 1925) told of hearing the tornado 5-10 minutes before it arrived. In its 5-mile path, the tornado touched the ground in only a few places, but it destroyed barns and fruit dryers, removed buildings from their foundations, tore up trees in orchards and uprooted many large oak and fir trees. Fir limbs were found driven several feet into the ground almost a quarter mile from where any trees were growing. As it passed over the Willamette River, the tornado sucked up quantities of water and gravel high into the air. Damage was category 3.

*McMinnville*   Feb. 19, 1926 (scale unknown)
This a small tornado apparently felled many trees and destroyed a huge "dry house." From several accounts it seems that there may have been four or five separate whirlwinds in a group.

*Clatskanie*   Oct. 12, 1934 (scale unknown)
The *Oregon Journal*, October 12, 1934, briefly reported that a twister was seen near Clatskanie (about 40 miles east of Astoria). The tornado, which was about 30 feet wide, narrowly missed Olof Sodestrom who was, at the time, working in a field.

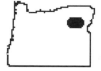

*Baker County*   Jun. 16, 1937 (scale unknown)
This seems to have been a very significant tornado. A barn was wrecked, a brick church was moved about 15 inches off its foundation, small buildings were turned completely over, and a garage was lifted and thrown to the side, leaving the car standing untouched where the garage had been. A cow was carried 60 feet through the air and deposited upside down without hair or skin! A women was injured when she was entangled by a barbed-wire fence during the storm. Damage was category 4.

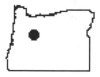

*Brownsville (20 miles SE of Albany)*   Sep. 8, 1938 (scale unknown)
The *Oregonian*, September 8, 1938, featured a photo of the writhing tail of a tornado dropping earthward from black thunder clouds in Brownsville. The tornado was first spotted south and east of Halsey. The central portion of the funnel was quite distinct from the walls and appeared translucent and of a light smoky blue color. The surrounding walls were much blacker and the extreme portion quite black and appeared like black puffs of smoke which climbed constantly upwards upon its twisting pillar

*Sherwood (Washington County)*   Oct. 1, 1940 (scale unknown)
A tornado which ripped a path across a cornfield near Scholb (Washington County) frightened residents of the area but did little damage. It passed with a roar over the Grover School, lashing a black tail groundward from the sky.

*Eugene*   Dec. 6, 1951 (scale: F1)
This small tornado moved along the ground for about 500 yards in a path 50 yards wide. It lifted a 30-by-32-foot barn 300 feet into the air, spreading timbers over a half-mile area. It lasted for only about 13 minutes.

*Seneca*   Jun. 25, 1952 (scale unknown)
The Burns *Times-Herald*, in its June 27 edition, reported that two days earlier a "twister" had struck in spots along a 20-mile path in the Logan Valley near Seneca.

*Corvallis*   Jan. 20, 1953 (scale unknown)
A "miniature tornado," which suddenly appeared out of dark clouds at 8 a.m., struck the downtown area. During its brief presence, it "exploded" one building, passed close to the Roosevelt school, then crossed the Willamette River before disappearing. Accompanying the tornado were rain and hail that fell in sheets, causing more damage to businesses than did the twister.

*Tualatin Valley about 15 miles west of Portland*   Oct. 22, 1954 (scale: F0)
This very small tornado occurred between Hillsboro and Orenco. It lasted less than 10 minutes and was only a few yards in diameter. It caused no damage.

*Sandy area*   Apr. 12, 1957 (scale: F1)
This small tornado was about 35 to 50 yards in diameter. It uprooted large fir trees and lifted them 40 feet into the air. A large barn was carried several hundred yards and roofs were torn off houses. The path was about 3 miles in length.

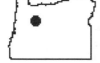

*Gilliam and Morrow counties*   Apr. 12, 1957 (scale: F0)
This moderate tornado occurred at almost the same time as the one mentioned above. It touched down west of Ione and rapidly moved towards Lexington. It was nearly a quarter mile wide in places and traveled on the ground for nearly 20 miles. Very little damage occurred because this area was mostly rangeland.

*Aumsville*   Mar. 8, 1960 (scale: F1)
A small but fairly violent tornado skipped over a path about a mile long, but only a few yards wide. It damaged several farms and uprooted some trees; category 3.

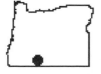

*Coquille*   Apr. 28, 1960 (scale unknown)
This small tornado was spotted 2 miles west of Coquille. The funnel, which lasted just a few minutes, reached halfway to the ground at its greatest extent. The top of the tornado, spinning violently, suddenly took on the appearance of a stopped-up air hose and withdrew first slowly then very rapidly. The base cloud then turned very dark and torrential rains began to fall.

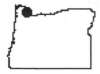

*10 miles south of Klamath Falls*   May 19, 1962 (scale: F1)
A very small but confirmed tornado moved through a farming area south of Klamath Falls, demolishing one hay barn and causing other slight damage, category 3/4.

*Rainier*   Nov. 10 1965 (scale: F0)
This small tornado began on the south bank of the Columbia River and proceeded to cross the river producing a small waterspout. Two buildings were damaged; category 3.

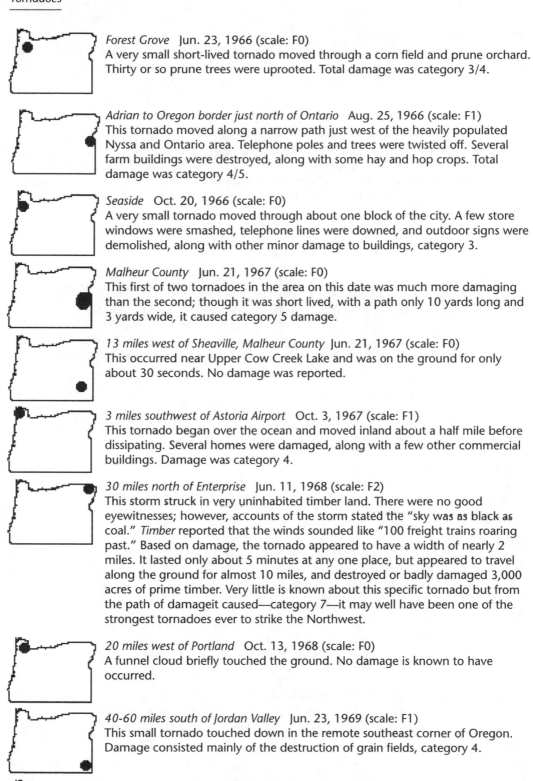

*Forest Grove* Jun. 23, 1966 (scale: F0)
A very small short-lived tornado moved through a corn field and prune orchard. Thirty or so prune trees were uprooted. Total damage was category 3/4.

*Adrian to Oregon border just north of Ontario* Aug. 25, 1966 (scale: F1)
This tornado moved along a narrow path just west of the heavily populated Nyssa and Ontario area. Telephone poles and trees were twisted off. Several farm buildings were destroyed, along with some hay and hop crops. Total damage was category 4/5.

*Seaside* Oct. 20, 1966 (scale: F0)
A very small tornado moved through about one block of the city. A few store windows were smashed, telephone lines were downed, and outdoor signs were demolished, along with other minor damage to buildings, category 3.

*Malheur County* Jun. 21, 1967 (scale: F0)
This first of two tornadoes in the area on this date was much more damaging than the second; though it was short lived, with a path only 10 yards long and 3 yards wide, it caused category 5 damage.

*13 miles west of Sheaville, Malheur County* Jun. 21, 1967 (scale: F0)
This occurred near Upper Cow Creek Lake and was on the ground for only about 30 seconds. No damage was reported.

*3 miles southwest of Astoria Airport* Oct. 3, 1967 (scale: F1)
This tornado began over the ocean and moved inland about a half mile before dissipating. Several homes were damaged, along with a few other commercial buildings. Damage was category 4.

*30 miles north of Enterprise* Jun. 11, 1968 (scale: F2)
This storm struck in very uninhabited timber land. There were no good eyewitnesses; however, accounts of the storm stated the "sky was as black as coal." *Timber* reported that the winds sounded like "100 freight trains roaring past." Based on damage, the tornado appeared to have a width of nearly 2 miles. It lasted only about 5 minutes at any one place, but appeared to travel along the ground for almost 10 miles, and destroyed or badly damaged 3,000 acres of prime timber. Very little is known about this specific tornado but from the path of damage it caused—category 7—it may well have been one of the strongest tornadoes ever to strike the Northwest.

*20 miles west of Portland* Oct. 13, 1968 (scale: F0)
A funnel cloud briefly touched the ground. No damage is known to have occurred.

*40-60 miles south of Jordan Valley* Jun. 23, 1969 (scale: F1)
This small tornado touched down in the remote southeast corner of Oregon. Damage consisted mainly of the destruction of grain fields, category 4.

*Southwestern Wasco County* May 11, 1970 (scale: F0)
This small tornado touched down just east of highway 26 about 10 miles northwest of Warm Springs. It lasted only a short time and caused no damage.

*McMinnville*   May 25, 1971 (scale: F0)
This was a small slow-moving tornado which touched down near a rural home. It unroofed the barn and damaged the house, category 3. The tornado moved along a 0.4-mile-long path damaging fir trees before lifting back into the cloud base.

*Portland area*   Apr. 5, 1972 (scale: F1)
The tornado touched down near Portland at the south shore of the Columbia River damaging four pleasure boat moorages on Marine Drive, fifty cabin cruisers, boat houses and dock shelters. It then crossed the Columbia, drawing water up with it. The tornado continued on its 9-mile-long path in Washington, near Vancouver, where it caused six deaths, three hundred injuries, and $5-6 million in damage.

*50 miles northeast of Lakeview*   Sep. 21, 1973 (scale: F0)
This small tornado was observed from about 10 miles away as it crossed open, uninhabited country. Damage was category 1.

*Newport*   Dec. 13, 1973 (scale unknown)
This apparent tornado ripped through Newport in the evening with the passage of a squall line. It tore off the roof of a real estate building, blew out several windows, damaged two other roofs, and moved a garage off its foundation.

*10 miles southwest of Nyssa*   Apr. 23, 1974 (scale: F1)
The tornado traveled along the Oregon-Idaho border, demolishing a large farm building and the machinery in it. It also lifted another small building completely off the ground. Damage was category 4.

*Eugene*   Aug. 18, 1975 (scale unknown)
This tornado occurred near Eugene but was not well documented. It apparently destroyed a metal building but caused no injuries. The amount of damage caused is unknown.

*Baker*   Sep. 16, 1975 (scale unknown)
This very small tornado only briefly touched down in an open field near Baker causing no damage.

*Tillamook*   Dec. 12, 1975 (scale: F1)
This was a moderate tornado that caused considerable damage—category 6—to the Tillamook area. The twister touched down near Tillamook and traveled along the ground for up to 2 miles. It passed very near KTIL radio station, which recorded 90 mph winds as it passed.

*Gresham*   Aug. 16, 1978 (scale: F1)
A small tornado touched down near Gresham causing some category 4 damage to buildings and crops. It was on the ground only briefly.

*Scappoose, Columbia County*   Aug. 20, 1978 (scale unknown)
This apparent tornado caused moderate (category 5) damage when it struck a mobile home, and scattered pieces for a quarter mile. However, no injuries or deaths occurred in the area.

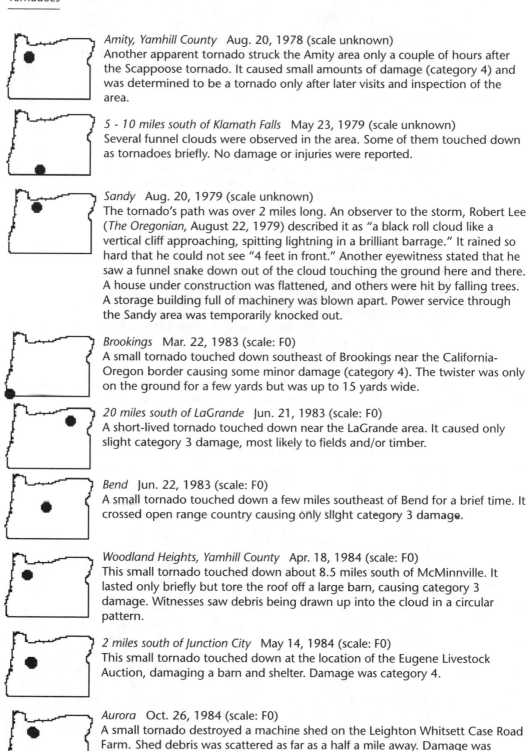

*Amity, Yamhill County*   Aug. 20, 1978 (scale unknown)
Another apparent tornado struck the Amity area only a couple of hours after
the Scappoose tornado. It caused small amounts of damage (category 4) and
was determined to be a tornado only after later visits and inspection of the
area.

*5 - 10 miles south of Klamath Falls*   May 23, 1979 (scale unknown)
Several funnel clouds were observed in the area. Some of them touched down
as tornadoes briefly. No damage or injuries were reported.

*Sandy*   Aug. 20, 1979 (scale unknown)
The tornado's path was over 2 miles long. An observer to the storm, Robert Lee
(*The Oregonian*, August 22, 1979) described it as "a black roll cloud like a
vertical cliff approaching, spitting lightning in a brilliant barrage." It rained so
hard that he could not see "4 feet in front." Another eyewitness stated that he
saw a funnel snake down out of the cloud touching the ground here and there.
A house under construction was flattened, and others were hit by falling trees.
A storage building full of machinery was blown apart. Power service through
the Sandy area was temporarily knocked out.

*Brookings*   Mar. 22, 1983 (scale: F0)
A small tornado touched down southeast of Brookings near the California-
Oregon border causing some minor damage (category 4). The twister was only
on the ground for a few yards but was up to 15 yards wide.

*20 miles south of LaGrande*   Jun. 21, 1983 (scale: F0)
A short-lived tornado touched down near the LaGrande area. It caused only
slight category 3 damage, most likely to fields and/or timber.

*Bend*   Jun. 22, 1983 (scale: F0)
A small tornado touched down a few miles southeast of Bend for a brief time. It
crossed open range country causing only slight category 3 damage.

*Woodland Heights, Yamhill County*   Apr. 18, 1984 (scale: F0)
This small tornado touched down about 8.5 miles south of McMinnville. It
lasted only briefly but tore the roof off a large barn, causing category 3
damage. Witnesses saw debris being drawn up into the cloud in a circular
pattern.

*2 miles south of Junction City*   May 14, 1984 (scale: F0)
This small tornado touched down at the location of the Eugene Livestock
Auction, damaging a barn and shelter. Damage was category 4.

*Aurora*   Oct. 26, 1984 (scale: F0)
A small tornado destroyed a machine shed on the Leighton Whitsett Case Road
Farm. Shed debris was scattered as far as a half a mile away. Damage was
category 4.

*Waldport*   Nov. 2, 1984 (scale: F1)
This tornado touched down near Waldport and proceeded to move through
town. It ripped several portions of a motel roof off, damaged several cars, and
overturned an RV. Damage was category 5.

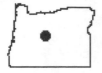

*Bend*   Aug. 22, 1989 (scale: F1)
This tornado touched down about 5 miles east of Bend. Two shed roofs were blown off, parts of which were never found. The tornado also uprooted juniper trees and embedded broken window glass into a chest of drawers in a house. Witnesses saw large metal roof pieces being rotated up into the sky. Damage was category 4.

*Eugene*   Nov. 24, 1989 (scale: F1)
The tornado touched down in the hills south of Eugene. It caused telephone pulls to break in half and uprooted several tall fir trees which fell on two houses and a camper causing significant (category 4) damage but no injuries.

*Umatilla County, near Pendleton*   May 1, 1991 (scale: F0)
This small tornado touched down in wheat fields near Pendleton causing little if any damage. It was visible from the National Weather Service office in Pendleton.

*Troutdale*   Nov. 12, 1991 (scale: F1)
This tornado caused significant (category 4)damage to 80 feet of fencing as it touched down near Troutdale. It also tore off part of a roof and ripped out the wall of a steel building.

*Tualatin*   Nov. 12, 1991 (scale: F1)
The second tornado of the day in Oregon touched down near an office district in Tualatin. It lifted two dumpsters and threw them into a parked van and sucked open an office door, ripping out the ceiling tiles. Damage was category 4.

*Silverton*   Nov. 12, 1991 (scale: F0)
The third tornado of the day in northwest Oregon! It was smaller than the other two but it ripped through a 700-square-foot barn causing significant (category 4) damage.

*Hells Canyon Dam*   Jul. 22, 1992 (scale: F0)
A family trying to escape the storm got into their car. The twister apparently went right over their car, blowing out the passenger windows, lifting it 2 or 3 feet, and pummeling it with debris. The car was totaled (category 3 damage) but there were no injuries.

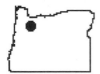

*Newburg*   Dec. 8. 1993 (scale: F2)
This was the most powerful tornado in Oregon in many years. Six veal calves were killed, a dairy farm was damaged, roofs were blown off some small buildings, and many trees were broken. People reported that the funnel was sucking water from the Willamette River as it moved northeast. There, it greatly damaged a mobile home park. A tree at least 2 feet in diameter was snapped off 6 feet above the ground and hit a two-story house. Total damage was category 6. Remarkably, no one was injured.

*Clatsop County, near Warrenton*   Feb. 13, 1994 (scale: F0)
A weak tornado touched down briefly at Kamper's West Park near Warrenton. It lifted twenty wooden picnic tables 40 feet into the air and deposited them 200 yards away. Damage was category 2.

*A few miles southeast of Hermiston*  Jul. 9, 1995 (scale: F0)
Workers at the Simplot Plant southeast of Hermiston spotted a tornado that touched down for about 2 minutes in a nearby wheat field, causing no damage.

## Scale

| Category | Speed (mph) | Damage | Description |
| --- | --- | --- | --- |
| F0, Gale tornado | 40-72 | Light | Some damage to chimneys and signs. Branches break off trees; shallow-rooted trees pushed over. |
| F1, Moderate tornado | 73-112 | Moderate | The lower limit (73 mph) is the beginning of hurricane wind speed. Surfaces are peeled off roofs; mobile homes pushed off foundations or overturned. Moving autos are pushed off the roads. |
| F2, Significant tornado | 113-157 | Considerable | Roofs are torn off frame houses and mobile homes demolished. Boxcars are pushed over, large trees are snapped or uprooted, and light-object missiles generated |
| F3, Severe tornado | 158-206 | Severe | Roofs and some walls are torn off well-constructed houses; trains are overturned. Most trees in forests are uprooted, heavy cars are lifted off ground and thrown. |
| F4, Devastating tornado | 207-260 | Devastating | Well-constructed houses are leveled; structures with weak foundations are blown off and travel some distance. Cars are thrown and large missiles generated. |
| F5, Incredible tornado | 261-318 | Incredible | Incredible tornado (261-318 mph); incredible damage. Strong frame houses are lifted off foundations and carried considerable distance to disintegrate. Automobile-sized missiles fly through the air in excess of 100 yards. Trees are debarked. Incredible phenomena will occur. |

## Damage

| Category | Cost | Category | Cost |
| --- | --- | --- | --- |
| 1 | Less than $50 | 6 | $500,000 to $5 million |
| 2 | $50 to $500 | 7 | $5 million to $50 million |
| 3 | $500 to $5,000 | 8 | $50 million to $500 million |
| 4 | $5,000 to $50,000 | 9 | $500 million to $5 billion |
| 5 | $50,000 to $500,000 | | |

# Windstorms

## The Columbus Day Storm
## and Other Large-Scale Events

When it comes to windstorms in Oregon, the Columbus Day storm of 1962 stands alone. Nothing before nor since has matched the intensity and damage of that storm, although a few have come close. The "storm" was actually three storms in quick succession. The first formed as a trough off the coast of Oregon on October 11; it moved northward, and then northwestward, and began to taper off on the 12th. The second (and most destructive) storm formed from the remnants of Typhoon Freda, which moved northeastward from the Philippines, nearing the west coast early on the 12th. As it approached California, the storm nearly stopped moving, intensified, and began to slowly move northward just off the coast. As it moved, it wreaked havoc from northern California to British Columbia.

*Damage to Van Buren Bridge, Corvallis, after 1962 Columbus Day storm. (OSU Archives, P95:458)*

The storm reached the Oregon coast on the afternoon of the 12th. The central pressure of the storm dropped lower and lower, finally reaching 28.42 inches. Winds were strong along the coast, but even stronger inland. At Mt. Hebo in the Coast Range west of Salem, measured wind speeds

reached 131 mph before the anemometer was destroyed by the winds. On the Morrison Street bridge in Portland, winds gusted to 116 mph; in Naselle, Washington, they reached 160 mph. Trees, houses, and power lines were destroyed throughout the state; in some cases residents were without power for two to three weeks. Giant towers over 500 feet high holding the main power lines into Portland were knocked down. The Red Cross estimated that 84 homes were completely destroyed, 5,000 severely damaged, and 50,000 moderately damaged. Twenty-three people died in Oregon alone, and damages were estimated at $170 million.

The third storm was similar to the first and caused very little damage. It is likely that all "vulnerable" objects had been toppled by the main second storm.

The Columbus Day storm is at the pinnacle of a type of weather event that is quite common in Oregon. Each year the state receives many of these "mid-latitude synoptic-scale cyclones"—in lay terms, big winter storms. These storms share several characteristics:

—They move in a general west-to-east direction, although they sometimes move northward or southward for short periods of time.

—They form over the North Pacific.

—They produce strong winds and significant precipitation; a high percentage of Oregon's annual precipitation comes from these storms.

—They occur primarily during the cool season, usually from October through March.

—They usually affect an area for one day (or part of a day) before moving on.

The Columbus Day storm had all of those characteristics, but many aspects of that storm were magnified. For example,

—Its central pressure was one of the lowest ever observed in this area.

—Its path of movement (northward along the coast) caused it to affect a wider area, for a longer period of time, than would a more typical eastward-moving system.

—It occurred very early in the season, before deciduous trees had lost their leaves. This caused much greater damage than if the leaves had already fallen.

—It was a very broad storm, covering an unusually large area.

—It reached its peak strength just as it reached the coast. All storms go through periods of growth, reach a peak, and then decay. The peak strength of the Columbus Day storm occurred as it reached our area.

*Later on the winds really started to get strong, and we could really hear them howling. My Dad and I were standing in the kitchen, looking out toward the barn. We heard a big noise and watched as the barn roof slowly lifted up, turned over upside down and then came crashing down on the ground, breaking into pieces. We heard the roofing starting to come off the house and were afraid the house would just collapse, so we hurried outside, across the yard, and into the field. It was dusty, but we felt safer there because nothing could fall on us. We turned so our backs were toward the wind and just stood there in the middle of the field. We had to lean at about a 30° angle to the wind to be able to stand in it, and we stayed that way for hours, just leaning into the wind. Finally in the evening it began to die down, so we went back to the house. Somehow the house had managed to survive the storm without much damage. In fact, we realized that day how well-built our house really was.*
—A Yamhill County farmer, describing the Columbus Day windstorm.

*Wind damage to automobile, Columbus Day storm, October 1962, Corvallis. (OSU Archives P82:78)*

Thus, all the elements came together in October 1962, producing what Howard Sumner of the Weather Bureau correctly called "one of the major weather catastrophes of the state's history," a statement which is every bit as true now as it was when Sumner uttered those words 35 years ago.

Since 1962, there have been many big windstorms in Oregon (see the list at the end of this chapter). The biggest recent one, in December 1995, closely resembled the Columbus Day storm. Although loss of life and total damages were considerably less in the 1995 storm, it established a new record low pressure observed anywhere in Oregon—28.51 inches at Astoria, breaking a record set in 1880.

# Western Oregon, January 9, 1880

Nearly lost in antiquity in the stories of Oregon's windstorms is the "Big Blow" that occurred Friday, January 9, 1880. In Portland, the early morning was exceptionally mild; a balmy breeze blew from the southeast. Suddenly, around 10:00 a.m., the barometric pressure dropped more than an inch to a low 28.56 inches of mercury at 1:20 p.m. The wind picked up to over 50 mph by 2:00 p.m.

Schools closed and children went scurrying home. Business people began lashing down signs that were swaying wildly. The tin roof on the New Market Theater loosened and part of it sailed away, slicing the tops of 26 chimneys. St. Matthew's Episcopal Chapel, located near the south end of First Street, blew down. William Aker's livery stable front crashed into the street. Bremen Hall, a saloon, collapsed and four men were pinned in the debris; one was taken out dead. The West Side railroad track from Portland to Independence was covered with so many trees that the train didn't run for five days.

An eyewitness to the storm, in a letter to *The Oregonian*, January 10, 1925, wrote:

> *I stood at the front windows of the St. Charles office and watched the furious assaults of the storm. Looking across the river, during times when it was possible, owing to the flying spray that often obscured the view, I saw tree after tree go down before the fury of the hurricane, for such it really was. At times the spray from the river seemed to rise to a height of a hundred feet in the air, and the waves of the Willamette ran like ocean combers.*

Since no bridges spanned the Willamette in 1880, it was impossible to cross the river for several hours. For about a week following the storm there was practically no wire communication of any kind and Portland was deprived of press dispatches. The newspaper depended on general news from the San Francisco papers which were brought in by coast steamships.

Reports of the storm from other parts of the state trickled in to Portland. From Salem, came word that parts of the roof of the State Capitol had blown off. The wind had raged for four hours with great violence, then suddenly died down, and snow had begun falling. The Capitol began to fill with snow, which soon melted, causing water to run through the building.

Reports came in from Silverton, Howell Prairie, Canby, and other places in the Willamette Valley. Scores of houses and barns were demolished or badly damaged. Virtually all fences that oriented west-east were toppled. From Mehama came correspondence to the *Oregon Statesman* (Salem) January 13, 1880, stating that the spray of the (Santiam) river was hurled 60 feet in the air.

There was considerable damage along the coast. At Newport, all but two boats were smashed to pieces. Every barn between Newport and Elk City was leveled.

At Coos Bay, a three-masted schooner dragged her anchor and was broken in two on the beach. Ocean waves crashed against Tillamook Rock where fifteen men were building a foundation for the lighthouse. There was great concern for their safety. It took nearly two weeks for a cutter to reach the rock through the rough waters that persisted after the great blow. The cutter found the men alive but hungry. Their food and their tools had been swept away, but they had remained safe in a cave blasted out at the rock's crest, 90 feet above the ocean.

One group of people benefited from the storm: the Siletz Indians. The *Oregon Statesman,* January 15, 1880 reported, "These half-starved creatures are around with their canoes fishing out dead carcasses of animals killed by the storm."

At Umatilla, instruments at the U. S. Signal Station clocked the winds as high as 60 mph at 2:00 p.m. and 80 mph at 5:00 p.m. From the morning of January 9 to the time the windstorm started the barometric pressure at Umatilla dropped from 30.00 to 28.28 inches. A news reported from Umatilla stated:

> *Boards, shingles, roofs, and debris were borne through the air with terrific violence. Great clouds of sand enveloped the doomed town. The waters of the Columbia (River) were lashed into angry waves and sheets of flying foam. . . . All buildings in town have patches torn from the roofs. Several buildings were severely damaged at Umatilla. At Weston several houses were blown down.*

Damage to Portland, with a population of 17,577 at that time, was estimated to have been $75,000. A Silverton resident since 1848 stated that he had seen nothing to compare with the January 9, 1880, storm. From Portland came the verdict that nothing resembling it had ever been witnessed before in the memory of the whites and that the oldest Indians testified that their aboriginal history or legends contained no recollections of such a violent windstorm.

## The Great Windstorm of April 1931

Although most of Oregon's damaging or violent winds come from the Pacific, there are times when a strong high pressure system lies east of the Cascades and a deep low is situated off the Oregon coast, and the pressure gradient will induce a rapid flow of air from east to west.

Such was the case in April 1931. A large pool of cool, dense air had settled over Alberta, Canada. At the same time a fairly deep low was entered to the south of Oregon. Winds began to blow hard about 10:30 p.m. Wednesday, April 21.

The next day, strong winds picked up the top soils in the semi-arid mid-Columbia Basin. Reports from Hood River and The Dalles indicated that residents of those cities, ". . . looked out upon a gray and dreary world—and

*Damage in Portland from the 1962 Columbus Day storm. (Oregon Historical Society, negative number OrHi 65299)*

wondered how long it would take [for] the eastern sections of Washington and Oregon to pass by." By the next day (Friday, April 23) the gusty gale had lasted 36 hours, and dust sifted down on cities, covering what were once emerald-green lawns, and crept under door sills, coating furniture and carpets with the fine silt. Residents breathed the dust, coughed, and sneezed.

Meanwhile, at 6:15 a.m on the 22nd, winds had temporarily reached what witnesses said were "near-cyclonic intensity" in the Camp Sherman area northwest of Sisters in central Oregon. The freakish winds swept along the west side of the Metolius River towards the small community of Camp Sherman. Fortunately, at that time of the year the many summer cabins along the Metolius River were unoccupied. In ten minutes, from 6:14 to 6:25 a.m., ten million board feet of virgin lumber was uprooted. Many year-round and summer residences were in splinters. Included in the destruction of summer homes was the lodge belonging to Henry L. Corbett of Portland, destroyed by fire which was started by a falling pine tree.

The windstorm skipped across the Metolius River and "tossed trees around as if they were matchsticks." One large pine toppled on the Camp Sherman store and pinned Evelyn Foster, the postmaster of Camp Sherman, who suffered a broken ankle. For a while, reports from Camp Sherman were sketchy. A contractor clearing the route for the new Santiam Highway reported hundreds of trees down near or on the road between Blue Lake and Sisters. People living along the Metolius River set up temporary quarters in nearby meadows.

As the strong winds continued over a wide region, other areas of Oregon, especially in the Mt. Hood National Forest, experienced extensive timber losses. One motorist, trapped by trees in front and behind, spent the night dodging trees "falling as thick as flies." At the Wapinitia Cutoff near Mt. Hood, trees were piled up as much as 20 feet deep across the highway. An estimated 75-100 summer homes in the Zigzag, Brightwood, and Government Camp areas were wrecked by falling trees. Relative humidity dropped as low as 8% at the Swan Island Airport in Portland. At Laurel Hill, near Mt. Hood, three hundred men fought a fire that had broken out.

Throughout many parts of Oregon, telephone and power lines were downed. Three deaths were reported in Washington and one in Oregon. Grains, fruit, and vegetables were ruined. So strong were the winds in the Willamette Valley that some houses near Brownsville rocked on their foundations. Near McKenzie Bridge, a Eugene youth, William Ludlow, was trapped for five hours in a cabin. Veteran woodsman Dee Wright heard faint cries for help, but the wind was so loud that it was some time before Wright could determine the source. Even then, it took Forest Service and highway crews much work to clear the highway to allow a rescue truck to reach the victim and take him to Eugene. Ludlow, unfortunately, died at the Eugene Hospital.

Dwellings in Lane County near Creswell, Veneta, and Cottage Grove were destroyed. Old-timers in the Valley commented that it was "the first time in their memory that dust had blown from eastern Oregon." Visibility near Amity (near McMinnville) dropped to one-quarter mile. In Eugene, wind gusts swept dust into the city. A weird coppery light was cast over the city as sunlight filtered through the dust. Eugene folks sneezed and rubbed their eyes.

In McMinnville, Linfield College professor Kenneth Derby measured dust that had fallen from 6:00 p.m., April 22 to 5:00 p.m., April 23. Professor Derby's calculations were that 48,400 pounds of dust, analyzed to consist of quartz in both irregular and round grains, had fallen per square mile of area sampled. Prorating this amount of dust over the area of Portland (66-86 square miles) the dust storm was depositing 1,618 tons of dust on the city every 24 hours. To haul away the dust would have required a train of 33 box cars loaded with nearly 50 tons each.

A Varney mail plane, which had left Pasco, Washington, on the 22nd, bound for Portland, climbed to 14,500 feet to surmount the dust cloud. The pilot lost sight of the ground and greatly underestimated the strong tail winds (over 70 mph). When he recovered his bearings, the waters of the Pacific Ocean came into view near Seaside! Five ships, sailing the eastern Pacific near Oregon, encountered the dust storm on April 22 and 23. One, the *Albertolite*, reported that "visibility [was] so low it necessitated navigating as in fog." Other reports contained references to a coating of fine brown dust on the entire ship. In Marshfield (Coos Bay), ships remained in harbor.

By Saturday, April 25, the windstorm was over. After three days' work, crews opened the Wapinitia Cutoff to one-way traffic. In Portland, dust had seeped under doors and windows to lie thick on rugs and furniture. The dust was also thick on lawns, flower beds, and porches. The sun, when glimpsed at all, was a sickly yellow. Portland residents prayed for rain!

## Western Oregon, December 11, 1995

On December 11, 1995, a large low pressure storm approached the southern Oregon-northern California coast and began to slow and deepen. Its central pressure at sea level dropped precipitously, and the National Weather Service began to issue high wind warnings for the coast and the inland valleys. Later that day, very high winds struck California, knocking down trees as far south as the Bay Area.

On the morning of the 12th, the area of highest winds reached the Oregon coast as the low, still offshore, moved northward. Late that morning, the wind at Sea Lion Caves near Florence topped out at 119 mph before problems developed with the anemometer (no wonder!). In Newport, a gust of 107 mph occurred downtown, while Astoria and Cape Blanco also had gusts of over 100 mph. Astoria set its record low air pressure that afternoon (comparable to the central pressure of a Category 2 hurricane!). Gusts in the Willamette Valley exceeded 60 mph. Hundreds of thousands were without power, there was widespread damage to homes, buildings, and boats, and four citizens lost their lives.

Roger Cunningham is a consultant who lives in Florence and maintains a home weather station and impeccable records. Roger describes what happened:

> The wind, of course, was the big story. In my three
> years with a good anemometer, I'd never exceeded 36
> mph—until about 9:45 a.m. on Tuesday, when the
> wind reached 37. Just after 10 a.m. it gusted to 42.
> The morning began with light winds, but I knew
> what was coming. When the electricity failed at 10:30

**Western Oregon, November 10, 1957**

*A strong storm brought high winds and heavy rain to most of western Oregon. In Troutdale, a rooster was blown through the plate-glass window of a bank, setting off the break-in burglar alarm. The rooster received only minor scratches, and was released by authorities after questioning.*

**Oregon, January 7, 1961**

*One of the worst windstorms in terms of loss of life, this storm affected all of western Oregon and large areas east of the Cascades as well. Three deaths occurred in Eugene, where a roof was torn off a house under construction, taking the workers with it. Two crab fishermen whose boat got into trouble near the mouth of the Columbia died, as did five Coast Guardsmen trying to rescue them.*

*a.m. my instrument went on battery power, so I had to keep the display blank most of the time to conserve battery. I checked the peak gust occasionally, and had a gust to 45 mph around noon and the biggest of all, 48 mph, just after 2 p.m. This peak level was very puny (fortunately!) compared to most of the coast, because I'm 2.5 miles inland in a protected area. The local cable TV office had a gust to about 85 mph 2 miles SSW of me. Sea Lion Caves, on a very exposed headland 250 feet in elevation about 8 miles NNW of me had a 119 mph gust. Newport, 50 miles N, gusted to 107 mph, and North Bend AP, 50 miles S, gusted to 86 mph.*

The very wet soil following an unusually rainy fall caused many large trees to topple over. In the Willamette Valley, it appeared that more trees were uprooted than snapped above ground. After foresters assessed the damage in remote areas, very large losses of standing timber were reported.

If not for accurate and timely forecasts, loss of life would probably have been far higher. But high wind warnings issued by the National Weather Service gave residents ample time to prepare (with help from the media, which faithfully broadcast the warnings). Dave Willson and Ira Kosovitz received awards from the American Meteorological Society for their predictions of the storm.

## Local Windstorms

Although most Oregon windstorms come from large-scale weather disturbances, and thus affect large areas (and provide ample warning), local windstorms are quite common. Occasionally these small-scale events produce winds that exceed hurricane strength, causing big-time damages, injuries, and even deaths. And unfortunately, it's usually impossible to forecast these events because they occur at scales well below those covered by forecasters. While they can "see" big storms developing, forecasters simply cannot predict strong winds over small areas, with only a few exceptions.

One of those exceptions is the Columbia Gorge. The most significant east-west gap in the mountains between California and Canada, the Gorge is a low-level passageway that funnels winds back and forth between western and eastern Oregon (and Washington). Wind direction depends solely on the pressure gradient. When pressure is relatively high to the east of the Cascades (and low to the west), winds blow from east to west (they always blow from high to low pressure); when the west is under high pressure and the east is low, winds blow from west to east. East to west, or "easterly" winds are most common during winter. Cold continental air over the Great Basin is usually accompanied (some might say caused) by high pressure. Over the Pacific, temperatures are much milder (averaging about 50°F, compared with typical sub-freezing temperatures on the eastside). This dramatic temperature gradient creates a strong pressure gradient, with much lower pressure over the warmer Pacific. Hence, there is a steady flow of air from east to west. In the summer, the temperature and pressure gradients reverse. While temperatures over the Pacific change very little throughout the year, inland summer temperatures are generally quite high; summer highs at Pendleton, for example, average about 85°F and are often above 90°F. The temperature differences produce remarkably consistent pressure differences (high to the west, low to the east) and thus steady west-to-east wind flow.

And this is where the "funnel" effect of the Gorge kicks in. The atmosphere is actually a very thin fluid, and behaves somewhat like water: it tends to stay level or stratified unless disturbed, it follows the path of least resistance, and it flows from high to low (pressure in the case of air, depth in the case of water). Imagine what would happen if there were a large, deep mass of water in eastern Oregon: it would flow downhill (to the west) until it encountered the Cascades; then it would funnel through the Gorge (moving much faster and with more turbulence through the narrow gap) until it reached the Willamette Valley, whereupon it would disperse and move more slowly. That's almost exactly what happens with cold, high pressure air as it moves westward in winter. Lacking the momentum to push its way over the Cascades, the cold air takes the path of least resistance and moves through the Gorge. Just as a narrow river canyon produces fast-flowing, turbulent rivers, so the Gorge creates strong winds that are quite gusty (a sign of turbulence). These cold east winds bring very cold air (and often ice; see the section on Ice Storms) to Troutdale, Portland, and other areas very near the Gorge. They frequently make driving within the Gorge a dangerous proposition, because of ice-coated roads and windy conditions. They have even inspired a name: Coho.

## The Name of the Wind: Coho

Until recently, Gorge east winds have been without an official name. However, during the month of November a Portland television station and *The Oregonian* teamed with the Oregon chapter of the American Meteorological Society for a "Name our East Wind" contest. Some 7,000 entries were submitted, with a total of 2,424 different names. The name "Coho" was judged to be the best name, since it is easy to pronounce (and spell); it's an indigenous name to the Pacific Northwest; Coho salmon are wild fast swimmers analogous to the wind; and it relates to the widely known westerly Chinook winds that are also a name of a salmon.

*Damage to greenhouses at North Willamette Experiment Station, Aurora, after 1962 Columbus Day storm. (OSU Archives P36:137)*

During the winter the "Coho" winds are predominantly from the east. These winds are "bora" winds, which are a type of down-sloping katabatic wind (katabatic means to fall.) Although down-sloping air is warmed by compression, "bora" winds are always much colder than the mild marine air they replace. The cold, dense air rushes through the Gorge being moderated only slightly along its journey to Portland. There it spills into the Portland area, chilling the air and turning any rain into freezing rain.

Since winds generally blow from high pressure to low pressure, the cold air is either pulled westward through the Gorge by approaching storms or pushed by high pressure inland. Once set in motion, these winds gain fierce speeds; they sometimes reach speeds of 80 mph, causing structural damage and blowing trucks off Interstate-84. While the Columbia River Gorge, the largest gap through the Cascades, is most prone to severe "boras," the winds can gain devastating speed even through the smaller gaps of the Washington Cascades. The winds can also add the final ingredient for severe ice and snowstorms. The combination of this arctic air and warm, moist air associated with Pacific storms can lead to paralyzing snow and ice storms. One of the most memorable such snowstorms hit Bonneville Dam on January 9, 1980, and dropped the greatest 24-hour snowfall ever recorded in Oregon of 39 inches.

Meanwhile, during the summer winds in the Gorge blow predominantly from the west. This is because the heated land surface over eastern Washington and Oregon induces lower pressure, known as a "heat low," while over the cold ocean waters of the Pacific, higher pressure resides. The wind blows from high pressure off the coast to low pressure inland. The winds in the summer are typically weaker, they are more consistent, and blow at speeds of 10 to 20 mph. However, if a strong "heat low" exists, winds can kick up to 50 mph and cause blowing dust.

The easterly "Coho" winds are not only stronger but more common, therefore there are an abundance of flagged trees (trees whose branches only grow on one side, away from the wind) in the Gorge. The wind blows at an annual average 13.0 mph at Hood River, Oregon. This compares to the notoriously windy Great Plains of Texas and Kansas where the average annual wind speed is 15 mph. —*Tye Parzybok, Research Scientist, Oregon Climate Service*

*Tree downed at Oregon State University after the Columbus Day Storm, 1962. (OSU Archives P82:78)*

Summer, with its warm inland temperatures, brings a reversal of the Coho winds, now mostly west-to-east (known as westerlies—so far they haven't been given a distinctive local name). In the middle of the Gorge, where winds are the steadiest and most reliable, sits the town of Hood River, until recently known primarily for its orchards (the beautiful Hood River Valley, less than 50 square miles in size, produces over $80 million per year in fruits, mostly apples and pears). But in the 1980s, as windsurfing became increasingly popular, its aficionados discovered something about the Gorge: in summer the strong, steady west winds blow just opposite to the current in the Columbia River. While west winds pushed the windsurfer to the east, his/her movement was compensated for by the westward flow of the river. At Hood River, a windsurfer could cross the mile-wide Columbia to White Salmon, Washington, turn around, return to the Oregon side, and end up in the same place where the journey began. And the process could be repeated hour after hour, day after day, through much of the summer.

Few places in Oregon have winds as reliable as those in the Gorge, but nearly every part of the state has been affected by strong local windstorms. In addition to the accounts below, there are many windstorm summaries in the accompanying table.

### Klamath Falls, July 5, 1970

A strong localized windstorm hit Klamath Falls during the afternoon of July 5. At a carnival site which was set up for the previous day's holiday, the winds toppled a double Ferris wheel, blowing it onto a truck and trailer. An employee standing nearby was injured when she was blown against an amusement park car†ride. Nearby, the roof was blown off a golf course clubhouse; it sailed over two rows of cars, smashing into the third row. At the Tackle and Saw Shop downtown, a boat was blown off the roof (we assume it was there for advertising display) and damaged a nearby car.

### Lane County, south of Eugene, November 24, 1989

The Eugene Weather Service Office Meteorologist-in-Charge, along with three other witnesses, reported strong winds associated with a funnel cloud between 40 and 60 feet in diameter that came within 30 feet of the ground in the hills south of Eugene. Winds from the thunderstorm broke power poles and pulled trees out of the ground (they fell on two houses and a camper and caused much damage.)

### Multnomah County, June 9, 1994

People at the scene described a funnel cloud between 50 and 75 feet wide and 300 feet high that hit two plastic skylights at a warehouse in Portland and spun them and other material in the air, 200 feet up. This wind was particularly unusual because it occurred on a warm sunny day of 80°F, not a typical situation for a funnel cloud.

# Significant Windstorms in Oregon

*Western Oregon*  Jan. 9, 1880
Winds in Portland ranged from 65 to 80 mph. Numerous buildings and trees, some 5 to 8 feet in diameter, were destroyed and damaged. Fallen trees stopped trains in most of northwest Oregon. The wind hurled debris through the air and injured many people.

*Coast and inland in northwest Oregon*  Jan. 20, 1921
At North Head (on the northern side of the mouth of the Columbia River) an official wind speed of 113 mph was recorded and Astoria reported gusts up to 130 mph. There were also hurricane-force winds along the entire coast and strong winds in the Willamette Valley. Buildings and timber were heavily damaged.

*Western and northeastern Oregon*  Apr. 21-22, 1931
Official wind speeds were only 27-36 mph, but unofficial reports were as high as 78 mph. These very strong winds caused extensive damage, especially in northern Oregon. Fruit orchards and timber experienced the most damage. Ships as far as 600 miles out at sea reported seeing dust settle on exposed areas many days after the storm.

*Western Columbia Gorge*  Dec. 20, 1935
Cold air from the interior Columbia Basin pushed westward through the Gorge. At Crown Point, Oregon, where the temperatures were between 30 and 34°F, winds from the east were so strong that they carried away all of the wind instruments. Pilots in the area estimated that wind speeds were about 30 mph at 4,000 feet but more than 50 mph at the surface. An observer estimated gusts up to 120 mph when the storm was at its peak. The average velocity at Crown Point, 58.2 mph, was the highest ever recorded for this station since it began operation in 1929. A trailer and a furniture truck full of furniture and kitchen stoves both blew over. Two cars had their tops completely removed.

*Most of Oregon*  Nov. 10-11, 1951
Widespread damage occurred to utility transmission lines, buildings, and timber from southerly and southwesterly winds of 40 to 60 mph with gusts of 75-80 mph.

*Most of Oregon*  Dec. 4, 1951
This storm was strongest along the coast, where wind observations were unofficially at 60 to 100 mph. In inland Oregon the unofficial reports showed wind gusts of 75 mph. Many buildings were damaged and power and telephone transmission lines losses were scattered throughout the state.

*Western Oregon*  Jan. 8-10, 1953
Winds reached 100 mph on the coast and 60 mph in the Willamette Valley and caused an estimated $1 million damage. Damage was especially sever to power lines outdoor signs, and roofs. Several large buildings were blown down along the coast. One person was killed.

*Western Oregon*   Dec. 6, 1955

This storm developed in the Pacific and brought very cold unstable air to the Oregon coast. The air produced strong winds with gusts up to 75 mph. Power failures were common because the wind blew trees onto the lines. Roofs and buildings were reported damaged. The wind collapsed a hanger in Lebanon and completely destroyed the small airplane inside. Lightning was also frequent in this storm; many trees were struck, but there were no lightning-related injuries or deaths. Heavy rains brought some rivers to flood stage as well as setting off mud slides that damaged roads. One person died as a result of this storm.

*Almost all of Oregon*   Dec. 21-23, 1955

High winds occurred throughout the state, causing problems with buildings and power and transmission lines. North Bend had sustained speeds of 70 mph with gusts of 90 mph, The Dalles had speeds of 66 mph, Pendleton had speeds of 61 mph with gusts of 69 mph. Others areas of the state reported speeds of 55-65 mph with much higher gusts. A man was killed when he stepped on a downed power line, another died when a tree fell on top of him and his bulldozer, and two others drowned on the Columbia because the wind capsized their boat. There was significant damage to farm machinery, buildings, and animals.

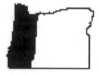

*Western Oregon*   Jan. 14-16, 1956

Beginning on the Oregon coast, this storm moved into all of western Oregon on the 15th and 16th. It included heavy rain and high winds with abundant snow east of the Cascades. Wind damage was mostly to utility poles and lines (causing damage estimated at $95,000), but there was also heavy damage because of mudslides. The rains and melting snow damaged roads and bridges.

*Most of Oregon*   Nov. 3, 1958

Every major highway in western Oregon was blocked by fallen trees at some point during this storm. Buildings, homes, and utility lines also suffered a lot of damage. Wind speeds of 51 mph were reported at the Portland Airport, with gusts up to 71 mph. Pendleton had its fastest speed of 51 mph, Astoria had a gust of 75 mph, Columbia Lightship had 90 mph, and Mt. Hebo Air Force base recorded a 131 mph gust on an unofficial instrument.

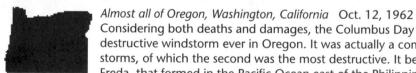

*Almost all of Oregon, Washington, California*   Oct. 12, 1962

Considering both deaths and damages, the Columbus Day storm was the most destructive windstorm ever in Oregon. It was actually a combination of three storms, of which the second was the most destructive. It began with Typhoon Freda, that formed in the Pacific Ocean east of the Philippine Islands. Freda headed east, then west, then south and on the afternoon of October 12th the huge storm arrived off the Oregon coast and stretched from northern California to British Columbia. In Oregon the winds were 131 mph on Mt. Hebo and 116 mph on the Morrison Bridge in Portland. The central pressure dropped to 28.42 inches. The Weather Bureau Airport Station at Portland reported its fastest wind speed of 73 mph with a peak gust of 79 mph. Several hundred thousand people were without power for hours, others for two to three weeks. The Red Cross estimated that 84 houses were destroyed, 5,000 were severely damaged, and between 40,000 and 50,000 were slightly damaged. Total damage was estimated at $170 million for Oregon, where an estimated 23 people were killed as a result of this storm.

*Coast and northwestern Oregon*   Mar. 27, 1963
With 100 mph gusts (unofficially), this storm was most severe along the coast; inland it was less intense but still caused widespread damage. Portland had wind speeds of 57 mph with a peak gust of 63 mph, Salem had winds at 39 and 68 mph, and Eugene had winds at 48 and 75 mph.

*Western and northern Oregon*   Oct. 2, 1967
Significant damage to agriculture, timber, utilities, and homes occurred with the highest wind speeds recorded since the Columbus Day storm. The Portland Airport recorded a top wind speed of 70 mph. The Oregon coast saw wind speeds of 100 to 115 mph. There was one fatality and about fifteen persons were seriously injured.

*Most of Oregon*   Mar. 25-26, 1971
This windstorm occurred when a storm center moved into northwestern Washington and the cold front headed east, bringing damaging winds to most of Oregon on the 26th. The greatest damage was in the Willamette Valley and counties along the Columbia River, though the coast did experience heavy damage as well. Roofs were blown off homes and several mobile homes and campers were blown over in the northern part of the valley. Windows and road signs were destroyed and falling trees damaged homes and power lines. In the valley and along the coast there were over six thousand power outages. A large ship and a barge broke loose from the Portland docks and a large semi-truck and trailer were blown over in Newport. There was also great destruction to standing timber in southern Lane County and northern Douglas County.

*Pacific Northwest*   Nov. 13-15, 1981
Back-to-back storms hit the Pacific Northwest with the highest winds since the Columbus Day storm of 1962. The November 13-14 storm did the most damage, with wind gusts including 75 mph at Astoria, 62 mph at Medford, and 92 mph at North Bend. The Willamette Valley had winds of 58 mph in Eugene and 71 mph in both Salem and Portland. The November 15 storm was weaker but added to the damage. Gusts to 60 mph were common throughout the state, with Portland officially recording 57 mph winds. Oregon's marinas, airports, and bridges suffered due to the high winds and large ocean swells. Fallen trees, live wires, blown roofs, and perilous helicopter rescues lead to $50 million in damages and eleven deaths.

*Northeastern Oregon*   Jan. 7, 1986
Strong winds tore pieces of the roof off two Lexington storage hangars and a 30-foot-wide strip from the Elgin High School gymnasium roof. Sustained winds of 80 to 90 mph occurred at Valley Air Service in LaGrande. Drifting snow accompanied this storm and forced the closure of Interstate 84 through Ladd Canyon.

*North and central Oregon coast*   Jan. 16, 1986
Winds of 75 mph stopped the transmission of power to five thousand people on the coast and damaged trees and buildings. Wind was probably the reason for a helicopter crash that killed a man.

*Oregon coast* Jan. 2-3, 1987 (1650 PST)
Because of a strong low pressure system that moved northward along the coast, strong winds hit Cape Blanco with a gust of 96 mph. The beach eroded and highways and beach houses were damaged due to the high winds and the record high tides for the year. There were several injuries that could have resulted in deaths.

*Southwestern Oregon* Mar. 4, 1987 (1200 PST)
A strong pressure gradient formed in front of a small low pressure system and cold front that traveled across the southwestern portion of Oregon. The winds were 70 mph in Ashland, 69 mph in Klamath Falls (the strongest in 25 years), and 85 mph in the Siskiyou Mountains. Trees were blown over and power failures occurred. Hangars, barns, and roofs were damaged and destroyed.

*Umatilla County* Dec. 6, 1987 (0939 PST)
The winds in the northeast mountains 50 east-northeast of Pendleton blew over a dead tree 18 inches in diameter which landed on top of a moving car, killing two people. One other death was recorded. Observed wind speeds in the area were 38 mph, but locally they were much higher.

*Oregon coast, northwestern Oregon* Dec. 6, 1987 (1800PST)
Low pressure moved up the coast with an active cold front that moved inland. On the coast the wind speeds were up to 60 mph and in Salem they were up to 47 mph. The ground was saturated from previously heavy rains and that in combination with the gusts of wind blew a tree onto a moving car in Mill City. Three children were killed and two other people in the car were injured.

*North and central Oregon coast* Mar. 22-23, 1988 (830-2100 PST)
Wind along the Oregon coast reached gusts of 55 to 75 mph. Mudslides closed roads and wind blew over trees. A death occurred when a tree fell near Ecola State Park (north of Cannon Beach) on top of a 15-year-old girl.

*Oregon coast* Mar. 9, 1989 (0130-2100PST)
Three men died when a small commercial fishing boat sank west of Newport. Seaside and Tillamook reported wind gusts of 71 and 70 mph, respectively.

*All of Oregon* Jan. 6-8, 1990
This windstorm began on the Pacific Ocean and moved toward land on the 6th. Heavy rain accompanied by winds exceeding 75 mph caused numerous trees to fall; they landed on cars, houses, and other buildings. A smaller storm the day before had weakened trees, a drive-in movie screen, radio towers, and barn roofs that then fell with the force of this bigger storm onto houses, cars, etc. Fifty-five million board-feet of lumber (worth over $20 million) blew down in the state and national forests of Oregon. Fatalities occurred when a tree fell on a girl in her back yard and when a man's car veered into the wrong lane during intense rain. At least nine people were injured. On January 8 and 9 winds reached 100 mph in Netarts and Oceanside (Tillamook County), the highest in 30 years.

*Lincoln County, south Cascades, Pendleton* Jan. 30, 1990
There was heavy snow and high wind all day, with most of the damage in the Lincoln City area. At Devils Lake a $25,000 fish-retaining structure was washed away by the wind and rough ocean waters. The south Cascades received 12 to 18 inches of new snow in 24 hours. Pendleton had winds of 54 mph.

*Oregon coast*   Feb. 9, 1990
In Netarts sustained winds were 40 mph with gusts up to 53 mph; at Astoria, winds gusted at 45 mph. High waves generated by the storm ripped a 64-foot salmon trawler from a dock and took the dock and four pilings with it.

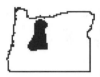

*West slopes, north Oregon Cascades*   June 21, 1990 (1500-1700 PST)
These winds were caused by thunderstorms that moved north along the Cascades with wind gusts that exceeded 60 mph. At McKenzie Bridge golfball-size hail and strong rain fell. A tree in Fisherman's Bend Campground fell because of the high wind and landed on a pickup truck where young children were trying to escape the rain, wind, and hail.

*Clatsop County, Wallowa County*   Dec. 4, 1990 (0100-1000 PST)
Wind gusts from this storm were typically around 65 mph, but caused extensive damage. One of these gusts caused the tower of the Astoria Flight Service Building to topple to the ground. Near Wheeler, the Paradise Cove Resort lost a 26-foot trailer to the wind as it was turned over, displacing two trailer spaces. The wind caused roof damage to the Joseph Elementary School and the Joseph Post Office and blew approximately 15 feet of wheeled irrigating line from a field to the road.

*Most of Oregon*   Jan. 11-12, 1991
The northern coast was struck first by strong winds which moved up the Columbia Gorge to northeastern Oregon. Wind gusts were 63 mph at Netarts, 57 mph at Seaside, and 52 mph at the mouth of the Columbia River. Northwest of Astoria a 75-foot-long trawler sank in the rough water. On the boat were a U.S. Coast Guardsman and four fishermen. Two of the fishermen were rescued; the remaining three people drowned.

*Cascades and northeastern Oregon*   Mar. 3, 1991 (945-1900PST)
This windstorm caused extensive damage. In Pendleton, where the wind was 48 mph and gusts were as high as 74 mph, an apartment building roof blew off and landed on a car in the parking lot . The roofs of Willowcreek Elementary School and Kays Cafe were also blown off (Kays Cafe roof landed on top of a neighboring building). Dust that was blown around because of the wind caused three car accidents. One was a four-car pileup, another was a two-car wreck, and the third happened when a trailer being towed fishtailed because of the wind, broke away, and ripped out its rear axle. Amazingly, no one was hurt. Wind speeds ranged from 44 to 52 mph with gusts from 54 to 74 mph.

*Oregon coast*   Nov. 15-16, 1991 (1300-2400PST)
This was a slow-moving, windy frontal system that blew over a 6-ton trailer in Clatsop County, knocked over the transmitter of a radio station, destroyed numerous signs in Lincoln County, blew off the roof of a mobile home, damaged two other mobile homes, and downed trees which then damaged houses and boats, closed roads, and turned off the electricity for thousands. Waves just offshore were measured at 25 feet. The storm also produced lightning.

*North-central and northeastern Oregon* Dec. 12, 1991
This windstorm caused extensive damage, with gusts up to 70 mph from Bend to LaPine. In Sunriver between six and eight hundred trees fell, many onto power lines and buildings. A construction worker was injured when a tree or parts of a tree fell on his shoulder, breaking it. At the Osprey Inn an 80-foot-tall tree snapped in half and fell into the Inn. The Grange Hall near Bend lost its roof to the wind and a storage building was left without its doors or its metal roof. Many other roofs were also destroyed. At the same time, people had to find shelter from the blowing dust.

*Southwestern Oregon, northeast mountains* Dec. 9-10, 1992
This was one of many strong storms this month. The winds were fastest along the south coast, with gusts of 110 mph near Brookings, and high gusts also reported at Cape Blanco (96 mph), Sea Lion Caves (78 mph), and Gold Beach (72 mph). Many locations reported winds of 40 mph for extended periods of time and gusts up to 60 mph. By the time the storm reached northeastern Oregon the winds were still 60 to 80 mph; damage was widespread.

*Oregon coast* Jan. 31, 1992 (530-1700 PST)
Gusts of 97 mph were reported at Oceanside, with 85 mph at Cape Blanco. In Clatsop County a mill lost many logs when they rolled off their piles and a United Parcel Service truck was blown over on its side.

*Oregon coast, northern Oregon* Jan. 19-20, 1993 (2200-1300PST)
A low pressure center moved northward just inland of the coast producing winds of up to 100 mph that blew down trees and caused thousands of power outages all along the coast. One power company had damages exceeding $1 million from to this storm. The most severe winds were in the Nehalem River valley (in the northern Coast Range). About $3 million of trees (some old growth) fell during the storm; many landed on top of houses and cars. Tillamook had the highest reported gust for this storm at 98 mph. Northeastern Oregon experienced winds of 70 mph and a foot of snow fell in the Cascades.

*Northern Oregon* Dec. 7-10, 1993
Intense rain and strong winds accompanied this Pacific storm. It did not cause significant damage except to power lines (the power went out in many areas). The highest winds, 70 to 80 mph gusting to 103 mph, were at Timberline Lodge ski resort (6,000 feet high on Mt. Hood); the Elkhorn Mountains in northeastern Oregon were also hit very hard. Many coastal areas reported 70 to 80 mph gusts. This storm also caused an F2 tornado in Yamhill and Washington counties

*Eastern Oregon* May 15, 1994
Trees, power lines and poles, and billboards fell due to strong winds in eastern Oregon. Blowing dust caused many car accidents. Winds of 55 mph, gusting to 65, were reported at Ontario Airport. The Treasure Valley agricultural area's irrigation ditches and dams were plugged up with tumbleweeds and water. No one was seriously injured.

*Statewide*   Dec. 12, 1995

This large offshore storm moved slowly up the Oregon coast, following the path of the Columbus Day storm. Record low barometric pressures occurred at Astoria (28.53 inches). The WillametteValley had 60 mph winds, but the coast was the hardest hit with gusts over 100 mph recorded from Newport to Cape Blanco. Sea Lion Caves near Florence recorded the storm's highest gusts (119 mph) before the anemometer broke. Wet soil from earlier rains could not hold trees in place so primary damages included homes, buildings, and boats. Four people were killed and twenty injured.

*Western Oregon*     Nov. 19, 1997

A potent Pacific storm system lashed western Oregon with high winds on November 19. The storm intensified offshore, maintained its strength and slowly moved northward, parallel to the coast. Wind gusts reached 89 mph at Florence, 80 mph at Netarts and Newport, and 52 mph in the Willamette Valley (Salem). Damage from the storm included several small airplanes flipped at the Albany airport; numerous trees toppled, especially in the Newport and Swiss Home areas; and beach erosion along the southern coast.

# Cold Weather

*Silver Creek Falls State Park (south falls), January 1949. (Photo by Wanda Gifford; OSU Archives P218:16)*

Winter in Oregon is characterized by wet, somewhat cold weather in the western third of the state, and drier, much colder weather east of the Cascades. The same (infrequent) storms that bring snow to western Oregon also provide the coldest temperatures. But in eastern Oregon, where snow dominates during winter, "cold" is much, much colder than in the west.

When Oregonians think "cold weather," the little town of Seneca generally comes to mind. Not only does Seneca share Oregon's all-time record cold temperature (with Ukiah), the temperatures there get cold *a lot*. Here is a description of "Oregon's icebox."

## Seneca

The town of Seneca is nestled in the Bear Valley, a high-elevation bowl in the mountains of eastern Oregon. The Silvies River flows through the valley on its way southward, but other than the small gap in the mountains through which the river flows, Bear Valley is surrounded by mountains, with some peaks exceeding 8,000 feet. On calm, clear nights (frequent in this region), cold air flows steadily downward, pooling in the valley below; this is generally called the "frost hollow" effect. Seneca, at about 4,700 feet, is in the lowest part of the valley, and the recipient of much of the cold air. As a result, Seneca often records the lowest temperatures in Oregon. Cold weather can occur any time of year, and freezing temperatures in summer come as no surprise to residents. Small wonder, then, that Seneca is widely known as "Oregon's icebox."

Lumber executive and weather hobbyist E.W. Barnes described Seneca's climate in 1932, one year after the installation of the first certified thermometer: "Seneca . . . is in

Bear Valley, which is a sort of 'draw' or funnel where cold air settles and makes a business of being cold. In the old stagecoach days passengers used to dread the part of the trip through the valley. A few miles away the temperature is moderate." (*The Oregonian*, December 2, 1932, quoted in Johnson 1994).

**Table 31. Seneca records since 1948**

| Lowest Temperature | | Consecutive days below 0°F | |
|---|---|---|---|
| Year | Temp (°F) | Year | Days |
| 12/23/83 | -48 | 1/1/86 | 21 |
| 2/6/89 | -48 | 2/5/72 | 12 |
| 1/26/57 | -43 | 2/4/79 | 12 |
| 2/4/85 | -43 | 1/7/60 | 11 |
| 1/22/62 | -41 | 1/12/74 | 11 |
| 12/30/78 | -41 | 1/20/85 | 11 |
| 12/9/72 | -40 | 1/4/79 | 10 |
| 1/1/79 | -40 | | |

Thus, it is fitting that Seneca shares Oregon's all-time cold temperature record. In February 1933, both Seneca and Ukiah (a nearby station in a similar high valley) reached -54°F (see story below). At Seneca, that temperature has been approached a number of times since. Table 31 lists the lowest temperatures in Seneca since 1948 (when digital records begin), as well as the longest streaks of consecutive days below 0°F.

Johnson (1994) quoted a number of Seneca residents who recalled dealing with the extreme cold in the old days. Leo "Duce" McKrola, a timber worker, remembers the sounds that occur when trees are felled when it's very cold: "They crack and pop, the timber does. It's just like cutting an icicle." His wife Kathryn recalls trying to wash her children's clothes and "hanging up those clothes and bringing them back in frozen and standing 'em up around the heater."

In an effort to help Leo avoid frostbite, Kathryn would "take my worn-out nylons, then I'd cut the tops off and tie a knot in the topnotch and he'd wear that over his head." Many of the men had similar devices, said Leo, because "a tin hat gets awful cold, just like an icicle on top of your head." The only problem with the head-warmer was that "it was so slick that your tin hat wouldn't stay on very good, you'd turn your head a little bit, and it was always falling off."

Doris Barott "Dodie" Lohf, whose father Howard was the Seneca weather observer during the 1933 event, remembers winter car troubles as being just an accepted part of life. "Sometimes you'd get the cars started but they wouldn't shift gear because they were so frozen . . . I mean, sometimes you start 'em, sometimes you don't and if it's three or four days you just don't start 'em . . . and you just stay in."

# Other Notable Cold Spots

Several other locations in Oregon rival Seneca for the title "Oregon's icebox." Meacham, Drewsey, and Ukiah are high-elevation sites in eastern Oregon which share the "frost-hollow" effects that characterize Seneca. Johnson's (1994 and 1999) insights were helpful here as well.

Meacham lies in a small mountain valley in the Blue Mountains in northeast Oregon, east of Pendleton. A classic frost hollow site, Meacham often is 10°F to 15°F colder than the nearby airport, which is just 250 feet higher in elevation. The coldest temperature recorded at the airport over a 25-year period was -23°F, while in town a reading of -52°F was recorded. Meacham is frequently mentioned by national news agencies as the coldest spot in the continental U.S. because it reports every day; although Seneca and other stations may be colder, their daily temperature reports are generally not received until the end of each month.

Drewsey is more than 1,000 feet lower than Seneca, and is generally milder. On occasion, however, Drewsey can be as cold as or colder than any site in Oregon. In 1924 Drewsey recorded a low of -53°F, the coldest ever reported in Oregon until Seneca and Ukiah reported -54°F nine years later. In 1984, Drewsey had Oregon's low for the year, -29°F, 5°F less than Seneca. And in 1990, Drewsey's -35°F extreme low was only 1°F milder than Seneca's -36°F.

*Steamer* Columbia *stuck in the ice on the Columbia River, January 1907. (Oregon Historical Society, negative number OrHi 67903)*

Ukiah, like Seneca, is in a river valley susceptible to cold air pooling. Its elevation, 3,340 feet, is even lower than Drewsey's, and its low temperatures are usually less extreme than Seneca's. But as in the case of Drewsey, when it gets cold in Ukiah it gets really cold. In February 1933, Ukiah tied Seneca's -54°F for Oregon's all-time low mark. Temperatures below -30°F are not uncommon. In an average year, Ukiah experiences thirteen sub-zero days, while Seneca averages twenty-four.

## Frozen Rivers

Prior to the establishment of dams, river levels varied much more than they do at present. Summer dryness produced low river flows that lasted well into autumn and early winter. Since winter storms produce snow, not rain, in much of the state, river levels rise only moderately during winter. But come spring, warm temperatures begin to melt the snow pack, often very suddenly. Historically, Oregon's greatest stream flows (and most of the floods) occurred in spring (see Floods chapter).

In the post-dam era, water levels remain much more uniform throughout the year. Flood-control practices have significantly reduced the magnitude of the big spring peak. They have also increased the levels during what was the low flow period.

In the past, when very low winter river levels corresponded with unusually cold temperatures, rivers often froze. At times, the ice thickness was enough to permit walkers (or even drivers) to cross the rivers. Some of the pictures in this section, taken near the turn of the century, show the Columbia frozen over. Since the 1930s, when the first dams were built, high winter flows make it highly unlikely that such incidents would recur.

# The Winter of 1861-62

By all accounts, the winter of 1861-62 was one of the deadliest, most extreme, and most unpleasant winters in Oregon's history. Cold, snowy weather characterized much of the winter, but there were also several very large floods. One of these, on December 12, was the largest on record for the Willamette River. The towns of Champoeg, Orleans, and Syracuse were all completely destroyed (see Flood chapter).

Low temperatures were just as impressive as the flood waters, especially in eastern Oregon and Washington. Following are excerpts from several books and diaries based on eyewitness accounts of that severe winter.

### From "Experiences of Thomas H. Brent"

In the fall of 1861, with Henry and William Hall (now prominent citizens of Grant County, Oregon) and George Byers, Brent went to the Walla Walla valley, taking one hundred head of milk cows for the purpose of establishing a dairy.

Having but little money, he hauled, with an ox-team, cordwood and lumber from the Walla Walla River and the Blue Mountains into the town of Walla Walla, while one of his comrades served as cook in a hotel. At that place he celebrated his twenty-first birthday, in honor of which the party feasted on stewed prairie-chicken with dumplings and roasted squash.

Between Christmas and New Year the weather turned intensely cold (the thermometer touching 35°F below zero), and it so continued until the coming of the Chinook winds about the middle of March. Snow fell throughout the valley to a depth of 3 feet, becoming so crusted that a man could walk on it, and remained in that condition more than two months; while in the mountains the fall was 10 to 12 feet.

Cattle perished by thousands, scarcely any surviving. Of those brought by Brents, the Halls' and Byers, only two were alive at the end of the cold spell. Soon after the storm began they had slaughtered one of the animals, which, with a sack of middlings, furnished them one meal of porridge a day; with the exception of a black-tailed deer shot by Mr. Brents, they had no other food during the winter.

They lived in a small unfurnished box house of inch lumber, unbattened, without floor, door, or chimney, and but partly covered. The fire was built on the frozen ground and the smoke easily found an outlet through the uncovered space above.

—Clinton Snowden, "Experiences of Thomas H. Brent in the winter of 1861," *History of Washington*, p. 314.

## Sherman County, Oregon

The severe winter of 1861-62 brought tragedy to the country as evidenced by an episode that has been remembered in various forms. There was scant provision for travelers, stage stations were far apart and there were none across the breadth of Sherman County.

There were neither homesteads, nor towns, nor sheep camps. Carson Masiker tells the story of the death of many members of a party bound for The Dalles from the Idaho mines with the accuracy of one who heard it directly from survivors. One of Emmitt Miller & Co.'s stages on their line running from Walla Walla to The Dalles, was snow-blocked at Well Spring, 16 miles east of Willow Creek. The passengers resolved to go on:

> John Jaggers was carrying 36 pounds of gold dust . . . he gave out and was afraid to trust anyone with his gold. He wrapped himself in a blanket and put his gold between his feet and his companions covered him with blankets. The next day he was found frozen stiff.

Sixteen passengers at Tom Scott's wanted to go on, which they did. Only one of them, a thinly clad youth of eighteen, got through because, so the story recounts, he did not drink any whiskey. When he arrived at Graham's he told of the others and men went out after them. Two were at the mouth of Spanish Hollow with frozen feet and eventually came in unaided.

Two others were found at Murray Springs, having left one Johnathan Mulkey who was found frozen down. He died at Deschutesville. Seven finally made it to safety. The next spring one was found near Rufus, another 20 miles up the Deschutes, one near the John Day and some were never found.—Giles French, "The winter of 1861-62," *The Golden Land*, p. 32-33

## A Washington perspective

The history of our state for twenty years was dated from the hard winter of 1861-62. Snow began falling about the middle of December and in two weeks had covered the state with a blanket varying from 2 to 6 feet. A day or two of warm weather melted the top snow then set in the longest and most severe cold spell recorded before or since.

A hard crust was frozen on top of the snow. East of the Cascade range the cold spell lasted fifty-four days with temperatures in Yakima and lower Columbia valleys falling to 32°F below zero and staying there for forty days. In the Okanogan valley and upper Columbia River valleys north of Spokane it was recorded as low as 52°F below for more than three straight weeks, congealing the mercury in the thermometers.

West of the Cascades the cold was not so severe but pioneers at Cowlitz Landing near Kelso and at Bellingham report that the snow lasted until well into April.

So abundant had been the bunchgrass in previous years that cattlemen had not taken the precaution to put up hay for feed. Cattle were not able to get food through the crust of snow and 90% of the cattle in the state starved to death.

Stories are told of people taking meat from the frozen cattle, drying it, rolling it in ground wheat and feeding it to the cattle. Others made a rich soup and let the cattle drink this in an effort to save them. Near Waterville seed wheat was fed to the cattle while it lasted but this small supply did not last long enough to save the cattle.

Many tales are told of burning rail fences and homemade furniture in order to keep warm. One woman had ice frozen on her floor from the condensed steam of her teakettle. In attempting to melt this she poured hot water on it and soon had a skating rink over a large part of the floor.

Mr. Van Sycle of Prosser who bought the Hudson's Bay Company's land near Wallula, in piling up the bones of the cattle on his land two summers afterwards had a pile as large as an average house. As soon as the cold weather abated somewhat the men took the hides from the cattle. A pioneer woman in Douglas County wrote that for years men in buying cowhide boots would smell them first.—"The Winter of 1861," The New Washington Historian.

## Another Washington account

Among the first to take claims east of the Cascades was Merill Short, who has left this account of a winter adventure in Klickitat County:

> We removed to Klickitat County before the severe winter of 1861-2, the severest winter that has ever been known in this western country, to white or red man. The ground was covered with snow from 1 to 3 feet deep for fifty days, and forty-two days of that time the mercury was 32°F below zero. There was a crust of sleet on top of the snow from 2 to 4 inches thick.
>
> A great many men perished in the snow, although the country was then but sparsely settled. A party of eleven men started from the John Day's River, where the old emigrant road crosses that stream, for The Dalles, all being on foot and the snow nearly 3 feet deep. It was 39 miles to the nearest house, or place of refuge. Nine out of the eleven died—four died on the way, and five after reaching their destination.
>
> Some of them had both hands and feet amputated. My brother-in-law, M. L. Alphin, had a brother in the company, Marion Alphin, who died in the snow in a canyon near the John Day's River. My brother-in-law lived at The Dalles, 22 miles from Columbus, which was near my place. He started to look for his brother, and reached my house, but the weather being so bitterly cold and the snow so deep he could go no further.
>
> He insisted on my going back, with him, and as my wood was nearly gone, and my flour was fast disappearing, and the weather still getting colder, I determined to do so. I had one horse that had got along pretty well, considering the scarcity of food and the terrible weather, so we made ready to start on our perilous journey. We had then but one child, aged 22 months.

*We breakfasted before daylight, and put my wife and child on
the horse, and strapped as many blankets around them as they
could manage, and started for The Dalles. The snow being deep
and the trail bad, we traveled very slow. We had a hard day's
journey, and when night came upon us we had not made over 12
miles of the 22, but had to stop.*

*We had reached an old shack, one end of which had been torn
away, but poor as it was it was undoubtedly the means of keeping
us alive; for we surely should have perished had we not found
shelter of some kind, and wood to make a fire. We soon had a
roaring fire, which we made from the floor of the building. We
wrapped my wife and the child in the blankets and they managed
to get a little sleep. My brother-in-law and myself stayed up all
night keeping the fire going.*

*That night was one of the coldest of all that winter, and the
coldest, I think, ever known in Washington. Early the next
morning we resumed our journey and' traveled hard all day, and
reached The Dalles late that evening, having eaten nothing since
our early breakfast before starting out from our home. I had no
overcoat, and my brother-in-law wore only as an extra wrap a sort
of cloak, and that he used to wrap the child in before the journey
was completed. [June 15, 1893.]*

—Clinton Snowden, "The Winter of 1861-62," *History of Washington*, p.
53-56.

# February 1933

February of 1933 was one of the coldest ever in Oregon. Seasonable
temperatures in the first several days of the month followed a mild January
in what had been an unremarkable winter. In the meantime, however,
record cold was occurring over Siberia. Strong west winds carried this frigid
air mass toward Alaska, where additional records were set early in the
month. Then an area of high pressure began to build in the Gulf of Alaska.
Clockwise wind circulation around the high caused air to flow southward
from Alaska, across western Canada, and directly into eastern Oregon.
Figure 23 is a weather map for 3,000 meters (about 10,000 feet) on
February 9, 1933, showing pressure-height lines. At this level in the
atmosphere, winds move parallel to the pressure-height lines. If we trace a
path parallel to these lines from Seneca toward the north (the direction
from which the winds were moving), it points directly back to interior
Alaska. Small wonder, then, that extreme cold occurred. Figure 24 is a copy
of the original Seneca observation form (kindly provided by Johnson,
1999). Note the -54°F reading on the 10th, but also how quickly things
warmed up the next day: the high on the 11th was 45°F, an increase of 99°F
in only 36 hours!

*Figure 24. Weather map for February 9, 1933 showing pressure at 3,000 meters (about 10,000 feet) above sea level. Winds at this height flow parallel to lines of equal pressure. The approximate wind direction is denoted by large arrows, and the location of Seneca is shown. Note how the winds brought air directly from Alaska and northwestern Canada to the Seneca vicinity on this day. The following morning, Seneca recorded its record -54°F.*

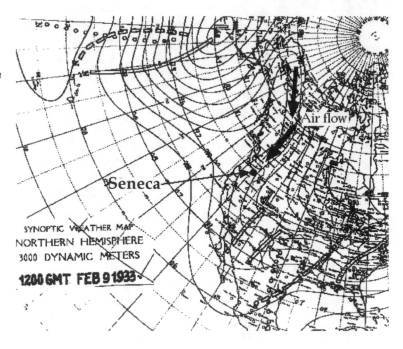

Seneca

Air flow

SYNOPTIC WEATHER MAP
NORTHERN HEMISPHERE
3000 DYNAMIC METERS
1200 GMT FEB 9 1933

*Figure 25. A copy of the original observation form for Seneca, February 1933. The -54°F temperature on the 10th is circled. Note how quickly temperatures moderated; by the afternoon of the 11th, the temperature was up to 45°F, a rise of 99°F in less than 36 hours.*

## COOPERATIVE OBSERVERS' METEROLOGICAL RECORD:

Month of February, 1933 ; Station, Seneca ; County, Grant

SENECA   OREGON   Hour of Observation, Sunset

State, Oregon ; Latitude, ; Longitude, ; Time used on this form,

| | TEMPERATURE | | | | PRECIPITATION | | | | DEPTH OF SNOW ON GROUND AT TIME OF OBSERVATION | PREVAILING WIND DIRECTION | CHARACTER OF DAY, SUNRISE TO SUNSET | MISCELLANEOUS PHENOMENA |
|---|---|---|---|---|---|---|---|---|---|---|---|---|
| DATE | MAXIMUM | MINIMUM | RANGE | SET MAX | TIME OF BEGINNING | TIME OF ENDING | AMOUNT | SNOWFALL IN INCHES | | | | |
| | 1 | 2 | 3 | 4 | 5 | 6 | 7 | 8 | 9 | 10 | 11 | |
| 1 | 35 | 17 | 18 | 7 | | | | | 18.3 | W | P. Cloudy | |
| 2 | 37 | 18 | 14 | 27 | | | | | 18.3 | SW | " | |
| 3 | 27 | -10 | 37 | 7 | | | | | 18.3 | SE | Clear | |
| 4 | 24 | -11 | 35 | 12 | | | | | 18.3 | SE | P. Cloudy | |
| 5 | 28 | -6 | 34 | 10 | 7 PM | 10 PM | .03 | 1.2 | 19.3 | W | " | |
| 6 | 25 | -8 | 33 | 12 | | | | | 19.3 | N.W. | " | |
| 7 | 22 | -26 | 48 | 10 | | | | | 19.3 | N | " | |
| 8 | 18 | 8 | 10 | 12 | 1 AM | 12 Noon | .09 | 1.8 | 20.0 | N | Cloudy | |
| 9 | 15 | -11 | 31 | -10 | | | | | 19.9 | N | " | |
| 10 | -1 | -54 | 43 | -16 | | | | | 19.9 | W | " | |
| 11 | 45 | -16 | 61 | 29 | 8 PM | 12 Noon | .41 | 2.1 | 21.5 | N | Cloudy | |
| 12 | 40 | -1 | 41 | 31 | | | | | 21.3 | N | " | |
| 13 | 31 | 22 | -36 | 67 | 10 | | | | 21.3 | N | " | |
| 14 | 33 | 4 | 29 | 20 | | | | | 21.7 | SW | P | |
| 15 | 48 | 2 | 46 | 30 | Nite + Day | | .90 | 8.0 | 22.0 | NE | P. Cloudy | |
| 16 | 42 | -5 | 47 | 31 | | | | | 26.5 | SW | P | |
| 17 | 31 | -17 | 48 | 19 | | | | | 25.0 | W | Cloudy | |
| 18 | 34 | 9 | 25 | 22 | | | | | 25.5 | W | Clear | |
| 19 | 40 | 10 | 30 | 29 | | | | | 23.5 | W | " | |
| 20 | 36 | 2 | 34 | 30 | | | | | 22.5 | SW | P. Cloudy | |
| 21 | 41 | 29 | 12 | 35 | | | | | 20.0 | N | " | |
| 22 | 41 | 26 | 15 | 36 | | | | | 18.5 | N | " | |
| 23 | 38 | 22 | 16 | 23 | | | | | 18.5 | N.W. | " | |
| 24 | 35 | -6 | 41 | 28 | | | | | 18.5 | N.W. | Clear | |
| 25 | 42 | 0 | 42 | 32 | | | | | 17.5 | SW | " | |
| 26 | 34 | 10 | 24 | 22 | | | | | 17.0 | S | P. Cloudy | |
| 27 | 38 | -8 | 46 | 27 | | | | | 16.5 | S | " | |
| 28 | 41 | 17 | 24 | 36 | Nite | 3 PM | .08 | 1.0 | 17.0 | S | Cloudy | |
| 29 | | | | | | | | | | | | |
| 30 | | | | | | | | | | | | |
| 31 | 927 | -46 | | | | | | | | | | |
| Sum | 484 | -24 | 914 | | | | 1.5 | 14.1 | 570.7 | N | | |
| Mean | 34.7 | .99 | | | | | | Aver. 20.4 | | | | |

### TEMPERATURE
Mean maximum, 34.7 33.1

Mean minimum, -9 -1.6

Mean, 15.8

Maximum, 48 ; date, 15

Minimum, -54 ; date, 10

Greatest daily range, 98 67

### PRECIPITATION
Total, 1.51 ; inches ; greatest in 24 hours .90

Date, 15

### SNOW
Total snowfall, 14.1 inches

On ground 15th, 27.0 inches

At end of month, 17.0 inches

### NUMBER OF DAYS—
With .01 inch or more precipitation, 5

Clear, 5 ; partly cloudy, 16

Cloudy, 7

### DATES OF—
Fog { Light, Dense,

Killing frost,

Thunderstorms,

Hail { Light, Moderate, Heavy,

Sleet,

Auroras,

BEST AVAILABLE RECORD

### REMARKS:

* Reading of maximum thermometer immediately after setting.
† Including rain, hail, sleet, and melted snow.
‡ Thunderstorms, halos, auroras, etc.

(IN TRIPLICATE)   See cover for instructions.

Howard Cold, Cooperative Observer.

Post Office Address, Seneca Oregon

# Significant Cold Weather Events in Oregon

*Pacific Northwest*   Dec. 22, 1861
A very snowy winter, and the snow did not disappear from the valleys and lower foothills until late February and mid-March. The temperatures ranged from 0°F to 30°F below zero. Over ten thousand cattle in eastern Oregon and Washington starved to death.

*Portland (and probably well beyond)*   January 1868
An intense cold period caused the Columbia to freeze over at Portland. Pedestrians and sleighs were able to cross the river between Portland and Vancouver.

*Wasco County and Columbia Gorge*   Dec. 8-28, 1885
Intense cold followed a big snowstorm. On December 17, Portland had a temperature of 10°F with 6 inches of snow on the ground.

*Portland*   Jan. 1890
Portland temperatures for January 3-6, respectively, were 18°F, 15°F, 12°F, and 20°F.

*All of Oregon*   Jan. 11-19, 1916
Severe cold weather and excessive snowfall affected all of Oregon. This was the coldest January since record keeping began, with an average departure from normal of -9°F. Hermiston dropped to -27°F on the 17th and 19th. Portland got as low as 13°F, Government Camp -2°F, and McMinnville 2°F.

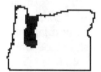

*Willamette Valley*   Dec. 9-21, 1919
This was the coldest December since records began in 1890. The Columbia River froze over, closing navigation from the confluence with the Willamette River upstream. During the week of January 10-17 the Willamette River froze at Portland and Vancouver. Corvallis set its all-time record of -14°F on the 21st.

*All of Oregon*   Dec. 15-26, 1924
This was the coldest December ever in Oregon, with the two-week cold period one of the longest and most severe ever. Most streams and rivers were frozen and blocked with ice. Automobiles were driven across the Willamette River at Portland. The lowest temperature, -53°F at Drewsey and Riverside, was a state record until 1933.

*All of Oregon*   Jan. 20-25, 1927
A generally mild month contained six very cold days. Portland's snowfall (16 inches) was the most since 1919, and temperatures stayed below freezing day and night for five days. Western Oregon low temperatures were in single digits at many locations. Ukiah was the coldest official spot at -46°F. Harney Experiment Station reached -36°F and Madras -32°F.

*All of Oregon*   Jan. 1930

Cold which began on the 5th and continued until nearly the end of the month was the most persistent since statewide records began in 1890. Snow was widespread and deep, and extended to the coast.The Columbia River was entirely frozen above the mouth of the Willamette, but kept open by icebreakers below Portland. Forest Grove at -8°F on the 21st was the coldest westside location, while east of the Cascades Danner reported a low of -52°F, Blitzen was -50°F, and Ukiah was -45°F.

*All of Oregon*   Feb. 9-10, 1933

This was the coldest February to date for eastern Oregon, and the second coldest for Oregon overall. Seneca and Ukiah reached -54°F, all-time records for Oregon, and Meacham dropped as low as -52°F. Many western Oregon locations reached single digits, including Forest Grove (9°F), Prospect (2°F), and Cascade Locks (6°F).

*All of Oregon*   Jan. 1937

The statewide mean temperature was the lowest since statewide records began in 1890. The lowest temperature was at Austin, -52°F on the 8th. Austin's monthly average temperature for the month was an even 0.0°F. Prospect (-12°F) and McKenzie Bridge (-3°F) had the lowest temperatures west of the Cascades. Newport and Astoria dropped to 7°F, and Astoria had over 7 inches of snow. Ice covered the Columbia River and some appeared on the Willamette.

*All of Oregon*   Jan. 1943

After a mild first half of the month, a severe cold wave struck, with northeast Oregon hit hardest. Meacham reported a low of -47°F, Seneca -42°F, and Austin -39°F. West of the Cascades, McMinnville and Hillsboro dropped as low as -2°F.

*All of Oregon*   Jan. 9-10 and 24-25, 1949

Western Oregon temperatures were the coldest ever recorded in 60 years of record; eastern Oregon's were the lowest since 1937 and the second coldest ever. Crater Lake froze over. Danner's -36°F on the 25th was the coldest January temperature in Oregon since 1943. Monthly mean temperature statewide was 12.9°F below normal.

*All of Oregon*   Jan. 29-Feb. 4, 1950

Very cold weather occurred over all of Oregon, causing widespread damage to fruit trees, especially in the northeast. The lowest temperature was -42°F at Fox, and some western Oregon temperatures were very low as well: Hillsboro was -10°F, Dallas -11°F, and Salem -10°F.

*All of Oregon*   Jan. 24-31, 1957

This was the coldest weather since 1950 in Oregon. Pendleton was -22°F, Hermiston -31°F, Bend -23°F, Seneca -43°F and Ukiah -41°F. Willamette Valley stations dropped into the single digits. Portland had twelve consecutive days when the temperature did not go above freezing.

*All of Oregon*   Dec. 7-13, 1972

Severe wintry weather brought widespread snow, followed by intense cold. In the Willamette Valley, temperatures were the coldest since 1924. Salem set its all-time record with a -12°F reading on the 8th. Seneca was the coldest in the state at -40°F. Newport (1°F) and Gold Beach (17°F) set all-time records.

*All of Oregon*   Dec. 1985
Crater Lake froze over for the first time since 1949. Wildlife suffered greatly because of continued cold since November 1994.

*All of Oregon*   Feb. 1-8, 1989
Wind chill was between 30°F and 60°F below zero. Extensive damage occurred in homes and businesses because of frozen pipes, there were numerous power outages, and several boats sank on the Columbia River because of ice. Three people died in car accidents and two froze to death.

*All of Oregon*   Dec. 1990
A very cold Arctic air mass reached Oregon on Dec. 19, bringing snow, ice, and record-setting cold temperatures. New all-time cold records were set at Cove (-24°), Clatskanie (1°), and Elgin (-31°). Ties for the record occurred at Astoria (6°), Arlington (-7°), Heppner (-15°) and Enterprise (-30°).

*Oregon Cascades*   Apr. 3-4, 1993
Icy cold weather gave the southern Cascades between 1 and 2 feet of snow during this storm. Crater Lake had about 2 feet of new snow in these two days.

*All of Oregon*   Dec. 1998
Temperatures were generally below normal for the month, mainly due to the very cold period just before Christmas. Even coastal locations were cold: Astoria had four consecutive days during which temperatures never rose above freezing. Tillamook had a low of 10°F on the 23rd. Coquille had lows of 16°F or below on four consecutive days. In eastern Oregon, the coldest temperatures were reported at Austin (-24°F), Seneca (-20°F), Halfway (-19°F), and Long Creek (17°F).

# Thunderstorms

The West Coast has the lowest incidence of thunderstorms in the continental U.S., with an average of less than ten days per year. West of the Cascades and Sierra Nevadas such storms are particularly rare. In the Willamette Valley, for example, a period of several years often elapses with no significant thunderstorms. East of the mountains, however, the situation is quite different.

A thunderstorm is a local storm produced by cumulonimbus clouds and containing lightning and thunder. The storm may consist of a line of clouds, a cluster, or a single cumulonimbus. Thunderstorms are most common during the warmer months. They occur when warm, usually humid air rises in an unstable environment. Upward motion may be triggered by uneven surface heating, terrain, or converging air masses. Once triggered, upward motion is enhanced as rising air condenses and releases its stored heat.

Cool marine air tends to keep western Oregon temperatures moderate through most of the summer., but the Cascades prevent this marine air from penetrating into eastern Oregon. As a result, eastside temperatures are generally quite high throughout the summer and can become excessive (with the record-setting 119°F at Pendleton and Prineville representing the most extreme cases). On the other hand, eastern Oregon is generally quite dry, since the Cascades effectively block marine moisture as well. Thus, summer days east of the Cascades are often warm, dry, and clear.

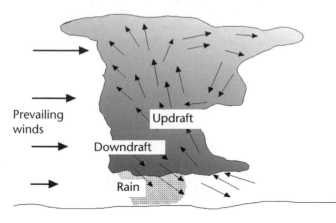

Figure 26. Idealized diagram of thunderstorm structure, showing wind flow, updrafts and downdrafts, and typical rainy areas.

But every so often, warm, humid air finds its way into eastern Oregon, typically from the south or southeast, by way of California or Nevada, or from the southwest, from the eastern Pacific by way of northern California. As this warm, humid air reaches eastern Oregon, low-level heating or the presence of mountains causes it to rise. Rising air cools, and since cooler air can hold less water in the form of water vapor, it eventually cools to the point of saturation, and condensation occurs. This results in several things:

—Cloud formation.

—Precipitation (water or ice droplets, which may or may not reach the ground).

—Release of large amounts of latent heat, which warms the air and intensifies the rising motion.

The air will usually continue to rise until water vapor is exhausted; in some cases the cloud tops will exceed 25,000 feet. Beneath the cloud, rain or hail are usually observed, and are sometimes very intense. Thunderstorm clouds usually move due to upper-level winds, but they occasionally remain stationary for extended periods of time. When they do, heavy rains can fall in a small area for an hour or more, causing local flooding—the dreaded thunderstorm flash flood. (For a description of some Oregon flash floods, see the Floods chapter.)

One of the biggest problems in documenting thunderstorms is that they are not measured in a well-defined way. Temperature, precipitation, and winds, for example, are measured explicitly and reported in specific ways; they are known as "weather elements." We may disagree on what constitutes a "hot day," but 80°F is always 80°F. Thunderstorms are large, complex systems made up of a lot of weather elements: winds, lightning, hail, rain, and so on, all in different combinations. Sometimes they produce dry lightning events or start forest fires. They may produce hail which destroys crops. If they're really strong, tornadoes and other life-threatening severe weather may occur. But it is extremely difficult to compare thunderstorms or specify their intensities.

The table describes some of the most damaging or spectacular thunderstorms that have affected Oregon. Others are listed in the Tornado chapter or the Flood chapter (and some are listed in more than one chapter). Doubtless there are many others not listed here, and some of those occurred in such remote areas that perhaps no one even knows how strong they were!

# Significant Thunderstorms in Oregon

*Willow Creek, Heppner*   Jun. 14, 1903
This intense thunderstorm which included heavy rain and hail hit Heppner hardest. The barren terrain surrounding the town allowed the massive amounts of rain to run off into the Willow Creek watershed. Severe flash flooding occurred along the creek, which the storm quickly turned into a wall of water that completely washed away the town, drowning 225 people (see Floods chapter).

*Wheeler County, Mitchell*   Jul. 13, 1956
A localized but powerful thunderstorm formed northeast of Mitchell. Bridge Creek, a 12-inch-deep stream flowing through the center of town, became the site of a surging wall of water that swept away many structures, bridges, and sections of highway. Since the observing station was washed away, there was no official record of the rainfall; however, through careful surveying it was later estimated that in 4 inches of rain fell in 50 minutes.

*Most of Oregon*   Jul. 22, 1959
Strong thunderstorms accompanied by lightning and hail caused widespread forest fires. The largest was a 25,000 acre blaze in Lake County.

*Western and Central Oregon*   Sep. 10, 1959
Lightning caused fires in much of the state. Near Lakeview, a fire burned over 1,200 acres, destroying an estimated 4 million board feet of pine timber.

*Most of Oregon*   Jun. 17-18, 1961
Strong winds, hail, and heavy rains affected many parts of the state. One man was killed by a falling power line; a drive-in theater screen collapsed. There were many grass and forest fires and considerable crop damage due to hail.

*Most of Oregon*   Aug. 14-16, 1961
Lightning touched off more than 700 fires in Oregon, the largest 20,000 acres near Jordan Valley. A cloudburst above Ione sent a wall of water into the business district. High winds caused extensive damage in the Umatilla area.

*Northern Oregon*   Aug. 1-2, 1965
Strong thunderstorms, with lightning and heavy rains, produced numerous fires and localized flooding. Mudslides buried highways and railroad bridges in some locations. Three people died as a result of the storm.

*Cascade Mountains*   Aug. 10-11, 1967
Strong thunderstorms produced lightning and hail. More than four hundred fires in forests and grasslands were started by lightning strikes.

*Cascade Mountains*   Jun. 2, 1970
Thunderstorms occurred throughout the Cascades, producing more than ninety lightning-caused fires. Extensive damage occurred in the Medford area as well, including a complete halt to Sheriff's office radio communication for 2 hours.

*Southeastern Oregon*   Aug. 9-10, 1972
Evening thunderstorms caused over sixty fires, covering as much as 13,000 acres. High winds and hail caused extensive crop damage and power outages.

*Grants Pass*   Sep. 23, 1972
Lightning from a severe thunderstorm struck a 15-year-old boy who was carrying a box of dynamite at a logging operation. The dynamite exploded, killing the boy and injuring two others.

*Eastern Oregon*   Jul. 12, 1975
A severe thunderstorm brought more than 1 inch of rain to the Klamath Falls area in about an hour. Lightning was widespread. Substantial damage occurred in Wallowa County, mostly from flooding; Ukiah had 2.28 inches of rain, most of it in a few hours.

*North-central Oregon*   Aug. 7, 1976
Strong storms, with heavy rains, caused widespread damage. Antelope received 2.71 inches of rain; Condon, Fossil, and Prineville had more than 1.5 inches.

*John Day area*   Jul. 13, 1982
A severe thunderstorm produced three-quarter inch hail, 100 mph winds, and more than 1 inch of rain in 15 minutes. Parked aircraft were damaged, many trees uprooted, and power lines downed.

*Umatilla County*   Aug. 9, 1982
A severe thunderstorm with winds exceeding 100 mph caused power outages and many acres of crop damage. A tornado was reported near Walla Walla, Washington.

*Morrow and Union counties*   Jun. 13, 1984
Thunderstorms accompanied by hail, strong winds, and heavy rain nearly washed away a highway near Harmden and inundated several homes. Extensive crop damage also occurred.

*Western Oregon*   Jul. 24, 1984
Strong thunderstorms originated in Deschutes County, crossed the mid-Willamette Valley, and continued on to the coast, producing lightning, high winds, and isolated heavy rains. A wind gust of 61 mph was reported in Lincoln County.

*Baker and Umatilla counties*   Oct. 1, 1984
Lightning knocked out power over a wide area. Downpours occurred in many areas (Ukiah had more than 1 inch of rain in less than an hour). Heavy rains and hail damaged wheat and barley fields.

*Northwestern Oregon*   May 20, 1986
Lightning struck and killed a man as he was moving irrigation pipes in a field.

*Eastern Oregon*   Aug. 10-17, 1986
Lightning storms caused many forest fires in Baker, Gilliam, Grant, Harney, Lake, Malheur, Umatilla, Union, and Wallowa counties. Hundreds of thousands of acres of forest and range lands were burned, with total damage estimates greater than $6 million.

*Southwestern Oregon*  May 7, 1987
Strong thunderstorms in the interior of southwestern Oregon brought 60-70-mph winds that tore galvanized roofing and heavy air conditioning units off a large chicken farm near Eagle Point (in Jackson County). In the same area, many barns and trees were blown down and damaged. Fires started in the foothills near Roseburg with lightning strikes.

*Douglas, Jackson, Deschutes, and Crook counties*  Jul. 1, 1987
Intense thunderstorms involving hail and lightning started numerous fires in the Umpqua and Rogue River National Forests and on state and county property. The most severe fire lasted five days. The hail came with 1-2 inches of rain in the Bend-Prineville-LaPine area. Three-quarter-inch hail damaged wheat fields.

*Southwestern Oregon*  Aug. 30-31, 1987
Over the Siskiyou Mountains in Josephine, Jackson, Jefferson, Klamath, Douglas, eastern Lane, and western Deshutes counties dry thunderstorms developed. Well over a thousand lightning strikes were reported, and over nine hundred fires. Those fires continued into September and burned more than 130,000 acres of forest. This was Oregon's second worst fire; the worst of the century was the Tillamook Burn in the 1930s.

*Union County*  Mar. 26, 1988
Thunderstorms originated in the northeast mountains and moved into Union County with intense winds that blew over trees, pushed branches through the wall of a house, destroyed a garage, and damaged the cars inside. Three-quarter-inch hail was reported.

*Northeast Oregon*  Jun. 26, 1988
There were thunderstorms all over Baker, Union, and Wallowa counties. The heavy rain and three-quarter-inch hail damaged crops and caused flooding in Baker and Enterprise. A highway completely washed out. One radio operator said that Baker experienced 2 inches of rain from this storm.

*Portland metropolitan area*  Apr. 25, 1989
Thunderstorms from the Cascades and moved into Portland in the afternoon. A Horizon Airlines commuter plane was hit by lightning multiple times as it was flying at 3,500 feet above sea level in an attempt to land at the Portland Airport. The single injury was to a 13-year old boy who was standing in the playground of his school when the ground near him was struck by lightning.

*Klamath County*  Aug. 8, 1989
A thunderstorm with forceful rain, wind thought to be 75 to 100 mph, and hail the size of marbles (3 inches deep on the ground) struck Merrill and lasted for about 20 minutes. Potato and grain fields were damaged by the hail, as well as thousands of trees (a hundred were pulled out of the ground).

*Jackson County*  Sep. 29, 1989
Lightning injured two men who were knocked to the ground as they were pouring cement in Ashland.

*Cascades*  Jun. 21, 1990
A series of thunderstorms, with golfball-size hail and 60 mph wind gusts, moved northward along the Cascades, mostly in eastern Lane and Linn counties. Three children were injured in Marion County when strong winds smashed a tree onto the truck where they were hiding from the storm.

*Hood River, Wasco counties*   Jul, 11, 1990

Thunderstorms were severe all over Oregon on this date but the one in these two counties was particularly destructive. It was accompanied by strong and steady winds at 60 mph at Foreman's Point. In The Dalles the wind was forceful enough to knock three concrete walls down.

*Eastern Malheur County*   Aug. 20, 1990

High winds and large hail severely damaged onion, bean pod, sugar beet, and alfalfa crops near the Oregon-Idaho border. Damage to the onions allowed a fungus to attack the crop, adding to the destruction of the storm. In Idaho, one house was flooded with mud 1 foot deep.

*Oregon coast and western interior*   Mar. 2-3, 1991

High winds and severe thunderstorms were widespread. Winds were 51 mph in Gold Beach with a peak of 91 mph. Cape Arago had wind gusts up to 54 mph, Netarts had a gust of 62 mph and Astoria 59 mph. A woman in North Bend fell to the ground and broke her hip. In Port Orford the roof of a house flipped over and a satellite dish was pulled out of the ground. Scaffolding tipped over on top of three cars in Eugene and a sailboat capsized on the Columbia River near Portland during 41 mph winds.

*Jackson County*   Sep. 2, 1992

A man who was sitting under a tree in Rogue River was killed when lightning bounced off an object and hit him.

*Central Oregon*   Jul. 29, 1997

Heavy rain from a thunderstorm filled underpasses in Bend up to the windows of stuck cars. Lightning strikes knocked out power to at least a thousand customers from Bend to Terrebonne. Some phone service was also down for a while. Flooding and power outages occurred as far north as Madras.

*Central and eastern Oregon*   May 4, 1998

There were numerous thunderstorms and record-setting rains in May, but the worst storm occurred on the 4th. La Grande and Prineville reported 1-inch hail, Bend had 60 mph wind gusts and heavy rain, and Union received .75 inches of rain in 20 minutes. Prineville had over an inch of rain in 20 minutes, with widespread rock- and mudslides.

*Union County*   July 2, 1998

Up to 1.50 inches of rain fell in 20 minutes in La Grande, and 0.25 inches of rain fell in only 2 minutes. Wind gusts to 50 mph were also reported. The result was a flooded underpass and several inches of water flowing along La Grande streets. Eight hundred to a thousand residents had power outages for several hours. The storm nearly wiped out crops in a strip $1^1/2$ to 2 miles wide by 6 to 7 miles long between Island City and Cove.

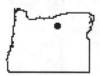

*Condon*   July 27, 1998

A thunderstorm moved through Condon and produced heavy rain and strong wind. Local rain gages measured up to 2.25 inches of rain in less than 2 hours. Several basements and downtown businesses, including the post office, were flooded. The wind also broke tree branches.

# Rainstorms

During winter, Oregon lies in the path of cool, moist air, with frequent storms, propelled by the jet stream across the Pacific. These mid-latitude storms produce most of western Oregon's precipitation, and a goodly share of that which falls in the east. Rain falls at lower elevations, with snow in the mountains.

On occasion, a surge of tropical moisture finds its way northward, merging into mid-latitude storms and greatly increasing their supply of water vapor. Some people have taken to calling this phenomenon the "Pineapple Express," since it appears to originate in the vicinity of Hawaii (at least on satellite pictures which show only the northeast Pacific). In actuality, the moisture more often originates in areas closer to the equator. When a North Pacific storm is "supercharged" by these warm, moist surges of air, the rainfall totals can be impressive indeed. In fact, Oregon's biggest rainstorms (and most of its biggest floods) have occurred under just such situations. We distinguish here between these large-scale storms (generally winter events) and local thunderstorm rains, which can be very intense but are quite localized (and are discussed in the previous chapter).

*Another rainy Oregon day. (OSU Archives, P94)*

# Curry County, January 1953

January 1953 was one of the wettest months on record in western Oregon. Monthly precipitation totals in the state included a monsoon-like 47.73 inches at Valsetz. East of the Cascades, the weather was generally dry; January precipitation totaled a scant 0.19 inches at the OO Ranch, south of Burns. But the westside was uniformly very wet.

Hardest hit by the heavy rains was the southern Oregon coast—especially in Curry County. In Gold Beach, 15.32 inches of rain fell between January 16 and 19. Slides along coastal highway 101 isolated the city and the only means of getting in and out was by light aircraft. A Piper Cub landed at Leith Airport on Tuesday (20th), the first vehicle of any kind to reach Gold Beach since Saturday (January 17). Thereafter, according to the *Curry County Reporter* for Thursday January 22, ". . . there has been a continuous shuttle service of single engine aircraft between Gold Beach and Crescent City and Coos Bay, carrying stranded passengers in and out and bringing in Gold Beach's first supplies in four days."

For a period of three days, communication with the "outside world" was by ham radio operators. On Monday, January 19, telephone communications were established with Crescent City. Two days later, telephone calls were possible to places north of Gold Beach. Although lacking fresh vegetables, fruit, and eggs, the food supply at Gold Beach was considered "adequate." Bread and yeast for the bakery were airlifted in beginning Wednesday, January 21.

The *Curry County Reporter* for January 22 described how two sackloads of mail were delivered to Gold Beach on January 18. Nick Turner, contract mail carrier, made his way from Brookings via mail truck, jeep, and car but mostly "by means of a stout heart and a pair of good Curry County legs." The first 5 miles out of Brookings was managed by truck. A break in the road necessitated a trek by foot, in the wind and rain, up Carpenterville Mountain. After walking 3 to 4 miles, Nick got a ride in a jeep from Stanley Colgrove. The two shoveled their way through slides and fallen trees. They detoured across open country where the road had completely washed out, by now in the darkness with fog and rain. A big slide just south of the Pistol River bridge stopped the jeep for good. Nick started out again with the mail sacks, using the still-intact bridge to cross the Pistol River. He then managed to pick up another ride. Then, stated the *Curry County Reporter*, "the whole road had dropped out into nothing," and Nick was forced to walk again. Added the Gold Beach newspaper:

> *He clambered up the mountain around the slide, covered with mud and soaking wet, and walked and climbed his way over 5 miles of the worst destruction he had ever seen. The worst slide, he reported, was just before he got to Cape Sebastian where 50 yards of road had dropped out of sight down the mountain. Just beyond the first slide near Belle Turner's ranch he was picked up by his*

*Figure 27. An infrared satellite picture of a typical Pacific winter storm approaching the Oregon coast. The locations of the surface low and the frontal boundaries are shown. Higher, rain-producing clouds appear brighter (due to lower temperatures) than low, fair-weather clouds.*

wife—and finally arrived in Gold Beach with the mail sacks after a six-hour trip.

Reserved and quiet as usual, Nick had little to say about his exploit except that he was glad the wind was blowing in the right direction. "Blew me right into Gold Beach," he said. "If it had been coming the other way, I might have ended up in Crescent City."

## Weastern Oregon, November 18-19, 1996

Record-breaking precipitation throughout much of Oregon caused local flooding, landslides, and power outages over much of the state. The rain resulted from a broad upper-air weather system of moist subtropical air which originated over the tropical Pacific. The air mass reached central California over the previous weekend, producing daily rainfall amounts exceeding 8 inches. Gradually the system moved northward, reaching southwestern Oregon on the 17th and spreading to the remainder of the state the following day. High rainfall amounts were reported throughout the state.

The Elk River Fish Hatchery reported a one-day total of 11.65 inches on the morning of the 19th. This was the highest daily total ever reported at an official Oregon weather station.

**Table 32. All-time one-day precipitation records**

| Location | Amount (inches) | Records began | Old record (inches) | Year set |
|---|---|---|---|---|
| Bandon | **6.25** | 1948 | 5.61 | 1987 |
| Corvallis | **4.45** | 1889 | 4.28 | 1965 |
| Corvallis Water Bureau | **6.29** | 1948 | 5.23 | 1996 |
| Langlois | **7.33** | 1956 | 7.04 | 1961 |
| Madras | **3.07** | 1952 | 1.71 | 1995 |
| North Bend | **6.67** | 1931 | 5.60 | 1981 |
| Port Orford 5E | **11.65** | 1971 | 9.40 | 1981 |
| Portland | **2.70** | 1939 | 2.48 | 1948 |
| Redmond | **2.38** | 1948 | 1.81 | 1969 |
| Roseburg | **4.35** | 1931 | 3.28 | 1965 |

—Port Orford 5E = station 5 miles east of Port Orford

Unofficial reports from locations in the mountains of southwest Oregon exceeded 20 inches. All-time one-day precipitation records were set at many locations. Some of these are shown in Table 32.

*Figure 28. Infrared Satellite Image, February 5, 1996*

*Figure 29.*
*Stream flow*
*records for*
*Johnson Creek*
*(top) and Rogue*
*River (bottom)*
*during the*
*November 1996*
*flood event (from*
*U.S. Geological*
*Survey).*

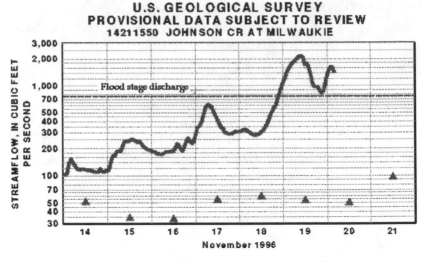

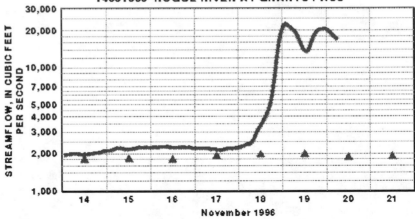

Flooding occurred widely in western and central Oregon. River rises were exceptionally fast, due to the intense rainfall. Figure 27 shows stream flow on Johnson Creek, southeast of Portland, and the Rogue River at Grants Pass for the week of the flood (courtesy US Geological Survey). Both exceeded flood stage. The Rogue, in particular, rose very quickly on the 18th, increasing by a factor of 10 in one day.

Mudslides killed five people in Douglas County in two separate incidents. At Hubbard Creek, west of Roseburg, four people were killed when a mudslide demolished a house. On a highway adjacent to state highway 38, a woman was killed when her car was swept into the Umpqua River.

# Significant Rainstorms in Oregon

*Western Oregon* Dec. 12-13, 1882
Portland, had 7.66 inches of rain in one 24-hour period and the two-day total was 10.75 inches. It is not known how widespread precipitation approaching this intensity may have been due to the very few observing stations at that time. From the limited information available, however, it appears that the heavy rainfall was only in northwest Oregon.

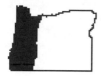

*Western Oregon* Jan. 28-Feb. 3, 1890
Very heavy rainfall fell over most of western Oregon, particularly along the coast and in the Willamette Valley. The seven-day totals ranged from 15 to 20 inches along the coast with 26.52 inches at Glenora in Tillamook County. Rainfall in the Willamette Valley was generally between 10 and 15 inches, while 5 to 10 inches fell in the southwestern interior valleys. Precipitation east of the Cascades was light.

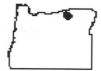

*Heppner* Jun. 14, 1903
A strong thunderstorm, accompanied by extremely heavy rain and hail, caused a flood that inundated Heppner, Oregon (see flood chapter). There are no rainfall records available for this storm because the weather observing station was completely destroyed and the observer and his entire family drowned.

*Northwest Oregon* Nov. 18-24, 1909
This was actually two storms following each other in rapid succession with no significant break in the weather between the first and second. During the seven-day period, rainfall totals were 10 to 20 inches along the coast, 4 to 6 inches in the western inland valleys, 7 to 14 inches along the western Cascades slopes, and only 1 to 3 inches in eastern Oregon. Along the coast and in the upper western Cascades, 24-hour totals of 4.50 to 5.50 inches were common. At least 80% of the stations west of the Cascades received 1 inch or more and 24-hour totals of at least 2 inches, with several stations receiving 3 inches or more.

*Northern Oregon* Nov. 19-21, 1921
Unusually heavy rainfall occurred over most of the state, but the heaviest was over the northwest and north-central Oregon. 1- and 3-day totals, respectively, included Portland (4.13 and 6.71 inches), Welches (6.55 and 11.93 inches), Hood River (4.05 and 8.64 inches) and The Dalles (4.20 and 8.90 inches).

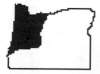

*Northwest Oregon* Dec. 26-30, 1937
Two-thirds of the observing stations in northwest Oregon reported 24-hour rainfall totals of 2 inches or more and at least a third of those stations had 24-hour rainfall totals of 3 inches or more. 1- and 5-day totals, respectively, included Falls City (5.50 and 15.35 inches), Headworks (4.20 and 10.17 inches), Portland (5.01 and 9.34 inches), and Valsetz (7.86 and 24.00 inches).

*Most of Oregon* Dec. 26-29, 1945
During the peak of this storm (on the 27th and 28th), western Oregon 24-hour rainfall totals were generally 3 to 5 inches. Illahe, in eastern Curry County, reported a 24-hour rainfall total of 8.25 inches, and received 12.91 inches during the entire storm. Rainfall totals were high in central Oregon as well. Several observing stations in north-central Oregon reported 24-hour rainfall totals of 3 to 5 inches, and storm totals of 4 to 6 inches.

*Most of Oregon*   Oct. 26-29, 1950
All of Oregon was affected, but the southwest of the state and the higher elevations of the Cascades were hit the hardest. In western Oregon, storm totals generally ranged between 10 and 12 inches in the extreme south, gradually decreasing to near 4 inches at the Columbia River. About one-fourth of observing stations in eastern Oregon reported 24-hour rainfall totals that were greater than the normal for the entire month of October.

*South coast*   Jan. 16-19, 1953
The heaviest rain fell over the south coastal areas, where 24-hour rainfall totals were generally 4 to 8 inches, and storm totals of 15 to 20 inches were common. Denmark recived 8.07 inches in one day and 16.24 inches for the storm. Gold Beach had 6.46 and 16.41 inches, and Illahe 7.17 and 17.37 inches (1-day and storm total).

*Western Oregon*   Nov. 22-24, 1953
All of western Oregon was hit, but the heaviest rains occurred over the south coast, where, at the peak of the storm, most observing stations reported 24-hour rainfall totals of 4 to 7 inches and 72-hour totals of 6 to 10 inches. Widespread heavy flooding occurred in all southwest Oregon streams and in most tributaries and the Willamette River.

*Mitchell*   Jul. 13, 1956
A small but very intense thunderstorm occurred just north and east of Mitchell, located in north-central Oregon in Wheeler County. The region is drained by Bridge Creek, which flows through the center of Mitchell and is usually less than 12 inches deep during July. Within minutes, Bridge Creek became a raging torrent of water that swept buildings away easily. The raging water completely destroyed or heavily damaged twenty buildings in the town center, and washed out several bridges and sections of highway. The observing station was carried away in the flood so no record of actual rainfall is available. Immediately after the flash flood, a United States Geological Survey worker visited the region. After careful surveying, he estimated that about 3.5 inches of rain fell in fifty minutes, and nearly 4.0 inches fell at the storm's center.

*All of Oregon*   Feb. 8-10, 1961
Heavy rains affected the entire state and caused widespread flooding. Numerous sites had more than 4 inches of rain in one day, topped by 7.04 inches on the 9th at Langlois.

*Rogue Valley*   Dec. 2, 1962
The heaviest rains since 1955 caused severe flooding, especially in the Medford area. Medford's total precipitation for the day was 3.30 inches.

*All of Oregon*   Dec. 20-24, 1964
The December 1964 rainstorm was probably the most severe rainstorm to ever occur over central Oregon, and among the most severe over western Oregon since the late 1870s. Several observing stations across central Oregon recorded two-thirds of their normal annual rainfall in just five days. Scores of stations set new records for both 24-hour totals and December monthly rainfall totals (see flood chapter).

*Western Umatilla County*  Jul. 26, 1965
Heavy rains sent a wall of water 8-10 feet high and 200 feet wide down Spears Canyon west of Pendleton. Estimates of the amount of rain exceed 3 inches in several hours.

*Northern Oregon coast*  Dec. 1-7, 1970
Intense storms produced 6 to 14 inches of rain in coastal sections and 6 to 9 inches of snow at higher elevations. A station 13 miles northeast of Tillamook reported 4.40 inches on the 6th and 12.32 inches for the week.

*Oregon coast, Coast Range, and Cascades*  Dec. 27-31, 1970
Two major Pacific storms produced high winds and abundant rains. Port Orford had 13.54 inches of rain in four days, and Valsetz had over 5 inches on the 30th.

*Western Oregon*  Mar. 1-3, 1972
Three days of heavy rains produced widespread flooding, especially in coastal areas. Highest 3-day totals included 10.78 inches at Port Orford 5E (including over 7 inches in one day), 9.96 inches at Illahe, and 8.08 inches at Gold Beach.

*Western Oregon*  Aug. 16, 1972
Unusually severe summer rains occurred over most of western Oregon. Eugene had a 24-hour total of 1.41 inches, and Crater Lake had more than 1 inch of rain mixed with wet snow.

*Western Oregon*  Dec. 16-24, 1972
A series of five storms with intense rain and heavy winds blasted Oregon. Rainfall totals were 8-13 inches along the immediate coast and in the northern Cascades and 18-22 inches in the higher elevations of the Coast Range. Laurel Mountain, Nehalem 9NE, Port Orford, and Valsetz all topped 5 inches on the 21st alone.

*All of Oregon*  Jan. 13-17, 1974
A series of storms brought unusually heavy rains and major flooding. Port Orford 5E received 9.01 inches of rain in one day and 19.97 inches in four days. Many Willamette Valley sites had one-day amounts exceeding 3 inches. Sexton Summit had 5.25 inches in one day and over 11 inches in three days.

*Western Oregon*  Jul. 17, 1974
An unusually powerful Pacific storm produced heavy rains. Otis had 3.05 inches, most of it in a 12-hour period. Tillamook, Valsetz, and Cloverdale all had more than 2 inches.

*North-central Oregon*  Aug. 7, 1976
Strong storms, with heavy rains, caused widespread damage. Antelope received 2.71 inches of rain; Condon, Fossil, and Prineville had more than 1.5 inches.

*Most of Oregon*  Dec. 13-15, 1977
Several powerful storms raked western Oregon. Portland's 2.59 inches in 24 hours was a new record for December. Valsetz had 5.68 inches on the 13th, Bend 1.43 inches on the 15th, Elgin 1.83 inches on the 13th.

*Western Oregon*   Aug. 24, 1978
A wet Pacific storm dumped considerable rain throughout western Oregon. Gold Beach had 3.17 inches, Brookings 2.81 inches, and Laurel Mountain 2.05 inches.

*All of Oregon*   May 4-5, 1979
A late "winter-like" storm produced abundant rain throughout the state. Port Orford 5E had 3.70 inches in one day, Laurel Mountain had 3.05, Cave Junction had 2.20, and Cherry Grove had 2.15.

*Eastern Oregon*   Aug. 13-14, 1978
Thunderstorms strengthened by Pacific moisture produced abundant rainfall. Nearly every location in Malheur County received more than 1 inch, topped by 1.92 inches at Vale. Huntington had 1.86 inches, and Owyhee Dam and Rockville had 1.85.

*All of Oregon*   Dec. 24-25, 1980
The big "Christmas storm" brought high winds and heavy rain to the entire state. Valsetz reported 7.20 inches on the 25th, Salem had 2.16 inches, Corvallis Water Bureau 4.30 inches, and many locations in eastern Oregon had more than 1 inch.

*Most of Oregon*   Feb. 13, 1984
A strong Pacific storm brought intense rains. Port Orford 5E had 6.93 inches for the day, and many other western Oregon locations exceeded 3 inches. In eastern Oregon, several locations exceeded 1 inch.

*Eastern Oregon*   Aug. 30-31, 1984
Strong winds, lightning, and hail accompanied the very heavy rains. Rock Creek had 2.56 inches of rain, Alkali Lake had 2.50 inches, nearly ten other stations reported more than 2 inches.

*Western Oregon*   Jun. 6-7, 1985
A late storm laden with tropical air brought abundant rains, especially along the coast. Valsetz had 6.40 inches and Port Orford 5E 5.08 inches; several other coastal sites exceeded 3 inches, and some Willamette Valley stations had more than 2 inches.

*Western Oregon*   Feb. 22-23, 1986
A strong storm laden with tropical moisture pounded western Oregon. Port Orford 5E had 6.05 inches of rain on the 23rd, and other 1-day totals included Valsetz at 4.03 inches, Lemolo Lake at 3.60 inches, and Bonneville dam at 3.21 inches.

*Northwest Oregon*   Nov. 23-28, 1986
Several powerful storms dumped heavy rain on much of western Oregon. Astoria had 4.19 inches on the 24th (a new November 1-day record). Port Orford 5E had 7 inches on the 27th.

*All of Oregon*   Jan. 6-9, 1990
A series of big, wet, windy storms pounded Oregon. Astoria received 4.53 inches of rain on the 9th, and Tillamook, Illahe, Laurel Mountain, and Cave Junction all exceeded 4 inches in one day. In eastern Oregon, Paisley had 2.38 inches on the 8th and Bend 1.87 inches the same day.

*Eastern Oregon*   May 18-20, 1991

Strong storms produced abundant rain and local flooding. La Grande had 2.30 inches on the 20th,Milton Freewater 2.09 inches on the 19th, and Hart Mountain 1.95 inches on the 18th.

*Northwest Oregon*   Feb. 23, 1994

An intense frontal band that stalled across northern Oregon caused heavy rain resulting in local urban flooding,  high winds, and heavy snow. The affected area stretched from the Portland metropolitan area across Mt. Hood and the Columbia Gorge in the northern Oregon Cascades to the Pendleton area. Portland International Airport recorded 2.46 inches of rainfall in 24 hours, which caused localized urban flooding in the Portland area. Heavy rain in the Columbia Gorge caused a landslide that temporarily closed the Columbia River Scenic Highway near Crown Point.

*Western Oregon*   Oct. 26-27, 1994

A very wet storm, augmented by tropical moisture, dumped large amounts of rain. Portland Airport set a new 24-hour record with 2.24 inches. Laurel Mountain reported 8.90 inches in one day, Otis had 6.21 inches, and Headworks had 6.80 inches.

*Northwest Oregon*   Nov. 26, 1994

A major winter storm brought very heavy precipitation and high winds. 24-hour totals included 2.33 inches at Portland Airport, 5.14 inches in Gresham, 7.70 inches in Sandy, and 3.05 inches at Hood River (tying the all-time 24-hour record).

*Northwest Oregon*   Nov. 27-30, 1995

A strong storm pummeled Washington and affected northwest Oregon as well. Astoria had over 8 inches in the four days, Government Camp had two days with more than 4 inches, and Seaside had 3.97 inches on the 29th.

*Northern Oregon*   Feb. 5-9, 1996

A series of intense surges of subtropical moisture inundated western Oregon. The combination of record-breaking rain, warm temperatures, and a deep snowpack led to severe flooding throughout northern sections of the state. Record-setting 4-day totals were observed, topped by Laurel Mountain's 27.55 inches. Other 4-day all-time records included 8.88 inches at Astoria, 8.10 inches at Corvallis, and 7.00 inches at Portland Airport.

*Western and central Oregon*   Nov. 18-19, 1996

Intense subtropical rainfall produced widespread flooding and record-setting precipitation—this may have been the wettest single day in Oregon's history. The Elk River Fish Hatchery near Port Orford reported 11.65 inches on the morning of the 19th, the highest total ever received at an Oregon NOAA station. All-time 1-day records were set at many locations, including North Bend, Roseburg, Corvallis, Salem, and Redmond.

*Western and central Oregon*   Aug. 20-21, 1997
The remnants of Tropical Storm Ignacio moved northward along the California coast and into Oregon, producing large amounts of rain in some areas. San Francisco reported 0.97 inches for August 19, the largest one-day total ever recorded there for any day in August. Many western Oregon locations received over an inch of rain.Events such as this are very rare in Oregon. The combination of a tropical storm, unusually warm offshore waters, and an approaching low pressure trough seldom occurs. In this case, it ended a prolonged dry spell (over forty days in much of western Oregon).

*Coos and Curry counties*   Jan. 3, 1998
A strong Pacific storm produced significant rainfall, very intense at times. Sixes reported 4.20 inches of rain in 24 hours, and Port Orford received 2.26 inches in just 8 hours.

*Eastern Oregon*   May 23-28, 1998
Widespread storms produced abundant rainfall and local flooding. Imnaha received 3.10 inches of rain on the 23rd. Springs and streams flowing out of canyons flooded and left 12- to 18-inch-deep ruts in some roads. LaPine and Ashwood had 1.5 inches on the 28th, and Prineville 2 inches the same day.

*Central and northwest Oregon*   Dec. 27-28, 1998
A surge of subtropical moisture brought very heavy rain, accompanied by high winds. In Corvallis, the 3.43 inches of rain on the 28th was the highest total for any day in December since records began in 1889. Laurel Mountain reported 7.42 inches, and Port Orford, Belkap Springs, and Detroit Dam all had more than 5 inches.

# Hot Weather

Despite Oregon's reputation as a mild, wet state, hot weather is common during long summer days. This is especially true in eastern and southern Oregon, where the valleys are sheltered from the moderating effects of the Pacific Ocean. However, much of eastern Oregon lies at high elevations, tempering daytime highs. For every thousand feet of elevation gain, temperatures decrease by 3-5°F. Thus, locations such as Bend, at about 4,000 feet, are 12-20°F cooler than they would be if the city were at sea level. Nonetheless, there are low-elevation sites in eastern and southern Oregon, and they can get very hot indeed. Even higher locations can get very hot on occasion.

Oregon's hottest weather occurs when strong high pressure over the state brings descending, warming air and clear skies. Winds from the east or south are customary during such periods. Sometimes heat waves in Oregon are very short-lived; in other cases, hot weather can persist for many days. In the following sections, Oregon's hottest days and longest heat waves are described.

*(OSU Archives, P94#9)*

## Record Heat

The hottest days recorded in Oregon occurred in 1898. In late July, temperatures began to build slowly, then quickly, and on the 29th Prineville topped out at 119°F, an all-time record for Oregon. However, the record was to be short-lived. Following a slight moderation in temperatures (Prineville was down to 101°F by August 3), things heated up again. Prineville reached 111°F on August 7, but then Pendleton tied the new record of 119°F on August 10. Within a week temperatures were back into the 80s throughout eastern Oregon, and they have never again matched the temperatures recorded on those days.

**Table 33. Oregon high temperature records by month**

| Month | Temp. (°F) | Station | Year |
|-------|-----------|---------|------|
| Jan. | 82 | Fremont | 1934 |
| Feb. | 85 | Coquille | 1992 |
| Mar. | 99 | Merlin | 1900 |
| Apr. | 102 | Marble Creek | 1906 |
| May | 108 | Blitzen | 1924 |
|  |  | Pelton Dam | 1986 |
| June | 113 | Blitzen | 1932 |
| July | 117 | Umatilla | 1939 |
| Aug. | 119 | Pendleton | 1898 |
| Sept. | 111 | Illahe | 1955 |
| Oct. | 104 | Dora | 1980 |
| Nov. | 89 | Mitchell | 1936 |
| Dec. | 81 | Dayville | 1897 |

There have, however, been some near-record days. Many of the highest single-day values were recorded at Umatilla, on the Columbia River, not far from Pendleton. Before the Umatilla station closed in 1965 it had reported temperatures of 117°F, 115°F (three times), and 114°F (four times). West of the Cascades, the highest temperature recorded was 115°F in Medford on July 20, 1946; Medford reached 114°F in 1941.

Although the Oregon coast is associated with generally mild weather, some extreme high temperatures have been reported. Along the immediate coastline temperatures seldom reach 90°F, but a short distance inland much higher readings can occur. Illahe is in Curry County about 25 miles from the coast. Temperatures there have reached 110°F on some occasions, and have been as high as 107°F as late as September and 98°F in October. Brookings, which is on the extreme southern Oregon coast, is notorious for unusually high temperatures, even during winter. Brookings' temperatures have been the subject of several technical reports discussing "the Brookings effect."

## Runs of Consecutive Extreme Days

During most summers, Oregon does not experience lengthy periods of extreme high temperatures. Marine air intrusions, although much milder and less frequent than in the cool season, move onshore often enough to prevent heat waves from lasting more than a few days in most cases. This is especially true west of the Cascades, where only coastal mountains separate inland areas from the cool Pacific. However, the Cascades serve as a major climatic barrier between coastal areas and the eastern two-thirds of the state. Much of the marine air is blocked by the Cascades and prevented from reaching the eastside, and any air that does cross the Cascades is greatly modified, becoming warmer and drier. As a result, eastern Oregon heat waves are likely to last longer and be more intense than those west of the Cascades.

Since air temperatures typically decrease with increasing elevation, highest air temperatures generally occur at low elevations. Most of eastern Oregon is above 4,000 feet, so high temperatures are considerably lower than in the low-elevation deserts of the southwestern U.S. (such as the infamous Death Valley which is actually below sea level). In some places, however, deep river valleys in eastern Oregon have much lower elevations, producing Oregon's hottest summer temperatures. Pendleton, Ontario, and Hermiston, for example, frequently experience hot temperatures in summer.

The title "Oregon's Heat Wave Capital" should probably be reserved for Ontario, which is in the Snake River valley at an elevation of about 2,200 feet. There are several NOAA weather sites in the Ontario area; radio station KSRV is usually the warmest. During clear summer periods, temperatures often exceed 90°F and remain that way day after day. In 1967, KSRV's maximum temperature was 90°F or more on 74 consecutive days (June 28 through September 10). An even more significant heat wave occurred in 1971, a warm summer throughout Oregon. On July 20, the high temperature reached 102°F, and the high did not drop below 100°F again until August 21. That string of 32 consecutive days is believed to be the longest ever recorded in Oregon.

Spray, in the John Day River valley at about 1,800 feet in elevation, has also experienced a number of remarkable heat waves. During that same hot period in 1971, Spray had 26 consecutive days (July 20 through August 15) with temperatures of 100°F or more, and in 1961 there were 48 days in a row of 90°F or more. The Spray station is no longer in operation, but during the 1937-78 period when it collected weather data it was frequently the hot spot in Oregon. Its all-time record high (116°F on August 4, 1961) was the fourth highest ever recorded in Oregon.

Although most of western Oregon experiences relatively mild summer temperatures, a few inland valley locations can get quite warm. Medford and Grants Pass in the Rogue valley of southwestern Oregon are generally the warmest westside locations. Medford has had as many as 34 consecutive days of 90°F or more (July and August 1961), and Grants Pass as many as 32 (July and August 1971). Medford has had ten consecutive days of 100°F or more on several occasions, the most recent in 1967.

# Significant Hot Weather Events in Oregon

*Oregon coast*   Feb. 19, 1896
A very warm period on the coast, with Langlois reaching 80°F.

*All of Oregon*   May 12, 1897
A warm period throughout Oregon. Vernonia was the highest at 106°F.

*Eastern Oregon*   Dec. 28, 1897
An unusual December warm spell. Dayville, at 81°F, was the hot spot.

*Eastern Oregon*   Jul.-Aug. 1898
The highest temperatures ever recorded in Oregon occurred during this period: 119°F at Prineville on July 29 and at Pendleton August 10.

*Eastern Oregon*   Jun. 14, 1903
The same day as the Heppner flood, hot weather affected many parts of eastern Oregon, topped by Coyote (Morrow County) at 110°F.

*All of Oregon*   Mar. 7-9, 1905
An early heat wave affected the entire state. The coast was the warmest area, with Marshfield (Coos County) the highest at 68°F on the 7th.

*All of Oregon*   Jul. 20-23, 1905
High temperatures prevailed throughout the state. Umatilla was 115°F on the 21st, and Pendleton and Blalock reported 114°F.

*Eastern Oregon*   Aug. 1-2, 1907
High temperatures in eastern Oregon included 115°F at Huntington, the second of three consecutive days above 110°F.

*Eastern Oregon*   Jul. 15-16, 1911
Exceptionally high temperatures throughout the area, including 115°F at Blalock, 112°F at Ella, and 110°F at Hermiston, Grants Pass, Echo, Pilot Rock, and Medford.

*Eastern Oregon*   May 15-16, 1924
A brief period of very hot weather, topped by 108°F at Blitzen on the 16th.

*All of Oregon*  Jun. 29-30, 1924
Hot weather affected the entire state. Echo was the highest at 112°F on the 16th. Rogue Valley stations topped 105°F, several Willamette Valley sites were over 100°F, and several eastern Oregon sites reached 110°F.

*All of Oregon*  Jun. 20-25, 1925
In a record-setting warm month, this period was the warmest. McMinnville and Oakridge reached 110°F on the 24th.

*Western Oregon*  Apr. 26-28, 1926
The hottest period in the warmest April on record to that date. McMinnville reached 99°F on the 27th, nearly every Willamette Valley site exceeded 90°F, and coastal sites were generally over 80°F.

*All of Oregon*  Jun. 23-26, 1926
It was hot everywhere. Coastal stations reached 90°F, Willamette Valley was over 100°F, the Rogue Valley topped 105°F, and Echo reached 109°F.

*All of Oregon*  Jul. 9-11, 1926
Another widespread heat wave. Echo hit 114°F on the 11th, Umatilla was 113°F, Pilot Rock  was 111°F, and McMinnville was 110°F.

*All of Oregon*  Jul. 21-26, 1928
A very hot period with many new records established. Pilot Rock and Echo hit 116°F on the 25th, and The Dalles was 115°F the same day. Grants Pass was 114°F on the 23rd.

*Western Oregon*  Nov. 2, 1929
Unusually warm weather, with Brooking reaching 88°F and Ashland and Medford 80°F.

*Western Oregon*  Oct. 1-3, 1932
Temperatures were in the 90s in much of western Oregon. Jacksonville reached 100°F on the 3rd.

*All of Oregon*  Jan. 24-31, 1934
An unusually warm week in an exceptionally mild month, this period was topped by Fremont's 82°F on the 31st and 78°F at Brookings on two different days.

*All of Oregon*  Mar. 9, 1934
In the warmest March on record to that time, North Bend and Powers reached 88°F on the 9th and numerous other stations topped 80°F.

*All of Oregon*  Oct. 7-10, 1936
A record-setting warm period for October, highlighted by Powers' 103°F on the 9th, and 98°F at Oakridge the same day.

*All of Oregon*   Sep. 12-14, 1937
One of the greatest September heat waves ever, this featured 108°F at Oakridge on the 14th and 105°F in Riddle the same day.

*All of Oregon*   Jul. 27, 1939
Umatilla reached 117°F on the 27th, Arlington and Hermiston were 112°F, and Illahe reached 109°F.

*All of Oregon*   Jun. 19-24, 1940
In this, the twelfth consecutive warmer than average month, Owyhee Dam and Kingman reached 110°F on the 19th, and Huntington was 108°F the same day.

*All of Oregon*   Feb. 9-13, 1943
The first of two very warm periods in a warm month, with Powers recording the highest temperature, 81°F on the 13th.

*All of Oregon*   Sep. 4-8, 1944
Temperatures over 100°F occurred over most of the state. Oakridge was 107°F on the 5th, and Drain reached 106°F the same day.

*All of Oregon*   Jul. 19-22, 1946
Very hot statewide. Medford reached 115°F on the 20th, Lakecreek and Illahe were 112°F, and Talent recorded 111°F. Even coastal sites were hot: on the 19th, Tillamook was 96°F and Seaside 93°F.

*All of Oregon*  Apr. 13-15, 1947
Temperatures were consistently in the high 80s and lower 90s, led by Lakecreek's 98°F on the 14th.

*All of Oregon*   Sep. 1-3, 1950
Temperatures were above 90°F virtually everywhere in the state except at high elevations. The Dalles topped out at 107°F on the 3rd.

*All of Oregon*   Jun. 8-11, 1955
Highs were in the 90s along the coast, and over 100°F in some inland valleys and much of eastern Oregon. Illahe had a high of 111°F on the 8th.

*All of Oregon*   Sep. 3-6, 1955
It was hot everywhere but at the coast. Illahe's 111°F on the 3rd was the highest September temperature ever recorded in Oregon. Pendleton (102°F), Bend (98°F) and Sexton Summit (97°F) also set all-time September records.

*Eastern Oregon* Jul. 18, 1960
Spray reached 115°F on the 18th.

*All of Oregon* Jun. 16, 1961
It was warm throughout the state; in fact, it was the second warmest June in Portland since records began. It was 110°F in Spray on the 16th and Arlington on the 27th, and 107°F-109°F in several other eastern Oregon locations.

*All of Oregon* Aug. 6, 1961
It was hot statewide. Spray was 116°F on the 6th, the fourth highest temperature ever in Oregon; Pendleton and Arlington were 115°F on the 4th. Portland topped 100°F, and Medford was 106°F. Spray was 90°F or more for 48 straight days.

*All of Oregon* Jul.-Aug. 1967
An unusually long heat wave, lasting from mid-July through mid-August. Medford had ten consecutive days when the temperature was above 100°F, Ontario had 74 consecutive days of 90°F or more (Jun. 28 - Sep. 10).

*All of Oregon* Feb. 26-29, 1968
This was the warmest February on record at many locations. Powers reached 81°F on the 29th, Canary and Tidewater 80°F.

*All of Oregon* Jul.-Aug. 1971
Like the 1967 event, this was a heat wave notable for lengthy periods of extreme temperatures. Ontario was 100°F or more for 32 straight days (Jul. 20 - Aug. 21), Spray for 26. Pilot Rock's 111°F on August 1 was the hottest day.

*All of Oregon* Apr. 23-28, 1977
A very warm April, with western Oregon temperatures in the 80s and eastern Oregon in the 90s, topped by Spray's 96°F on the 24th.

*All of Oregon* Oct. 1-5, 1980
Temperatures were mostly in the 90s statewide with a few higher values. Dora was 104°F on the 3rd and Fremont 104°F a day later, and Powers was 103°F on the 3rd.

*South coast* Dec. 15, 1980
A mid-winter coastal heat wave. Port Orford was 80°F on the 15th, Brookings reached 79°F, and Bandon 77°F.

*Western Oregon* Aug. 8, 1981
One of the warmest periods on record west of the Cascades. Medford topped out at 114°F on the 8th. Corvallis set its all-time record (108°F) the same day.

*All of Oregon* May 25-28, 1983
These were unusually warm May temperatures, including 106°F at McKenzie and Oakridge on the 28th, and 105°F at Estacada and Arlington.

*Oregon coast* Feb. 18-20, 1988
The coast warms up: it was 83°F at Brookings on the 19th, 80°F at Powers, 78°F at Tidewater.

*All of Oregon*  Jul.-Aug, 1990
Extended very warm conditions occurred throughout the state. The Willamette Valley was over 100°F on a number of days, southern Oregon above 105°F.

*Western Oregon*  Jun. 21-23, 1992
Many records were set, including June records of 111°F at Medford and 105°F at Salem. Cave Junction reached 109°F, Lost Creek Dam 107°F.

*All of Oregon*  Jul. 20-25, 1994
Multi-day hot spell, with Medford reaching 109°F on the 21st, Arlington 111°F on the same day, and Pelton Dam 114°F twice.

*All of Oregon*  Jul. 28-Aug. 11, 1996
High temperatures statewide, including 113°F at Pelton Dam on the 11th, 109°F at Dayville the same day, and 107°F at several southwest Oregon locations.

# Drought

D rought is a periodic climate cycle that affects virtually all regions and countries on earth. The natural world has adapted to these dry periods, although not without changes in plant and animal populations. Steadily rising human populations, coupled with increased demands for water for agricultural, domestic, industrial, recreation, and power generation purposes, have made water an increasingly scarce and precious resource.

To study drought and its effects on Oregon, we begin by defining drought, discuss ways to monitor its behavior, and describe ways in which drought has affected Oregon in the past.

*In 1992, ongoing drought conditions caused lake levels statewide to drop to very low (sometimes unprecedented) levels. At Detroit Lake, the water level dropped low enough to expose stumps of old trees which had occupied the valley before the dam was built—their first appearance above water in about 40 years. Drawing by John R. Taylor.*

# Drought Definitions

The *American Heritage Dictionary of the English Language* defines drought as follows:

> *drought (drout) n. Also drouth (drouth). 1. A long period with no rain especially during a planting season. 2. A dearth of anything; a scarcity.*

The first definition is a concise statement describing a meteorological phenomenon and includes a major effect of droughts (agriculture), but begs more questions than it answers:

—What is meant by a long period?

—Does a period with only a little rain qualify as a drought?

—What about other forms of precipitation, namely snow?

—Some areas on earth commonly receive little or no rainfall for extended periods. Are these always drought periods?

Clearly a more precise definition is necessary for our purposes. Van Havel and Carriker (1957) defined drought in terms of its effects on plants as a period with "sufficient moisture not available in the root zone for plant growth and development."

Palmer (1965) described drought in meteorological terms:

> *An interval of time, generally months or years, when actual moisture supply consistently falls short of the climatically appropriate moisture supply.*

This definition, unlike the dictionary definition, includes a consideration of climatic normals in its description. Thus, a period of very dry weather that might be common or even normal in Death Valley can be seen as atypical on the Oregon coast, and thus would constitute a drought. Palmer also defines the time scale of a drought as being seasonal, annual, or of multi-year duration. Finally, his definition encompasses all aspects of water supply (precipitation, streamflow, groundwater, etc.). It thus serves as a solid, useful definition of meteorological drought.

What remains is to define "climatically appropriate." Clearly this varies from one location to the next and should encompass a sufficient period of time to avoid short-term variations. Climatologists generally define "normal" as a thirty-year average. It is the custom in the United States to use a given thirty-year average for ten years, whereupon the averaging period is moved forward to the most recent thirty-year period. Since 1991, for example, the 1961-90 average has represented "normal." In a few years, new normals will be calculated (for the 1971-2000 period).

In addition to "agricultural" and "meteorological" droughts, one might define "regulatory" drought. Drought is one of many natural disasters that may trigger availability of funds or other assistance from federal or state agencies. It is therefore necessary to define drought in a manner that enables responsible agencies to declare a drought situation. The Oregon Drought Plan includes the following statement;

> *The Legislative Assembly finds that an emergency may exist when a severe, continuing drought results in a lack of water resources, thereby threatening the availability of essential services and jeopardizing the peace, health, safety, and welfare of the people of Oregon.*

This definition is the basis for drought declarations or terminations by the governor.

## Quantifying Drought

Accurate determination of the existence of a drought requires an objective criterion for defining the onset, continuation, or end of a drought period. The ideal approach is to develop an established numeric drought index; values above some threshold would indicate near-drought or drought conditions, while values below the threshold would correspond to periods with adequate or surplus water. Various indices exist for defining drought, although some were designed for identifying meteorological drought while others were intended for agricultural or hydrological drought.

One of the earliest drought indices in this country was established in 1905 by the U.S. Weather Bureau, which defined drought as "any period of 21 or more days with rainfall 30% or more below normal." This proved to be a very liberal definition since it identified sixty-two "droughts" in a thirty-three year period in the District of Columbia. Van Bavel and Carriker (1957) defined drought in terms of its effects on agriculture. They identified drought as a period with "sufficient soil moisture not available in the root zone for plant growth and development." This method proved to be fairly sensitive to precipitation; even a few hundredths of an inch of rainfall could be sufficient to end such droughts. In addition, this method completely ignored the effects of low winter precipitation.

The most widely used drought index is that developed by Palmer (1965), who defined "meteorological drought." Palmer's method, which is still in widespread use, was based on precipitation, runoff, evaporation, and soil moisture. It provided numeric values ranging from -4 (extreme dryness) to +4 (extremely wet), with 0 representing normal conditions. Palmer's method has been shown to work reasonably well in many parts of the country, particularly the Midwest. However, it has several major shortcomings especially when applied to the high-relief areas in the western states. The Palmer index reacts very slowly to changes in water availability. It is also very complicated to use and works poorly in areas with significant elevation changes, since it handles snowpack very inadequately. These deficiencies of the Palmer index have given other researchers incentive to develop more effective techniques.

*Technically, the SPI is the number of standard deviations that the observed value would deviate from the long-term mean, for a normally distributed random variable. Since precipitation is not normally distributed, a transformation is first applied so that the transformed precipitation values follow a normal distribution.*

*The SPI was designed to explicitly express the fact that it is possible to simultaneously experience wet conditions on one or more time scales, and dry conditions on other time scales, often a difficult concept to convey in simple terms to decisionmakers.*

One of these was the method developed by Shear and Steila (1974), which used the same basic input parameters as the Palmer method but seemed to work more effectively. It proved to be sensitive to short-term changes in water availability and is much simpler to use and apply. In addition, this method yields numeric values that are in the same units as precipitation, and therefore has actual meteorological significance, unlike the nondimensional values produced by the Palmer index.

The poor performance of the Palmer index in mountainous areas was the incentive for the development of the Surface Water Supply Index (SWSI). Developed jointly by the U.S. Soil Conservation Service and the Colorado Division of Water Resources, SWSI is based on precipitation, reservoir storage, and either snowpack (winter) or stream flow (summer). SWSI produces the same units as the Palmer index, but appears to respond much more appropriately to changes in available moisture.

The Standardized Precipitation Index (SPI) was formulated by the Colorado Climate Center in 1993. The purpose is to assign a single numeric value to precipitation, for comparison across regions with markedly different climates. The SPI is normalized so that wetter and drier climates can be represented in the same way, and wet periods can also be monitored using the SPI. (See the sidebar for the technical details of how the SPI operates.)

McKee et al. (1993) used the classification system shown in Table 34 to define drought intensities resulting from the SPI. They also defined the criteria for a "drought event" for any of the time scales. A drought event occurs any time the SPI is continuously negative and reaches an intensity where the SPI is -1.0 or less. The event ends when the SPI becomes positive. Each drought event, therefore, has a duration defined by its beginning and end, and an intensity for each month that the event continues. The accumulated magnitude of drought can also be measured. The authors called this the Drought Magnitude (DM), and it is the positive sum of the SPI for all the months within a drought event.

**Table 34. SPI values**

| SPI values | Drought category | Time in category |
|---|---|---|
| 0 to -0.99 | Mild Drought | 24% |
| 1.00 to -1.49 | Moderate Drought | 9.2% |
| 1.50 to -1.99 | Severe Drought | 4.4% |
| 2.00 or less | Extreme Drought | 2.3% |

Table 34 also shows the percentage of time that the SPI is in each of the drought categories based on an analysis of stations across Colorado. Because the SPI is standardized, these percentages are expected from a normal distribution of the SPI. The 2.3% of SPI values within the Extreme Drought category, for example, is a percentage that is typically expected for an "extreme" event (Wilhite 1995). In contrast, the Palmer index reaches its "extreme" category more than 10% of the time across portions of the central Great Plains. This standardization allows the SPI to determine the rarity of a current drought, as well as the probability of the precipitation necessary to end the current drought.

Other drought indices used to assess water availability (drought, floods, or in between) include the following:

## Percent of normal

The percent of normal precipitation is one of the simplest measurements of rainfall for a location. Analysis using the percent of normal is very effective when used for a single region or a single season but is also easily misunderstood and gives different indications of conditions depending on the location and season. It is calculated by dividing actual precipitation by normal precipitation—typically considered to be a thirty-year mean—and multiplying by 100%. This can be calculated for a variety of time scales, usually ranging from a single month to a group of months representing a particular season, to an annual or water year. Normal precipitation for a specific location is considered to be 100%.

One of the disadvantages of using the percent of normal precipitation is that the mean, or average, precipitation is often not the same as the median precipitation (the value exceeded by 50% of the precipitation occurrences in a long-term climate record). Precipitation on monthly or seasonal scales does not have a normal distribution, but use of the percent of normal comparison implies a normal distribution where the mean and median are considered to be the same. An example of the confusion this could create can be illustrated by the long-term precipitation record in Melbourne, Australia, for the month of January. The median January precipitation is 1.4 inches, meaning that in half the years less than 1.4 inches is recorded, and in half the years more than this amount is recorded. However, a monthly January total of 1.4 inches would be only 75% of normal when compared to the mean, and 75% of normal is often considered to be quite dry.

Because of the variety in precipitation records over time and location, there is no way to determine the frequency of

*Consequently, a separate SPI value is calculated for a selection of time scales, covering the last 1, 2, 3, 4, 5, 6, 7, 8, 9, 10, 11, 12, 15, 18, 24, 30, 36, 48, 60, and 72 months, and ending on the last day of the latest month. The SPI is calculated by taking the difference of the precipitation from the mean for a particular time scale, and then dividing by the standard deviation. Because precipitation is not normally distributed for time scales shorter than twelve months, an adjustment is made which allows the SPI to become normally distributed. Thus, the mean SPI for a time scale and a location is zero and the standard deviation is one.*

departures from normal; the rarity of an occurring drought is not known and cannot be compared with a different location. This makes it difficult to link a given value with a specific impact, inhibiting attempts to mitigate the risks of drought and form a plan of response (Willeke et al. 1994).

## Deciles

Arranging monthly precipitation data into deciles is another drought-monitoring technique that was developed by Gibbs and Maher (1967) to avoid some of the weaknesses within the percent of normal approach. This technique divided the distribution of occurrences over a long-term precipitation record into sections for each 10% of the distribution. They called each of these categories a "decile." The first decile is the rainfall amount not exceeded by the lowest 10% of precipitation occurrences. The second decile is the precipitation amount not exceeded by the lowest 20% of occurrences. These deciles continue until the rainfall amount identified by the tenth decile is the largest precipitation amount within the long-term record. By definition, the fifth decile is the median, and it is the precipitation amount not exceeded by 50% of the occurrences over the period of record. The deciles are grouped into five classifications, which are shown in Table 35.

**Table 35. Decile classifications for dry and wet periods**

| | | |
|---|---|---|
| Deciles 1-2 | lowest 20% | precipitation much below normal |
| Deciles 3-4 | next lowest 20 % | precipitation below normal |
| Deciles 5-6 | middle 20% | precipitation near normal |
| Deciles 7-8 | next highest 20% | precipitation above normal |
| Deciles 9-10 | highest 20% | precipitation much above normal |

The decile method is relatively simple to calculate, requires less data and fewer assumptions than the Palmer index, and provides uniformity in drought classifications. One disadvantage of the decile system is that a long climatological record is needed to calculate the deciles accurately.

## Drought Monitoring

At one time, the Oregon Drought Council was the primary drought assessment agency in Oregon. Comprising representatives of various state and federal agencies, the Council met monthly and reported to the Strategic Water Management Group (SWMG), which in turn reported to the Governor. The Drought Council played an important role in the 1992 drought, when Oregon successfully sought federal relief funds for the statewide drought emergency. Unfortunately, SWMG was disbanded several years later, and with it went the Drought Council.

The National Drought Mitigation Center (NDMC) was founded in 1995. It is housed in the Department of Agricultural Meteorology at the University of Nebraska-Lincoln, also home to the International Drought Information Center. It is the first research and development program to address drought as a national issue in the U.S.

## Drought in Oregon

A history of drought in Oregon reveals many short-term droughts and a few long-term events. In some cases, droughts have been widespread, affecting virtually the entire state. At other times, regional or local water shortages have occurred.

Figure 28 shows the monthly Palmer Drought Severity Index for the Willamette Valley from 1895 through early 1998. As stated earlier, the Palmer index is not the best water availability indicator for Oregon, but it has the advantage that data have been available for more than a hundred years. In western Oregon, the Palmer index is a good indicator of precipitation compared with normal (averaged over a period of about six months).

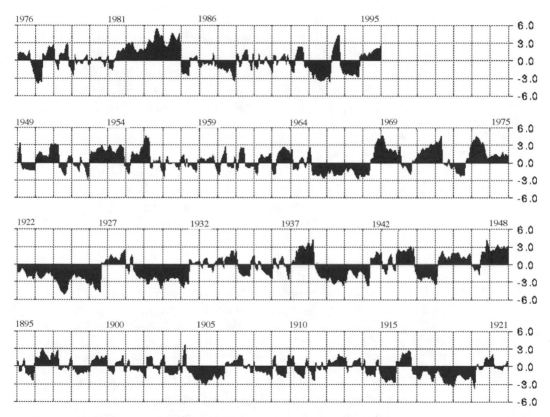

The figure shows some significant periods of water shortage:
—1904-05. A drought period of about 18 months.
—1917-31. A very dry period, punctuated by brief wet spells in 1920-21 and 1927.
—1939-41. A three-year intense drought.
—1965-68. A three-year drought following the big regional floods of 1964-65.
—1976-77. A brief but very intense statewide drought.
—1985-94. A generally very dry period, capped by statewide droughts in 1992 and 1994.

*Figure 30. The Palmer Index for the Willamette Valley. (National Climatic Data Center)*

# Effects of Droughts

Droughts have obvious effects on lake and river levels, cause significant harm to wildlife, and present major problems for farmers and ranchers. The greatest impacts, however, may be on forests. During the 1985-94 drought, trees were weakened by water shortages and tree pests proliferated. Spruce budworm and bark beetles ravaged large areas in Oregon, killing many trees. The forests became huge tinderboxes, ripe for major fires. The situation was not unlike what had occurred during the long dry period from the late teens throug the early 1930s. In the 1990s, Oregon was fortunate not to experience major forest fires. In the 1930s we were not so lucky.

## The Tillamook Burn

Between 1933 and 1951, the Tillamook Forest burned four times, with bizarre regularity, every six years. The fires burned over 350,000 acres of forest, and are collectively known as the Tillamook Burn.

The first fire started a little after one o'clock on the afternoon of August 14, 1933. Stewart Holbrook described the scene for the *American Mercury*:

> *Hundreds of men fought valiantly all night on that August 14, and for all the good they did they might as well have remained in their camps. The fire leaped into the tops of the trees and swept on with fearful speed, making its own wind as it went. Those great trees, many of them 300 feet high, burned like tremendous torches. I saw one great body of Douglas firs, each nearly 500 years old, burn savagely like so many huge columns of fat, spitting, crackling, then roaring like flame under a bellows.*
>
> *Smoke rolled and billowed above the flames. It formed, for two days, a pillar and mushroom that stood clear and white and terrible five thousand feet above the forest. Presently ashes were drifting through the screens of the windows in Portland homes, fifty miles away. The wind over the fire rose at last to a hurricane and the noise was greater than the sea pounding the Oregon shore. It rumbled and thundered and was marked by the deep booming of ancient trees uprooted by the gale and crashing down.*
>
> *Five hundred more men, then a thousand more, then two thousand were hurried to the lines that now formed a front along a hundred miles, and mariners far at sea saw dead embers fall on the decks of their ships, while the tides piled debris two feet deep along the Oregon beaches. Tillamook County, Oregon's great timbered pride, was going up in flame and smoke. I saw it burn and I never expect to see another sight like it. . . .*
>
> *A sudden shift of the wind, on the tenth day of the conflagration, brought immediate danger to Camp McGregor, logging headquarters of the Oregon-American Lumber Company.*

*An hour later the main body of the fire was only half a mile from the camp, and spot fires were springing up within a few yards of the buildings. Men fought these near fires, a rear-guard action, while wives and children were loaded aboard a logging train. The train pulled out just as the camp itself started to burn fiercely. It pounded down the mountain, rocked around curves and crossed dizzily high trestles that were beginning to smoulder, while back on the mountain the camp was going up in smoke.*

*The little hamlet of Elsie, set almost in the middle of this gigantic destruction, was soon surrounded by the fire, and for twenty-four hours it was believed that Elsie and all it contained had been wiped away. But through some quirk in the wind, Elsie survived. Not so another hamlet, Lukarilla. Settlers watched while Lukarilla, with its homes and barns and fences and one store, disappeared entirely. Strangely enough there was no loss of life here. Only one person died in all the fire, Frank Palmer, a CCC boy from Illinois, who was killed instantly when a big fir, uprooted by the wind, crushed him to earth.*

*The blaze burned itself out on August 24, after a fog blanket drifted in from the coast to smother it. In ten days it had killed twelve and one-half billion feet of fine timber. It burned over some 310,000 acres. How can one describe twelve and one-half billion feet of timber? There is no use piling it up, in Sunday-supplement style beside the Empire State Building, which it would put in shadow many times over. But perhaps it will mean something to know that during the year 1932, twelve and one-half billion feet of logs was enough to supply the needs of all the sawmills, lath mills, shingle mills and pulpwood mills in the forty-eight states.*

Drought, like floods, will doubtless return every so often to Oregon. During periods of plentiful water (such as we are experiencing in the late 1990s), it is easy to forget that fact. But unless we are prepared for water scarcity, we will encounter problems when drought reappears. Most Oregon state and local agencies have enacted comprehensive drought contingency plans. The only element missing is early assessment of drought, something at which the Drought Council excelled. If we were to suggest ways to improve Oregon's responsiveness to drought, we would begin by reestablishing the Drought Council!

# Significant Droughts in Oregon

*All of Oregon*   1928-1941
This was a prolonged statewide drought that caused major problems for agriculture. The only area spared was the northern coast, which received abundant rains in 1930-33. The three big Tillamook burns, the first in 1933, were the most significant results of this very dry period.

*Eastern Oregon*   1959-1964
Streamflows were low throughout eastern Oregon during this period, but areas west of the Cascades had few problems. Ironically, the driest period in western Oregon was the summer following the 1964 flood.

*Western Oregon*   1976-1981
Low streamflows prevailed during this period, but the worst year by far was 1976-77, the single driest year of the century. Portland Airport received only 7.19 inches of precipitation between October 1976 and February 1977, only 31% of the average of 23.16 inches for that period.

*All of Oregon*   1985-1994
This long-lasting drought was not as severe as the 1976-77 drought in any single year, but the cumulative effect of ten consecutive years with mostly dry conditions caused statewide problems. The peak year of the drought was 1992, when a drought emergency was declared for all of Oregon. In the 7-year period from 1986-1992, Medford received only five years' worth of precipitation, and other southern Oregon locations were nearly as hard hit. Forests throughout Oregon suffered from the lack of moisture; fires were common, and insect pests flourished.

**PART 6**

# Appendices

# Access to Data via the Internet

The Internet has become a widely used tool for obtaining information of various kinds. Weather and climate data and reports are available from a wide variety of public and private organizations. Below we list a few of our favorites. The URL (or Universal Resource Locator) is the Internet address used to access the site, via a Web browser.

**Oregon Climate Service**
http://www.ocs.orst.edu
Wide variety of Oregon weather and climate information and data sets, including extensive links to other sites.

**Western Regional Climate Center**
http://www.wrcc.sage.dri.edu
Information for the eleven western states.

**National Climatic Data Center**
http://www.ncdc.noaa.gov
National and international climate information.

**National Weather Service, Portland**
http://nimbo.wrh.noaa.gov/Portland
Local NWS headquarters, and a very complete Web site.

**Climate Prediction Center**
http://nic.fb4.noaa.gov
El Niño information and long-range forecasts (out to 15 months).

**The Weather Channel**
http://www.weather.com
In case you don't have cable TV.

**WeatherNet**
http://cirrus.sprl.umich.edu/wxnet
Probably the most complete set of weather-related links available anywhere.

**USDA NRCS Water and Climate Center, Portland**
http://www.wcc.wrcs.usda.gov
Snow, climate, and natural resources information.

**USGS Water Information**
http://h2o.usgs.gov
Stream flow data for the U.S.

**Oregon Home Page**
http://www.state.or.us
Plenty of Oregon info.

# Measuring, Archiving, and Delivering Weather and Climate Information in Oregon

## Organizations

Weather and climate data are collected from hundreds of locations in Oregon. A variety of agencies are involved in data collection, and many kinds of data are collected.

### National Weather Service (NWS)

According to its mission statement, NWS "provides weather, hydrologic, and climate forecasts and warnings for the United States, its territories, adjacent waters and ocean areas, for the protection of life and property and the enhancement of the national economy. NWS data and products form a national information database and infrastructure which can be used by other governmental agencies, the private sector, the public, and the global community." Currently there are three NWS offices in Oregon: Portland (the state headquarters), Medford, and Pendleton.

**History of the NWS.** The original weather agency operated under the War Department from 1870 to 1891 with headquarters in Washington, D.C., and field offices concentrated mainly east of the Rockies. Little meteorological science was used to make weather forecasts during those early days. Instead, weather that occurred at one location was assumed to move into the next area downstream.

The beginning of the National Weather Service we know today was on February 9, 1870, when President Ulysses S. Grant signed a joint resolution of Congress authorizing the Secretary of War to establish a national weather service. This resolution required the Secretary of War

> to provide for taking meteorological observations at the military stations in the interior of the continent and at other points in the States and Territories . . . and for giving notice on the northern (Great) Lakes and on the seacoast by magnetic telegraph and marine signals, of the approach and force of storms.

After much thought and consideration, it was decided that this agency would be placed under the Secretary of War because military discipline would probably secure the greatest promptness, regularity, and accuracy in the required observations. Within the Department of War, it was assigned to the Signal Service Corps under Brigadier General Albert J. Myer, who gave the National Weather Service its first name: The Division of Telegrams and Reports for the Benefit of Commerce.

From 1891 to 1940, the Weather Bureau was part of the Department of Agriculture. These first two decades of the 20th century had a remarkable effect on the nation's meteorological services. In 1902, Weather Bureau forecasts were sent via wireless telegraphy to ships at sea. In turn, the first wireless weather report was received from a ship at sea in 1905. Two years later, the daily exchange of weather observations with Russia and eastern Asia was inaugurated.

In 1910, the Weather Bureau began issuing weekly outlooks to aid agricultural planning. And in 1913, the first fire-weather forecast was issued. During these times, weather forecasters began using more sophisticated methods including surface weather observations; kite experiments to measure temperature, relative humidity and winds in the upper atmosphere; and, later, airplane stations.

Realizing that the Weather Bureau played an important role for the aviation community, and therefore commerce, in 1940, President Franklin D. Roosevelt transferred the Weather Bureau to the Department of Commerce where it remains today. During the late 1940s, the military gave the Weather Bureau a new and valuable tool—25 surplus radars—thus launching the network of weather surveillance radars still in use today. In 1970, the name was changed to the National Weather Service, and the agency became a component of the Commerce Department's newly created National Oceanic and Atmospheric Administration.

The advent of computer technology in the 1950s paved the way for the formulation of complex mathematical weather models, resulting in a significant increase in forecast accuracy.

**Modernization.** The National Weather Service is in the midst of a major modernization program that is offering more timely and precise severe weather and flood warnings for the nation. Recent advances in satellites, radar, sophisticated information processing and communication systems, automated weather observing systems, and high speed computers are the foundation of the modernization. The components of the modernization are the new Doppler Weather Surveillance Radar, the Automated Surface Observing System, a new generation of Geostationary Operational Environmental Satellites, National Center Advanced Computer Systems, and the Advanced Weather Interactive Processing System. The modernization also includes a new structure of field offices for the NWS, including Weather Forecast Offices and River Forecast Centers.

## National Climatic Data Center (NCDC)

NCDC is the world's largest active archive of weather data.

The Weather Bureau, Air Force, and Navy Tabulation Units in New Orleans, LA, were combined to create the National Weather Records Center in Asheville, NC, in November 1951. The Center was eventually renamed the National Climatic Data Center. The National Archives and Records Administration has designated NCDC as the Commerce Department's only Agency Records Center. NCDC archives weather data obtained by the National Weather Service, Military Services, Federal Aviation Administration, and the Coast Guard, as well as data from voluntary cooperative observers. NCDC has increased data acquisition capabilities to ingest new data streams such as NEXRAD and ASOS (see Types of Observations section).

Improving quality control and continuity of these new data sets as well as making them available in timely fashion has been paramount. As operator of the World Data Center-A for Meteorology, which provides for international data exchange, NCDC also collects data from around the globe. The Center has more than 150 years of data on hand with 55 gigabytes of new information added each day—that is equivalent to 18 million pages a day.

NCDC archives 99% of all NOAA data, including over 320 million paper records; 2.5 million microfiche records; and over 500,000 tape cartridges/magnetic tapes; and has satellite weather images back to 1960. NCDC annually publishes over 1.2 million copies of climate publications that are sent to individual users and 33,000 subscribers. NCDC maintains over five hundred digital data sets to respond to over 170,000 requests each year.

Data are received from a wide variety of sources, including satellites, radar, remote sensing systems, NWS cooperative observers, aircraft, ships, radiosonde, wind profiler, rocketsonde, solar radiation networks, and NWS Forecast-Warnings-Analyses Products. NCDC supports many forms of data and information dissemination such as paper copies of original records, publications, atlases, computer printouts, microfiche, microfilm, movie loops, photographs, magnetic tape, floppy disks, CD-ROM, electronic mail, on-line dial-up, telephone, facsimile, and personal visit.

The Center, which produces numerous climate publications and responds to requests from all over the world, provides historical perspectives on climate that are vital to studies on global climate change, the greenhouse effect, and other environmental issues. The Center stores information essential to industry, agriculture, science, hydrology, transportation, recreation, and engineering. This information can mean tens of millions of dollars to concerned parties.

NCDC's mission is to manage the nation's resource of global climatological in-situ and remotely sensed data and information to promote global environmental stewardship; to describe, monitor and assess the climate; and to support efforts to predict changes in the Earth's environment. This effort requires the acquisition, quality control, processing, summarization, dissemination, and preservation of a vast array of climatological data generated by the national and international meteorological services. NCDC's mission is global in nature and provides the U.S. climate representative to the World Meteorological Organization, the World Data Center System, and other international scientific programs. NCDC also operates the World Data Center-A for Meteorology.

### Western Regional Climate Center (WRCC)

The mission of the Western Regional Climate Center is to disseminate high-quality climate data and information pertaining to the western United States; to foster better use of this information in decision making; to conduct applied research related to climate issues; and to improve the coordination of climate-related activities at state, regional, and national scales.

The Western Regional Climate Center, inaugurated in 1986, is one of six regional climate centers in the United States. The regional climate center program is administered by NOAA. Specific oversight is provided by the National Climatic Data Center.

The WRCC exists to fill several roles:

—Serve as a focal point for coordination of applied climate activities in the West
- Federal resource management agencies
- Western committees and commissions

—Maintain links to other climate programs
- National Climate Data Center, Asheville, NC
- Regional climate centers
- State climatologists and state climate programs
- Climate Analysis Center, Washington D.C.
- National Weather Service

—Conduct applied research on climate issues affecting the West
- Impacts of climate variability in the western United States
- Quality control of western databases
- Relation of El Niño/Southern Oscillation to western climate
- Climatic trends and fluctuations in the West
- GIS and remote sensing

In support of these functions, WRCC maintains a historical climate database for the West.

## Oregon Climate Service (OCS)

OCS is located on the Oregon State University campus in Corvallis and is the state repository for weather and climate information. OCS's mission is fourfold:

—To collect, manage, and maintain Oregon weather and climate data.

—To provide weather and climate information to those within and outside the state of Oregon.

—To educate the people of Oregon on current and emerging climate issues.

—To perform independent research related to weather and climate issues.

**Linkages.** OCS acts as the liaison with:

—National Climatic Data Center

—Western Regional Climate Center

—National Weather Service

—Natural Resources Conservation Service

—Climate Prediction Center

—American Association of State Climatologists

—Other state climate offices

**Climate Data.** OCS maintains the most complete set of state weather and climate records in Oregon. A large amount of the data is stored in a computer-accessible format (hard disks and magnetic tapes) for easy retrieval and manipulation. In addition, various studies, reports, summaries, etc. are stored on paper and/or fiche.

**Services.** On average, OCS handles about six thousand telephone or mail data requests per year. OCS provides a full range of climate-related services to both the public and private sectors. Services/products include, but are not restricted to:

—Site-specific climate reports/summaries.

—Various statistical analysis's, such as means, extremes, probabilities, percentiles, threshold exceedances, etc.

—Climate tables/inventories.

—Precipitation maps.

—Customized research.

—Current climate data and information.

**Computing.** OCS uses state-of-the-art computers to store and manipulate climate data. A variety of UNIX, IBM-compatible, and Macintosh workstations are utilized. In addition, a comprehensive World Wide Web (WWW) site is maintained.

**Research.** OCS has been involved in numerous research projects undertaken by governments, universities, and private interests. Among these are:

—Climate variability studies.

—Precipitation mapping (PRISM).

—Quality control of data.

—El Niño/Southern Oscillation and its influence on western climate.

—Drought and flood studies.

—Climate change.

—Long-term/lead forecasting.

—Air quality studies.

—Wind modeling.

## USDA Natural Resources Conservation Service (NRCS)

NRCS installs, operates, and maintains an extensive, automated system to collect snowpack and related climatic data in the western United States called SNOTEL (for SNOwpack TELemetry). The system evolved from NRCS's congressional mandate in the mid-1930s "to measure snowpack in the mountains of the West and forecast the water supply." The programs began with manual measurements of snow courses; since 1980, SNOTEL has reliably and efficiently collected the data needed to produce water supply forecasts and to support the resource management activities of NRCS and others.

Climate studies, air and water quality investigations, and resource management concerns are all served by the modern SNOTEL network. The high-elevation watershed locations and the broad coverage of the network provide important data collection opportunities to researchers, water managers, and emergency managers for natural disasters such as floods.

# Types of Observations

L isted below are major types of collection platforms operating in Oregon. Federal agencies provide the bulk of weather and climate data collection, archiving, and delivery.

## NOAA Cooperative Stations

Cooperative stations are U.S. stations operated by local observers which generally report maximum/minimum temperatures and precipitation. National Weather Service (NWS) data are also included in this dataset. The data receive extensive automated and manual quality control. Over eight thousand stations are currently active across the country, more than three hundred in Oregon.

Despite all of the state-of-the-art technology associated with the modernization of the NWS, the cooperative program has remained virtually unchanged since its inception over a hundred years ago. Many cooperative stations in the United States have been collecting weather data from the same location for over a hundred years.

The first extensive network of cooperative stations was set up in the 1890s as a result of an act of Congress in 1890 that established the Weather Bureau, but many of its stations began operation long before that time. John Companius Holm's weather records, taken without the benefit of instruments in 1644 and 1645, were the earliest known observations in the United States. Subsequently many persons, including George Washington, Thomas Jefferson, and Benjamin Franklin, maintained weather records. Jefferson maintained an almost unbroken record of weather observations between 1776 and 1816, and Washington took his last weather observation just a few days before he died. Two of the most prestigious awards given to cooperative weather observers are named after Holm and Jefferson. Because of its many decades of relatively stable operation, high station density, and high proportion of rural locations, the cooperative network has been recognized as the most definitive source of information on U.S. climate trends for temperature and precipitation. Cooperative stations form the core of the U.S. Historical Climate Network and the U.S. Reference Climate Network.

Equipment to gather these data is provided and maintained by the NWS and data forms are sent monthly to the NCDC in Asheville, NC, where data are digitized, quality controlled, and subsequently archived. Volunteer weather observers regularly and conscientiously contribute their time so that their observations can provide the vital information needed. These data are invaluable in learning more about the floods, droughts, and heat and cold waves which inevitably affect everyone. They are also used in agricultural planning and assessment, engineering, environmental-impact assessment, utilities planning, and litigation and play a critical role in efforts to recognize and evaluate the extent of human impacts on climate from local to global scales. Many cooperative weather observers report daily precipitation to River Forecast Centers in support of the National Weather Service Hydrology Program.

## Historical Climatological Network

The 187-station daily dataset for the contiguous United States consists of three elements: maximum temperature, minimum temperature (both in °F), and precipitation (in hundredths of inches).

Stations in the Daily Historical Climatology Network include 138 long-term stations operated by cooperative (non-paid) observers. Additional stations, chosen from the first order NWS station network, were included to increase the spatial resolution. All stations were selected using the following criteria:

—A station's potential for heat island bias over time should be low.

—It should have maintained a relatively constant observation time.

—Reasonably homogeneous spatial distribution over the contiguous U.S.

The only Oregon stations in the 138-station dataset are Dufur and Grants Pass.

## Surface Airways Observations

These observations are collected at airport sites. In general, they are collected and administered by the Federal Aviation Administration (FAA) for NWS. Most of the stations are now automated, 24-hour stations which can be accessed via the Internet. Oregon stations are shown in Table 36.

## Instruments for Modernization (NWS)

New observing systems are the key to the ongoing modernization program of the NWS. Below are descriptions of three key measurement platforms as well as a software-hardware processing system.

### Automated Surface Observing System

The Automated Surface Observing System (ASOS) will relieve staff from the manual collection of surface observations. Over one thousand ASOS systems across the nation will provide data on pressure, temperature, wind direction and speed, runway visibility, cloud ceiling heights, and type and intensity of precipitation on a nearly continuous basis. The implementation status of ASOS is updated regularly.

## Table 36. Surface Airways Observations—Oregon stations.

| ID | Station Name | Latitude (degrees & minutes) | Longitude (degrees & minutes) | Elevation (feet) |
|---|---|---|---|---|
| 3S2 | Aurora State | 4525 | -12277 | 197 |
| 4BK | Brookings | 4205 | -12428 | 79 |
| 4LW | Lakeview | 4222 | -12035 | 4772 |
| 5J0 | John Day State Arpt | 4440 | -11897 | 3697 |
| AST | Astoria/Clatsop | 4615 | -12388 | 23 |
| BKE | Baker Municipal | 4483 | -11782 | 3369 |
| BNO | Burns Muni | 4358 | -11895 | 4169 |
| CVO | Corvallis Muni | 4450 | -12328 | 246 |
| CZK | Cascade Locks State | 4567 | -12188 | 151 |
| DLS | The Dalles Muni | 4562 | -12117 | 243 |
| EUG | Eugene/Mahlon Sweet | 4412 | -12322 | 374 |
| HIO | Portland/Hillsboro | 4553 | -12295 | 203 |
| JNW | Newport | 4458 | -12407 | 157 |
| KP88 | Rome | 4290 | -11765 | 3811 |
| LGD | La Grande | 4528 | -11800 | 2713 |
| LKV | Lakeview | 4217 | -12040 | 4726 |
| LMT | Klamath Falls/Kings | 4215 | -12173 | 4090 |
| MEH | Meacham | 4552 | -11840 | 4054 |
| MFR | Medford/Jackson Co. | 4237 | -12287 | 1328 |
| ONP | Newport Municip | 4458 | -12405 | 157 |
| OTH | North Bend | 4342 | -12425 | 13 |
| PDT | Pendleton Municipal | 4568 | -11885 | 1496 |
| PDX | Portland Intl Arpt | 4560 | -12260 | 39 |
| RBG | Roseburg Municipal | 4323 | -12335 | 525 |
| RDM | Redmond | 4425 | -12115 | 3077 |
| S47 | Tillamook | 4542 | -12382 | 36 |
| SLE | Salem/Mcnary | 4492 | -12300 | 200 |
| SXT | Sexton Summit | 4262 | -12337 | 3841 |
| TTD | Portland/Troutdale | 4555 | -12240 | 36 |

### NEXRAD

NEXRAD is the commonly used acronym for the Next Generation of Weather Radar which began to be tested and implemented by NWS and the FAA during the 1980s. These new Doppler radar systems, now more appropriately known as the WSR-88D (Weather Surveillance Radar - 1988 Doppler), have replaced the aging network of WSR-57 and WSR-74 radar systems which these agencies had been using for the previous several decades. The WSR-88D provides several advantages over the its older predecessors, including:

— Greater sensitivity.

— Higher resolution data.

— The ability to detect the relative motion of echoes within a storm.

— Multiple volumetric views of the atmosphere.

— Algorithms to estimate the amount of liquid in the atmosphere.

— Algorithms to estimate the amount of precipitation that has fallen.

NEXRAD sites in Oregon are associated with the NWS offices at Portland, Medford, and Pendleton.

### Geostationary Operational Environmental Satellites

The Geostationary Operational Environmental Satellites (GOES) will continue to be a major data source for severe weather and flood warnings, short range forecasts, cloud imagery, and atmospheric sounding data.

### Advanced Weather Interactive Processing System

The Advanced Weather Interactive Processing System (AWIPS) will be the nerve center of the operations at each Weather Forecast Office. AWIPS will be the data integrator receiving the high-resolution data from a multiple of sources. From this information base all warning and forecast products will be prepared.

# SNOTEL Data Collection Network

SNOTEL uses meteor burst communications technology to collect and communicate data in near-real-time. VHF radio signals are reflected at a steep angle off the ever-present band of ionized meteorites existing from about 50 to 75 miles above the Earth. Satellites are not involved; NRCS operates and control the entire system.

There are over six hundred SNOTEL sites in eleven western states including Alaska. The sites are generally located in remote high-mountain watersheds where access is often difficult or restricted. Access for maintenance by NRCS includes various modes from hiking and skiing to helicopters.

Sites are designed to operate unattended and without maintenance for a year. They are battery powered with solar cell recharge. The condition of each site is monitored daily when it reports on eight operational functions.

## Table 37. Current SNOTEL stations in Oregon

| ID | Station name | Latitude (degrees & minutes) | Longitude (degrees & minutes) | Elevation (feet) |
|---|---|---|---|---|
| 17D02S | Aneroid Lake #2 | 4513 | 11712 | 7300 |
| 19D02S | Arbuckle Mountain | 4511 | 11915 | 5400 |
| 18D09S | Beaver Reservoir | 4508 | 11813 | 5150 |
| 22G21S | Big Red Mountain | 4203 | 12251 | 6250 |
| 23G15S | Bigelow Camp | 4205 | 12321 | 5120 |
| 22G13S | Billie Creek Divide | 4225 | 12217 | 5300 |
| 21D33S | Blazed Alder | 4525 | 12152 | 3650 |
| 18E16S | Blue Mountain Spring | 4415 | 11830 | 5900 |
| 18E05S | Bourne | 4449 | 11812 | 5800 |
| 18D20S | Bowman Springs | 4522 | 11827 | 4580 |
| 22F03S | Cascade Summit | 4335 | 12201 | 4880 |
| 21F22S | Chemult Alternate | 4313 | 12148 | 4760 |
| 21D13S | Clackamas Lake | 4505 | 12145 | 3400 |
| 21D12S | Clear Lake | 4512 | 12143 | 3500 |
| 22G24S | Cold Springs Camp | 4232 | 12211 | 6100 |
| 18D08S | County Line | 4511 | 11832 | 4800 |
| 22E08S | Daly Lake | 4437 | 12203 | 3600 |
| 19E03S | Derr | 4427 | 11956 | 5670 |
| 22F18S | Diamond Lake | 4311 | 12208 | 5315 |
| 18E03S | Eilertson Meadows | 4451 | 11807 | 5400 |
| 18D04S | Emigrant Springs | 4533 | 11827 | 3925 |
| 18G02S | Fish Creek | 4242 | 11838 | 7900 |
| 22G14S | Fish Lake | 4223 | 12225 | 4665 |
| 22G12S | Fourmile Lake | 4224 | 12213 | 6000 |
| 18E08S | Gold Center | 4446 | 11817 | 5340 |
| 21D01S | Greenpoint | 4537 | 12142 | 3200 |
| 18D19S | High Ridge | 4541 | 11806 | 4980 |
| 21E06S | Hogg Pass | 4425 | 12152 | 4760 |
| 22F42S | Holland Meadows | 4340 | 12234 | 4900 |
| 21F21S | Irish Taylor | 4349 | 12157 | 5500 |
| 22E07S | Jump Off Joe | 4423 | 12210 | 3500 |
| 23G09S | King Mountain | 4203 | 12312 | 4000 |
| 18E18S | Lake Creek R.S. | 4411 | 11836 | 5200 |
| 22E09S | Little Meadows | 4437 | 12213 | 4000 |
| 18D06S | Lucky Strike | 4517 | 11851 | 5050 |
| 19D03S | Madison Butte | 4506 | 11930 | 5250 |
| 21E04S | Marion Forks | 4435 | 12158 | 2600 |
| 21E07S | McKenzie | 4412 | 12152 | 4800 |

*Table continues on next page*

| ID | Station name | Latitude (degrees & minutes) | Longitude (degrees & minutes) | Elevation (feet) |
|---|---|---|---|---|
| 17D06S | Moss Springs | 4516 | 11741 | 5850 |
| 21D08S | Mt Hood Test Site | 4520 | 12143 | 5400 |
| 17D18S | Mt. Howard | 4516 | 11710 | 7910 |
| 21D35S | Mud Ridge | 4515 | 12144 | 3800 |
| 21F10S | New Crescent Lake | 4329 | 12158 | 4800 |
| 22D02S | North Fork | 4533 | 12201 | 3120 |
| 20E02S | Ochoco Meadows | 4426 | 12020 | 5200 |
| 21D14S | Peavine Ridge | 4503 | 12156 | 3500 |
| 20G06S | Quartz Mountain | 4216 | 12047 | 5700 |
| 22F05S | Railroad Overpass | 4337 | 12208 | 2750 |
| 21D04S | Red Hill | 4528 | 12142 | 4400 |
| 22F43S | Roaring River | 4354 | 12202 | 4900 |
| 18F01S | Rock Springs | 4359 | 11851 | 5100 |
| 23D01S | Saddle Mountain | 4532 | 12322 | 3250 |
| 22F04S | Salt Creek Falls | 4336 | 12204 | 4000 |
| 21E05S | Santiam Junction | 4426 | 12156 | 3750 |
| 17D08S | Schneider Meadows | 4500 | 11709 | 5400 |
| 23D02S | Seine Creek | 4531 | 12317 | 2060 |
| 22G33S | Sevenmile Marsh | 4241 | 12208 | 6200 |
| 21F12S | Silver Creek | 4257 | 12111 | 5720 |
| 18G01S | Silvies | 4245 | 11841 | 6900 |
| 19F01S | Snow Mountain | 4357 | 11933 | 6220 |
| 19E07S | Starr Ridge | 4416 | 11901 | 5300 |
| 20G09S | Strawberry | 4206 | 12151 | 5760 |
| 20G02S | Summer Rim | 4242 | 12049 | 7100 |
| 22F14S | Summit Lake | 4327 | 12208 | 5600 |
| 21G03S | Taylor Butte | 4242 | 12124 | 5100 |
| 17D07S | Taylor Green | 4502 | 11732 | 5740 |
| 21E13S | Three Creeks Meadow | 4409 | 12138 | 5650 |
| 18E09S | Tipton | 4440 | 11822 | 5150 |
| 18D21S | Wolf Creek | 4504 | 11808 | 5700 |

Serious problems or deteriorating performance trigger a response from the NRCS electronic technicians located in six data collection offices.

The SNOTEL sites are polled by two master stations operated by NRCS in Boise, Idaho, and Ogden, Utah. A central computer at NRCS's National Water and Climate Center (NWCC) in Portland, Oregon, controls system operations and receives the data collected by the SNOTEL network.

Basic SNOTEL sites have a pressure-sensing snow pillow, storage precipitation gauge, and air temperature sensor. However, they can accommodate 64 channels of data and will accept analog, parallel, or serial digital sensors. On-site microprocessors provide functions such as computing daily maximum, minimum, and average temperature information. Generally, sensor data are recorded every fifteen minutes and reported out in a daily poll of all sites. Special polls are conducted more frequently in response to specific needs.

Table 37 lists current SNOTEL stations in Oregon.

## Snow Surveys

Manual snow surveys require two-person teams to measure snow depth and water content at designated snow courses. A snow course is a permanent site that represents snowpack conditions at a given elevation in a given area. A particular snowpack may have several courses. Generally, the courses are about 1,000 feet long and are situated in small meadows protected from the wind.

*Snow survey team, 1938, in the Oregon Southern Cascades. (Photo by J.G. Jones, USDA Soil Conservation Service. OSU Archives, P98:870)*

Measurements generally are taken on or near the first of every month during the snowpack season, though the frequency and timing of these measurements varies considerably with the locality, the nature of the snowpack, difficulty of access, and cost. On occasion, special surveys are scheduled to help evaluate unusual conditions. The manual surveys involve travel and work in remote areas, often in bad weather, but reliable data are obtained. Locations that are too hazardous or costly to measure on the ground can be equipped with depth markers that can be read from aircraft. Snow depth can be measured in this way with a high degree of accuracy. Although the amount of water in the snowpack is not measured, it can be reliably estimated from the observed snow depth.

NRCS conducts intensive training in snow sampling techniques, safety, and mountain survival. On-the-job training and an annual school develop the needed skills; the school has become known throughout the western United States and Canada for its unique training program offered to NRCS employees and others engaged in the cooperative surveys. A critical part of the training is the overnight bivouac in a snow shelter constructed by the student. Many graduates have credited this training with bringing them safely through unforeseen, hazardous situations.

## AgriMet

In 1983, in cooperation with the Bonneville Power Administration, the U.S. Bureau of Reclamation began "piggy-backing" a network of automatic agricultural weather stations onto Reclamation's regional Hydromet satellite telemetry network. The Hydromet network is a series of automated data collection platforms that provide information necessary for near-real-time management of Reclamation's water operations in the Pacific Northwest. As a subset of the overall Hydromet network, this agricultural network, dedicated to crop water use modeling and other agricultural applications, has been identified as AgriMet.

The present AgriMet network consists of 51 agricultural weather stations located throughout the Pacific Northwest (see Figure 29). Forty-nine are full AgriMet stations with two additional frost control stations (with fewer sensors). An additional ten stations east of the divide in Montana are managed by the U.S. Bureau of Reclamation Great Plains Region .

The network is sponsored by the U.S. Bureau of Reclamation with additional support from the Northwest Energy Efficiency Alliance, the USDA Agricultural Resource Service, the USDA Natural Resources Conservation Service, land grant universities, the Cooperative Extension System, electric utilities, power companies, and other public and private agencies and organizations.

Real-time AgriMet data are transmitted from individual stations to Reclamation's receive site in Boise, Idaho, through the GOES-8, GOES-9, and DOMSAT satellites. Each station transmits data at regular intervals of four hours. Data collection intervals within this four-hour period are dependent on the specific sensor equipment at each station. Types of data collected at each station vary. The data are processed on minicomputers running the OpenVMS operating system at the Boise site, then shared with other organizations and individuals participating in the AgriMet program. Access to the system is available by telephone modem, telnet, DECNET, and the World Wide Web.

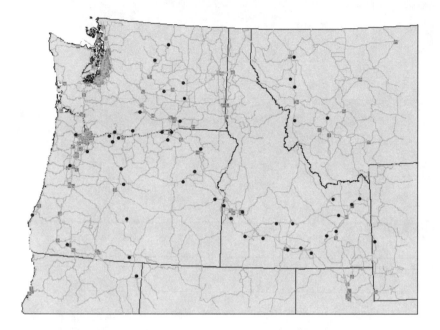

*Figure 31.*
*AgriMet stations*
*in Oregon.*

# Weather Observer's Report Form

As you read through The Oregon Weather Book, you may notice that we have left out an interesting or significant weather event. You might also have been a witness to such an event that occurred after this book was published. In either case, we encourage you to use the form below, or a similar form of your own design, to report weather events to us. If we use your reports in future editions of the Weather Book, we will give you credit and provide you with a free copy of the book. If more than one person writes about the same event, credit will go to the first one we hear from.

Thank you for helping make future editions of this book more complete and up-to-date!

-- -- -- -- -- -- -- -- -- -- -- -- -- -- -- -- -- -- -- -- -- -- -- -- --

## The Oregon Weather Book
## Weather Observer's Report Form

*Mail to:*                                                    *or fax to:*
Oregon Climate Service                          541-737-5710
316 Strand Ag Hall
Oregon State University
Corvallis  OR  97331

Date: _____          Location: _____

Description of what happened:_____

_____

_____

_____

_____

Your name: _____

Address: _____

_____

# Glossary

**Absolute humidity.** The density of water vapor in the air, expressed as the mass of water vapor in a given volume (e.g., pounds per cubic foot).

**Acid deposition.** Acidic particles (commonly sulfuric acid and nitric acid) deposited at the earth's surface. This can occur in dry form (dry deposition) or wet form (wet deposition).

**Acid fog.** See *Acid rain.*

**Acid rain.** Water in the atmosphere combining with gaseous pollutants, such as sulfur and nitrogen oxides, to create falling rain (or snow) acidic with a pH less than 5.0. *Acid fog* is made when fog droplets combine with the pollutants.

**Adiabatic process.** A process that occurs with no transfer of heat between the system (such as an air parcel) and its surroundings. In this process, compression will always produce warming, and expansion results in cooling. See also *Dry adiabatic rate, Moist adiabatic rate.*

**Advection.** The transfer of any atmospheric property horizontally.

**Advection fog.** Fog formed when warm, damp air travels over a cool surface and the air cools to below its dew point.

**Aerosols.** Very small suspended solid particles (dust, smoke, etc.) or liquid droplets from either natural or human sources, e.g., fossil fuel burning.

**Air mass.** A mass of air which has similar horizontal temperature and moisture properties.

**Air parcel.** An imaginary "box" of air a few feet on each side, used to explain and model the characteristics of sir.

**Air pollutants.** Airborne solid, liquid, or gaseous materials that have the potential to harm the health of humans and animals, to damage vegetation and structures, or to toxify the environment.

**Air pressure** (also *atmospheric pressure*). Pressure exerted by the weight of the air above a given point; most often measured in millibars (mb) or inches of mercury (in. Hg).

**Albedo.** The amount of radiation that returns from a surface compared to that which strikes it. High reflectivity equates with high albedo.

**Aleutian low.** Subpolar low-pressure area on mean sea level pressure charts centered near or south of the Aleutian Islands.

**Anemometer.** A device that measures wind speed.

**Aneroid barometer.** A liquid-less apparatus used to determine air pressure.

**Anticyclone.** A surface high-pressure area around which the wind blows clockwise in the Northern Hemisphere and counterclockwise in the Southern Hemisphere.

**Apparent temperature.** The "feel" of the air for various combinations of air temperature and relative humidity.

**Arid climate.** An extremely dry or "desert" climate. Temperatures can be very warm or quite cool, but precipitation is always low.

**Atmosphere.** The gases that encircle a planet, captured by the planet's gravitational force. The Earth's atmosphere is mainly nitrogen and oxygen. See also *Mesosphere, Stratosphere, Troposphere.*

**Atmospheric greenhouse effect.** The warming of the atmosphere caused by its absorbing and reemitting infrared radiation while allowing shortwave (ultraviolet) radiation to pass through. The gases mainly responsible for the Earth's atmospheric greenhouse effect are water vapor and carbon dioxide.

**Atmospheric models.** Mathematical equations or physical models used to simulate the atmosphere's behavior.

**Atmospheric pressure.** See *Air pressure.*

**Atmospheric stagnation.** A situation with light winds and slow vertical mixing that can lead to increased concentrations of pollutants. Air stagnations most often occur with fair weather, an inversion, and the sinking air of a high-pressure area.

**Aurora.** Gases in the nighttime sky, stimulated by solar energy, give glowing light shows in the upper atmosphere. The aurora borealis (northern lights) occur in the Northern Hemisphere; and the aurora australis (southern lights) in the Southern Hemisphere.

**Autumnal equinox.** The equinox around September 23 when the sun passes directly over the equator. This represents the beginning of autumn in the Northern Hemisphere and spring in the Southern.

**Backing wind.** Wind changing direction in a counterclockwise motion in the Northern Hemisphere (e.g., north to northwest to west).

**Barometer.** Instrument used to measure air pressure. Two widely used barometers are the mercury barometer and the aneroid barometer.

**Blizzard.** An intense storm with cold temperatures, winds in excess of 35 mph, and heavy snow either falling or blowing. When the snow stops falling, but the other conditions remain, it is called a *ground blizzard*.

**California current.** The southward-flowing ocean current that runs along the entire west coast of the United States down to Baja California.

**Cap cloud.** A smooth cloud in the form of a cap, on the top of a cumulus cloud.

**Carbon dioxide (CO2).** An odorless and colorless gas present in the atmosphere at a concentration of about 0.035% (350 ppm) of air at sea level. $CO_2$ is important in the earth's atmospheric greenhouse effect because it selectively absorbs infrared radiation. $CO_2$ in its solid state is called dry ice.

**Carbon monoxide (CO).** The toxic gas that is created with the unfinished combustion of fuels containing carbon.

**Celsius scale.** A temperature scale, designated by °C, where zero is assigned to the temperature at which water freezes and 100 to the temperature at which water boils (at sea level).

**Cirrus.** Thin, wispy white clouds made up of ice crystals and formed high in the atmosphere.

**Climate.** Weather events or measurements averaged over a period of time.

**Cloudburst.** An abrupt and severe rain shower.

**Cloud seeding.** A form of weather modification in which tiny particles (condensation nuclei) are injected into a cloud in order to speed up condensation and thereby enhance precipitation.

**Cold front.** A transition area, commonly a line, where a cold air mass moves into and replaces a warm air mass.

**Condensation.** The change of state from a gas to a liquid, e.g., water vapor to liquid water.

**Condensation level.** The height in the atmosphere at which rising air cools to the dew point and begins to condense. The base of a cumulus cloud marks this height.

**Condensation nuclei.** Tiny particles upon which water condenses in the atmosphere, such as dust or smoke particles.

**Conduction.** The transfer of heat from one substance to another, or within a substance, through molecular activity.

**Convection.** The transmitting and mixing of properties within a fluid. In meterology, convection refers to massive motion in the atmosphere in an upward or vertical motion.

**Convergence.** A condition that occurs when winds cause a horizontal net inflow of air into a region, often leading to rising air.

**Cooling degree-day.** A number representing the difference in degrees between an actual temperature and a base temperature, used as a measure of the amount of space cooling needed. For example, for a base temperature of 65°F, an average daily temperature of 70°F would represent 5 cooling degree-days. On the other hand, a temperature of 60°F would require 0, since the temperature is below the threshold. See also *Growing degree-day, Heating degree-day.*

**Coriolis force.** An apparent force whereby the rotation of an object (often the Earth) causes objects, wind, and ocean currents to move at right angles relative to the direction of rotation. The deflection in the Earth's Northern Hemisphere is to the right of the path of motion and to the left in the Southern Hemisphere.

**Corona (optic).** Colored concentric rings surrounding moons or the sun and caused by the light diffraction off uniformly sized water droplets.

**Cumulonimbus.** A very dense, tall cloud caused by intense convection, often associated with severe weather, such as thunderstorms, rain, lightning, and hail.

**Cumulus.** A rather dense cloud with a fluffy and rounded form. These clouds usually have an even base and then bulge in the upper part to resemble a pile of cotton balls. In calm weather they are called *cumulus humilis*. Cumulus clouds displaying obvious vertical growth are called *cumulus congestus* or *towering cumulus*. The largest, most violent cumulus are cumulonimbus.

**Cyclogenesis.** The growth and advancement of mid-latitude (extratropical) cyclones.

**Cyclone.** A violent storm in which the winds rotate around a central area of low pressure. In the Northern Hemisphere the winds blow counterclockwise and in the Southern Hemisphere clockwise.

**Daily range of temperature.** The maximum temperature minus the minimum for a particular day.

**Dendrochronology.** The study of past climate conditions using the annual growth rings of trees.

**Density.** The mass per unit of volume of a substance. Common units for air density are grams per m3 or kilograms per m$^3$.

**Deposition.** In subfreezing air, water vapor can change to ice without going through the liquid phase. The ice is deposited on surfaces such as buildings, trees, and wires.

**Depression.** See *Extratropical cyclone*.

**Dew.** Condensed moisture on objects near the ground when their temperatures are below the dew point of the surface air.

**Dew point (dew-point temperature).** The temperature to which air must be cooled (at constant pressure and constant water vapor content) for saturation and condensation to occur.

**Diffraction.** The process by which light bends around objects. Cloud droplets can bend sunlight into rings of light or colored bands.

**Doppler radar.** Radar which uses the Doppler shift to establish the velocity of falling precipitation either toward or away from the radar unit.

**Downburst.** A severe localized downdraft that can be experienced beneath or adjacent to a severe thunderstorm.

**Drizzle.** Very light rain.

**Drought.** A period of abnormally dry weather sufficiently long to cause serious effects on agriculture and other activities in the affected area.

**Dry adiabatic rate.** The rate of temperature change with elevation in an unsaturated air parcel. The adiabatic rate (cooling or warming) is about 5.5°F per 1,000 feet. See also *Adiabatic process*.

**Dry-bulb temperature.** The reading of the air temperature from a dry-bulb thermometer.

**Dust devil** (also *whirlwind*). A small, tornado-like funnel that rotates and pulls in dust and debris, usually on clear, dry, hot afternoons. Although dust devils can cause damage, they are much less intense than tornadoes.

**El Niño.** A situation in which the water off the coast of Peru and Ecuador warms more than usual, generally coinciding with cooler ocean temperatures in the western Pacific. This causes a shifting in wind and moisture patterns, causing significant changes in weather in the U.S. and worldwide. Major El Niño events occur irregularly, about once every three to seven years. In Oregon, El Niño events produce generally mild, dry winters.

**Energy.** The property of a system that enables it to do work. Some forms of energy are kinetic, radiant, potential, chemical, electric, and magnetic.

**Equinox.** See *Autumnal equinox, Vernal equinox*.

**Evaporation.** A change in state from the liquid phase to the gas phase, usually through warming of the liquid.

**Extratropical cyclone.** A cyclonic storm that most often forms along a front in middle and high latitudes. Also called a middle latitude storm, a depression, or a low. It is not a tropical storm or hurricane.

**Fahrenheit scale.** A temperature scale, designated by °F, where 32 is assigned to the temperature at which water freezes and 212 to the temperature at which water boils (at sea level).

**Flash flood.** A flood that rises and falls quite rapidly with little or no advance warning, usually as the result of intense rainfall over a relatively small area.

**Fog.** A cloud that forms at the Earth's surface.

**Freeze.** A situation where the air temperature of a region is below freezing for a substantial amount of time. This usually occurs when cold air is advected into an area and freezing conditions continue to develop into a deep layer near the surface.

**Freezing rain and freezing drizzle.**
Precipitation that falls and freezes when
hitting a cold surface, thereby coating
objects and the ground with ice.

**Front.** The line where two different air masses
meet. See also *Cold front, Occluded front,
Stationary front, Warm front.*

**Frost** (also *hoarfrost*). When the air
temperature falls below freezing, deposition
on objects will turn to ice.

**Frostbite.** Damage to exposed areas of the
body caused by the skin freezing.

**Funnel cloud.** A twisting cone-shaped cloud
protruding down from the base of a
thunderstorm. It becomes a tornado when it
touches the ground.

**Geostrophic wind.** A horizontal wind blowing
parallel to the isobars that results when the
Coriolis force balances the horizontal
pressure gradient.

**Graupel.** Small particles of ice that form in
clouds or snowflakes that become rounded
through collision with other ice particles,
and subsequent buildup.

**Green flash.** A greenish area that occasionally
can be seen on the top of the sun as it sets
or rises.

**Greenhouse effect.** See *Atmospheric greenhouse
effect.*

**Growing degree-day.** A form of degree-day the
threshold temperature of which is
established for different types of crops. See
also *Cooling degree-day, Heating degree-day.*

**Gust front.** A boundary between air masses
which causes a sudden increase in wind
speeds, and usually a change in wind
direction, as it passes.

**Hailstones.** Ice particles that vary in size from
centimeters to inches in diameter, and are
formed in strong convective storms, such as
cumulonimbus.

**Halo.** Ring that appears to circle the sun or
moon, caused by light refraction, generally
from ice crystals in the upper atmosphere.

**Haze.** Reduced visibility caused by tiny,
suspended particles, usually in or near
urban areas.

**Heat.** Energy that is transferred through
objects due to differences in temperature.

**Heat index (HI).** A way to express how the air
actually feels, based on a combination of air
temperature and relative humidity; hot days
feel hottest when humidity is high.

**Heating degree-day.** A number representing
the difference in degrees between an actual
temperature and a base temperature, used
as a measure of the amount of space heating
needed. For example, for a base temperature
of 65°F, an average daily temperature of
60°F would represent 5 heating degree days.
On the other hand, a temperature of 70°F
would require 0, since the temperature is
above the threshold. See also *Cooling degree-
day, Growing degree-day.*

**Heatstroke.** A physical complication caused by
the body overheating due to high
temperatures and humidity.

**High.** See *Anticyclone*

**Hoarfrost.** See *Frost.*

**Hook-shape echo.** An image viewed on a radar
screen that is hook-shaped; commonly
associated with tornado activities.

**Humidity.** The amount of water vapor in the
air.

**Hurricane.** An intense tropical cyclone with
winds 75mph or more.

**Hydrologic cycle.** A model that explains the
transfer of water through the earth, oceans,
and atmosphere.

**Hygrometer.** A device used to measure the
water vapor in the air.

**Hypothermia.** A condition in which the body
temperature is rapidly lowered to
dangerous, sometimes deadly, levels.

**Ice fog.** Fog that is formed from small
suspended ice particles at very low
temperatures.

**Ice nuclei.** Particles that start the ice crystal
formation process.

**Ice pellets.** See *Sleet.*

**Indian summer.** Summer-like dry and clear
conditions that extend into fall and usually
occur after a period of cool conditions.

**Infrared (IR) radiation.** Electromagnetic
radiation with wavelengths longer than
visible light and shorter than microwaves.
IR radiation is generally associated with
heat transfer.

**Insolation.** The incoming radiation from the
sun.

**Instrument shelter.** A structure to protect
weather instruments from direct sunlight
and precipitation.

**Intertropical Convergence Zone (ITCZ).** An
area of rising air and unsettled weather that
separates the southeast trade winds (to the

south) and the northeast trade winds (to the north). The ITCZ is usually near the equator, but moves northward and southward following the sun's zenith position with the seasons.

**Inversion.** An increase in air temperature with height. Warm air above cold air is known as a "stable" atmospheric situation, and often leads to buildup of air pollutants near the ground. See also *Radiation inversion, Subsidence inversion, Temperature inversion.*

**Isobar.** An imaginary line that passes through points of equal pressure.

**Isobaric map.** A map that shows temperature and winds on a constant pressure surface. Variations in pressure are shown by isobars.

**Isotach.** An imaginary line that goes through points of equal wind speed.

**Isotherm.** An imaginary line that goes through points of equal temperature.

**Jet stream.** High-speed winds near the troposphere that flow in a concentrated band. Generally represents the boundary between warm subtropical and cool polar air. Often known as the "storm track," since storms tend to follow its path as they circle the globe.

**Katabatic wind.** Wind that blows downslope; can be cold or hot depending on the season, but is generally quite dry.

**Kelvin.** A unit of temperature, denoted by K. A unit of 1 K equals 1°C. Zero K is absolute zero, and equals -273.15°C.

**Kinetic energy.** Energy that results from motion within a body or substance.

**Knot.** A unit that measures speed and is equal to 1 nautical mile per hour (1.15 mph).

**Koppen classification system.** A climate classification system based on seasonal and annual averages of temperature and precipitation.

**La Niña.** The counterpart to El Niño, which also causes weather and climate disruptions worldwide. Ocean temperatures off South America are cooler than normal, and temperatures near Indonesia are warmer than normal. In Oregon, La Niña winters are generally cooler and wetter than normal.

**Lake breeze.** Wind that blows off a lake onto the shore.

**Lake-effect snow.** Snow that occurs when cold dry air picks up moisture while passing over a lake, generally deposited downwind of the lake.

**Land breeze.** Wind that blows from land to sea, usually at night or in the cold season.

**Lapse rate.** The rate of temperature decrease with height.

**Latent heat.** Heat that is transferred by a substance when it changes its state through evaporation, condensation, or sublimation.

**Lenticular cloud.** A lens-shaped cloud formed by strong winds affected by terrain, usually mountains.

**Lightning.** An electrical discharge created by thunderstorms.

**Low.** See *Extratropical storm.*

**Mammatus clouds.** Clouds with large pouches hanging from the underside, often preceding severe weather.

**Marine climate.** A climate that is influenced mostly by the ocean. Temperatures are generally mild throughout the year and humidity high.

**Maritime air.** Air that has developed over a body of water and is generally mild and moist.

**Mean annual temperature.** A location's temperatures averaged over a year.

**Mean daily temperature.** The average of all hourly temperatures, or of the maximum and minimum temperatures, for a 24-hour period.

**Mercury barometer.** See *Barometer.*

**Meridional wind flow.** Wind with a predominant north-to-south or south-to-north direction. See also *Zonal wind flow.*

**Mesoscale.** The scale of meteorological conditions referring to areas from 1 km (0.62 mile) to 100 km (62 miles).

**Mesosphere.** The atmospheric layer above the stratosphere, extending from about 30 miles to about 50 miles above the Earth's surface.

**Meteorology.** The study of the atmosphere and everything in it, including weather and weather forecasting.

**Microburst.** Very localized downdrafts that occur in severe thunderstorms and are associated with strong rain and downward-moving air.

**Middle latitude storm.** See *Extratropical cyclone.*

**Millibar (mb).** A unit of atmospheric pressure. Standard sea-level pressure is 1,013.4 mb.

**Mixing depth.** The depth of the mixing layer.

**Mixing layer.** The unstable layer of air that is well mixed and extends from the surface up to the base of an inversion.

**Mixing ratio.** The ratio of the amount of water vapor in the air to the amount of dry air.

**Moist adiabatic rate.** The rate of temperature change in saturated air as it rises or descends. The rate of temperature changes varies somewhat, but is usually about 6°C per 1,000 meters (3.3°F/1,000 feet).

**Monsoon wind system.** Winds that switch directions between winter and summer. Most of the time the wind blows from land to sea in winter and from sea to land in the summer.

**Mountain and valley breeze.** A local wind system of mountain valleys where the wind blows downhill at night and uphill during the day.

**NEXRAD.** Acronym for Next Generation Weather Radar, the Doppler radar currently used by the National Weather Service. See also *Doppler radar.*

**Noctilucent clouds.** Thin, curvy, bluish clouds which form at altitudes of 50-55 miles above the surface, best viewed at twilight in polar latitudes.

**Occluded front (occlusion).** A front that occurs when a cold front overtakes a warm front.

**Offshore wind.** Wind that blows from land to the water.

**Onshore wind.** Wind that blows from the water to the land.

**Orographic uplift.** Air lifted over topographic features; when clouds form as a result they are called orographic clouds.

**Ozone (O3).** A gas form of oxygen found naturally in the stratosphere. Stratospheric ozone absorbs some of the sun's ultraviolet light and thus acts as a shield for the earth's surface. In the lower troposphere, however, ozone is a harmful air pollutant formed by chemical reactions involving pollutants emitted from fossil fuel combustion.

**Ozone hole.** A decreased amount of ozone in an area over the polar regions in the springtime.

**Pacific high.** Same as *Subtropical high.*

**Parcel of air.** A "section" of air that can be used to study or explain the characteristics of air.

**Particulate matter.** Particles in solid or liquid form that are tiny enough to stay suspended in the air.

**Photochemical reaction.** Chemical reaction in the atmosphere that involves sunlight. For example, ozone in the lower atmosphere is formed by sunlight reacting with nitrogen dioxide, followed by a chemical reaction to form ozone.

**Photochemical smog.** See *Smog.*

**Pollutant.** A substance released into the air, water, or land that destroys or alters the existing properties of the particular medium.

**Potential energy.** The energy an object possesses because of its position relative to other objects subject to gravitational effects.

**Precipitation.** Water, in any form, falling from the sky and reaching the surface.

**Pressure gradient.** The rate at which pressure changes along a horizontal distance.

**Pressure gradient force.** The force caused by differences in pressure in the atmosphere. Winds in the atmosphere are proportional to the pressure gradient.

**Pressure tendency.** The rate that pressure changes in a particular time period, usually three hours.

**Prevailing wind.** The most common wind direction at a given location and period of time.

**Probability forecast.** The forecast of specific weather conditions based on probability.

**Radar.** A device that uses reflection of microwaves to track moving or falling objects (e.g., rain).

**Radiation.** Energy that is in the form of electromagnetic waves, and can even travel in a vacuum.

**Radiational cooling.** A cooling of air near the earth's surface resulting from release of infrared radiation (cooling) by the earth.

**Radiation fog.** Fog that forms when radiational cooling brings the air temperature down to the dewpoint temperature.

**Radiation inversion.** An inversion caused by radiational cooling near the ground, resulting in warmer air aloft.

**Radiosonde.** A balloon equipped with a device that measures air characteristics and sends the data to a station at the ground.

**Rain.** Liquid precipitation consisting of large drops (as opposed to drizzle, the drops of which are very small).

**Rainbow.** A colored arc that is visible when the sun is at one's back, caused by light refracted by water droplets in a rain shower.

**Rain gauge.** An instrument used to determine the amount of precipitation.

**Rain shadow.** An area on the downwind side of a mountain that receives much less precipitation than the windward side.

**Reflection.** The process whereby some of the radiation striking an object is turned back.

**Refraction.** Bending of light as it passes through different environments.

**Relative humidity.** The ratio of the actual water vapor in the air to the amount the air could hold at the current temperature and pressure.

**Return stroke.** The lightning stroke that shoots upward from the Earth to the bottom of a cloud.

**Ridge.** An area of high pressure in the atmosphere.

**Rime ice.** Freezing of water drops upon impact on a cold object, leaving a layer of ice.

**Roll cloud.** A thick, roll-shaped cloud that forms in thunderstorms along the leading edge of the gust front.

**Rotor cloud.** A dynamic cumulus cloud the air of which rotates on an axis parallel to the leeward side of a mountain range along which it forms.

**Saturation (of air).** A situation in which the maximum possible amount of water vapor is present in air, for a given temperature and pressure.

**Saturation vapor pressure.** The maximum amount of water vapor that air can contain at the current temperature and pressure.

**Sea breeze.** Surface winds which blow from the ocean onto land.

**Sea-level pressure.** The pressure of the atmosphere at mean sea level.

**Semi-arid climate.** A dry climate that is not as dry as an arid climate. Short grass is the usual vegetation.

**Semipermanent highs and lows.** Regions of high or low pressure that stay at a certain latitude throughout much of the year.

**Sensible heat.** Heat that is "felt" and can be measured with a thermometer. See and contrast Latent heat.

**Sensible temperature.** The temperature that is felt by the body, as opposed to the measured temperature.

**Shower.** Precipitation that falls sporadically but often heavily.

**Sleet.** Precipitation consisting of small pellets of ice with diameters of less than one-quarter inch.

**Smog.** Polluted air with limited visibility, often formed through photochemical processes. Ozone is a primary component of photochemical smog.

**Snow.** Solid form of precipitation consisting of ice crystals.

**Snowflake.** The group of ice crystals that falls from a cloud.

**Snow flurry.** Sporadic snow showers.

**Snow grains.** A solid form of drizzle composed of tiny particles of ice.

**Snow pellets.** Ice crystals that stick together in a cloud to form balls of ice approximately $1/16$-$3/16$ inch in diameter.

**Snow squall.** A heavy shower of snow that limits visibility.

**Soundings.** Observations taken at different heights in the atmosphere that produce a continuous profile of temperature, humidity, or winds at different heights.

**Southern oscillation.** An alternation of surface air pressure in the east and west tropical Pacific Ocean associated with El Niño and La Niña conditions.

**Standard atmosphere.** Average temperature, pressure, and density of the Earth's atmosphere at various heights above sea level.

**Standard atmospheric pressure.** Average pressure of the atmosphere at various heights. Standard sea level pressure is 29.92 inches (measured in a barometer). In other units, standard pressure is 1013.25 millibars or 760 millimeters.

**Stationary front.** A front that remains more or less fixed in place, with winds blowing parallel to the front on either side (but in different directions).

**Station pressure.** The air pressure at a particular station.

**Storm surge.** Unusually high tide along a shore, caused by the winds of a strong storm (e.g., hurricane).

**Storm track.** See *Jet stream*.

**Stratocumulus.** A primarily low stratiform cloud with a rounded and bumpy appearance on the underside.

**Stratosphere.** The second layer of the atmosphere from the Earth, following the troposphere and preceding the mesophere. This layer extends approximately 6 to 30 miles above sea level, and is characterized by a temperature inversion.

**Stratus.** A layer of low, uniformly based gray clouds that often precipitate as drizzle.

**Sublimation.** A change of state from solid (e.g., ice) to gas (e.g., water vapor) without passing through the liquid phase.

**Subsidence.** Slow sinking of air, generally in association with high-pressure areas.

**Subsidence inversion.** A temperature inversion caused by air sinking and warming, with colder air below.

**Subtropical high.** A persistent high pressure area in the subtropical belt generally centered near 30° latitude.

**Subtropical jet stream.** A jet stream located in the subtropics, between 20° and 30° latitude.

**Summer solstice.** The day when the sun is at its highest point in the sky. This is about June 22 in the Northern Hemisphere, December 21 in the Southern.

**Sunspots.** Areas of high magnetic energy that are linked to "cooler" spots on the sun.

**Surface map.** A weather map showing the air pressure, winds, temperature, and other information at the Earth's surface.

**Synoptic scale.** The weather scale that includes large-scale storm systems, fronts, and other features, stretching over continent-sized areas.

**Temperature.** The average speed or kinetic energy of the atoms and molecules in a object or the heat measured by a thermometer.

**Temperature inversion.** An increase of air temperature with height, rather than the customary decrease.

**Thermal.** A parcel of warm air that rises when heated by the surface of the earth.

**Thermal lows, thermal highs.** The areas of high and low pressure that are predominately produced by surface heating or cooling.

**Thermometer.** An instrument used to measure temperature.

**Thunder.** The noise created when gases expand quickly near a lightning strike.

**Thunderstorm.** A localized storm that includes lightning and thunder, and often heavy winds and rain or hail.

**Tornado.** A violent, swirling column of air that extends from a cumulonimbus cloud and touches ground. See also *Funnel cloud*.

**Trace (of precipitation).** A precipitation total that is less than 0.01 inch.

**Trade winds.** Prevailing winds in the tropics that blow from east to west, and toward the ITCZ.

**Transpiration.** A transfer of water vapor from plants to the atmosphere through evaporation.

**Tropopause.** The boundary between the troposphere and the stratosphere.

**Troposphere.** The lowest layer of the atmosphere, from the Earth's surface to about 6-10 miles.

**Trough.** A region of low pressure in the atmosphere.

**Turbulence.** Gusts and eddies produced by irregular flow in the atmosphere.

**Twilight.** The times during the day when the sun is either just about to rise or has just set and the sky is not completely dark.

**Typhoon.** A hurricane in the western Pacific.

**Ultraviolet radiation.** The electromagnetic radiation the wavelengths of which are shorter than visible light but longer than X-rays.

**Upper-air map.** A map of temperatures, pressures, and winds in the upper atmosphere.

**Upslope precipitation.** The precipitation that is produced when damp air progressively rises along the terrain. Rising motion causes the air to cool, and when air temperatures drop to the dew point, condensation (and precipitation) result.

**Upwelling.** The rising of cold, deep ocean water toward the surface, usually caused by winds in the lower atmosphere.

**Urban heat island.** An increase in temperatures in urban areas compared to rural areas nearby, resulting from industrial, domestic, and transportation activities.

**Valley breeze.** See *Mountain and valley breeze*.

**Vapor pressure.** The pressure exerted by water vapor molecules in a given volume of air.

**Vernal equinox.** The date on which the sun's rays shine directly on the equator in the Northern Hemisphere spring (on or about March 20).

**Virga.** Precipitation that evaporates before reaching the Earth's surface.

**Visible image.** A satellite picture that shows the Earth's surface and atmosphere as it would appear from space in visible light (as from a black-and-white camera).

**Visibility.** The maximum distance one can see and recognize notable objects.

**Warm front.** A front where the warm air replaces the cold air.

**Warm sector.** The area of warm air located between a warm front and a cold front.

**Water equivalent.** The amount of water in frozen precipitation when it is melted. Usually 10 inches of snow will contain 1 inch of water.

**Waterspout.** A tornado-like column of swirling wind over the water that may suck water up into it.

**Water vapor.** Water that is in its gaseous form.

**Water vapor image.** A satellite picture that shows the total amount of water vapor in the atmosphere at every point in the image.

**Wave cyclone.** The extratropical cyclone that propagates and moves along a front producing wavelike formations in the front.

**Weather.** The properties of the atmosphere at a specific time and location.

**Weather elements.** The aspects of weather that describe the state of the atmosphere (precipitation, winds, temperature, and so on).

**Westerlies.** The winds that dominantly blow from the west in the middle latitudes.

**Wet-bulb tenperature.** The temperature measured by a thermometer with a wetted wick surrounding it, used to determine humidity or dew point of the air.

**Whirlwind.** See *Dust devil.*

**Wind.** Air movement caused by pressure differences in the atmosphere. See also *Geostrophic wind, Katabatic wind, Offshore wind, Onshore wind, Prevailing wind, Trade winds, Westerlies.*

**Wind-chill factor.** The combined cooling effect of temperature and wind speed, proportional to loss of body heat.

**Wind direction.** The direction that the wind is blowing from.

**Wind profiler.** A Doppler radar that measures the vertical profile of wind speed and direction.

**Wind rose.** A graph or diagram that shows the percentage frequency that wind blows from different directions and at different speeds.

**Wind shear.** The rate that wind speed or direction changes in a particular area, either vertically or horizontally.

**Wind vane.** An instrument used to determine wind direction.

**Windward side.** The side of an object facing the prevailing wind.

**Winter solstice.** The point at which the sun is lowest in the sky and over the latitude 23.5°S. This occurs around December 22 in the Northern Hemisphere, and June 22 in the Southern.

**Zenith.** The highest point in the sky reached by the sun or other heavenly bodies.

**Zonal wind flow.** Wind with a predominant west-to-east component. See also *Meridional wind flow.*

# Bibliography

Ahrens, C. Donald, 1993. *Meteorology Today,* Fifth Edition. West Publishing Company, Minneapolis/ St. Paul.

Bancroft, Hubert Howe, 1887. "History of Oregon." *In History of the Pacific states of North America,* A.L. Bancroft, San Francisco.

*Bend Bulletin,* December 11, 1919. Bend, Oregon.

Brogan, Phil, 1956. "The Case of the Brown Snow." *The Oregonian,* March 25. Portland, Oregon.

Clark, Donald H., 1853. "Remember the Winter of?" *Oregon Historical Quarterly.* Portland, Oregon.

Columbia Basin Meteorology Committee, 1969. *Columbia Basin Meteorological Handbook.* Portland, Oregon.

*Curry County Reporter,* January 22, 1953. Gold Beach, Oregon.1965.

Daly, C., R.P. Neilson, and Dl. L. Phillips, 1994. A Statistical-Topographic Model for Mapping Climatological Precipitation over Mountainous Terrain. *Journal of Applied Meteorology, 33*(2):140-158.

Department of Vocational Education, 1950. "One Day More: An Outline for Tourist Home Schools." Salem, Oregon.

Earley, Mollie, 1976. *In* Hays, Marjorie H., *The Land That Kept its Promise,* Lincoln County Historical Society, Newport, Oregon.

*Eugene City Guard,* January 22, 1887. Eugene, Oregon.

French, Giles, 1958. *The Golden Land: A Hsitory of Sherman County.* Oregon Historical Society, Portland, Oregon.

Gibbs and Maher, 1967.

Holbrook, Stewart. Article on the Tillamook Burn for the *American Mercury.*

Inwards, Richard, 1893. *Weather Lore.* Elliot Stock, London. Reprinted in 1994 by Senate, London.

Johnson, Bruce, 1994. Boom Days in Oregon's Coldest Town. *Cascades East,* Winter 1994-95.

Johnson, Bruce, 1999. Personal correspondence.

Johnson, Robert Underwood, 1923 . *Remembered Yesterdays.* Little, Brown, and Company, Boston.

Laskin, David, 1997. *Rains All the Time.* Sasquatch Books, Seattle, Washington.

McKee, T. B., N. J. Doesken, and J. Kleist, 1993. The relationship of drought frequency and duration to time scales. Preprints, 8th Conference on Applied Climatology, 17-22 January, Anaheim, CA, 179-84.

Nash, Wallis, 1878. *Oregon There and Back in 1877.* McMillan & Co., London. Reprinted by OSU Press, 1976.

Oliphant, J. Orin,1932. Winter Losses of Cattle in the Oregon Country, 1847-1890. *Washington Historical Quarterly.* 33: January 1932. p.8

Oliver, Egbert C., 1942. *The Oregonian,* March 1.

*Oregon Statesman,* January 13, 1880. Salem, Oregon.

Palmer, W. C., 1965. *Meteorological Drought.* Research Paper No. 45, U.S. Department of Commerce Weather Bureau, Washington, D.C.

Palmer, W. C., 1968. Keeping track of crop moisture conditions, nationwide: the new Crop Moisture Index. *Weatherwise,* 21: 156-161.

Redmond, K.T. and R.W. Koch, 1991. Surface climate and streamflow variability in the western United States and their relationship to large-scale circulation indices. *Water Resources Research, 77*(9):2381-2399.

Shear, J.A. and D. Steila, 1974. The assessment of drought intensity by a new index. *Southeastern Geographer, 13*(1), 195-201.

Snowden, Clinton, 1911. *History of Washington.* The Century History Company, New York.

Soth, Connie, 1987. "Nice Day in Oregon Should Include Raindrops, Wind, Umbrellas." *The Oregonian,* October 18, Portland, Oregon.

*The East Oregonian,* June 17, 1903.

*The New Washington Historian,* January, 1937, p. 11-12.

*The Oregonian,* February 27, 1904. Portland, Oregon.

*The Oregonian,* December 13, 1919. Portland, Oregon.

*The Oregonian,* January 10, 1925. Portland, Oregon.

*The Oregonian,* 1976. Portland, Oregon.

*The Oregonian,* May 9, 1986. Portland, Oregon.

*The Oregonian,* 1996. "In Oregon, Yule Be Damp." December 25, Portland, Oregon.

Thoele, Mike, 1986. *Eugene Register-Guard,* May 27.

Van Bavel, C.H.M. and J.R. Carriker, 1957. *Agricultural Drought in Georgia.* Georgia Agricultural Experiment Stations, Athens.

Wantz, J.W. and R.E. Sinclair, 1981. Distribution of extreme winds in the Bonneville Power Administration service area. *Journal of Applied Meteorology, 20*:1400-1411.

Wilhite, D. A. and M. H. Glantz, 1985. Understanding the drought phenomenon: the role of definitions. *Water International, 10*(3): 111-120.

Wilhite, D. A., 1995. Developing a precipitation-based index to assess climatic conditions across Nebraska. Final report submitted to the Natural Resources Commission, Lincoln, Nebraska.

Willeke, G., J. R. M. Hosking, J. R. Wallis, and N. B. Guttman, 1994. The National Drought Atlas. Institute for Water Resources Report 94-NDS-4, U.S. Army Corps of Engineers.

# Index